A Vindication of Monsters

Essays on
Mary Wollstonecraft And Mary Shelley

Compiled and Edited by

Claire Fitzpatrick

Preface by Sara Karloff

Introduction by Leslie S. Klinger

Foreword by Lisa Morton

A Vindication of Monsters:
Essays On Mary Shelley And Mary Wollstonecraft

ISBN-13: 978-1-922856-40-1

V1.0

This book was aided by a Grant from the Horror Writers Association.

Cover art/design and frontispiece artwork by Greg Chapman.

Printed in Palatino Linotype and Antique Book Cover

IFWG Publishing International
Gold Coast

www.ifwgpublishing.com

"Beware, for I am fearless, and therefore powerful."
–Mary Shelley

"Women do not want power over men. They want
power over themselves."
–Mary Wollstonecraft.

TABLE OF CONTENTS

Memoir

Mary Wollstonecraft Timeline

April 1759—**Mary's Birth.** Mary Wollstonecraft is born in the Spitalfields neighbourhood of London. She is the second of seven children of John Edward and Elizabeth Dickson Wollstonecraft.

Dec 19, 1774—**Moves to Hoxton.** After a series of moves around England as John Edward looks unsuccessfully for work, the Wollstonecraft's move to Hoxton, a London suburb. Mary Wollstonecraft befriends Mr and Mrs Clare, who become a second family to her and encourage her education.

Dec 19, 1775—**Meets Fanny Blood.** Wollstonecraft meets Fanny Blood, a young woman her age who becomes her best friend.

Dec 19, 1776—**Moves to Wales.** The Wollstonecraft's move to Wales.

Dec 19, 1777—**Back to London.** The Wollstonecraft's leave Wales and move to the Walworth suburb of London.

Dec 19, 1778—**Gets Her First Job.** Wollstonecraft moves to Bath to take a position as a companion to an elderly woman named Sarah Dawson. She and her ornery elderly client don't get along well.

Dec 19, 1781—**Returns to London.** Late in the year, Wollstonecraft moves back to London to care for her ailing mother.

Apr 19, 1782—**Mother Dies.** Wollstonecraft's mother Elizabeth dies. Her father remarries immediately, and Wollstonecraft moves in with the family of Fanny Blood, her best friend.

Dec 19, 1783—**Moves in With Sister.** In the winter, Wollstonecraft moves in with her sister Eliza, who has just given birth to a baby. Wollstonecraft notices that her sister is depressed and believes she is suffering at the hands of her husband, Meredith Bishop.

Jan 1, 1784—**Helps Eliza Flee.** Wollstonecraft takes her sister away from her unhappy marriage, leaving the baby behind. The baby dies in August. Because of the damage to her reputation, Eliza is unable to re-marry and spends the rest of her life impoverished.

Dec 19, 1784—**Opens School.** Fanny Blood, Eliza and Mary Wollstonecraft start a school for girls in Newington Green. Everina Wollstonecraft joins them soon after.

Nov 29, 1785—**Fanny Blood Dies.** Fanny Blood marries Hugh Skeys, becomes pregnant and sails to Portugal with him. Wollstonecraft accompanies her. Fanny Blood and her infant child die after complications from premature labour while she and Wollstonecraft are in Portugal.

Dec 1, 1785—**Closes School.** Wollstonecraft returns to London and finds her school has encountered massive financial problems in her absence. She is forced to close it the following year.

Dec 19, 1786—*'Thoughts on the Education of Daughters'.* Inspired by her experiences with her school, Wollstonecraft pens the feminist tract *Thoughts on the Education of Daughters*, a polemic about women's education. She takes a job as governess to the Kingsborough family to support herself.

Dec 19, 1788—**Publishes Novel.** Wollstonecraft publishes her first and only novel, *Mary, A Fiction*. She also publishes a children's book entitled *Original Stories from Real Life*.

Dec 19, 1789—**French Revolution.** The French Revolution begins, inspiring Wollstonecraft and other English intellectuals. She publishes *The Female Reader* under a male pseudonym.

Dec 18, 1790—*'A Vindication of the Rights of Man'.* Wollstonecraft pens a scathing rebuttal to conservative Edmund Burke's anti-revolution treatise *Reflections on the Revolution in France*. *A Vindication of the Rights of Man* brings Wollstonecraft her first real attention as a writer.

Dec 19, 1791—**Meets William Godwin.** Mary Wollstonecraft meets political philosopher William Godwin at a dinner party. The fiercely intelligent, opinionated pair get into an argument and leave irritated with each other. "The interview was not fortunate," Godwin recalls later.

Dec 19, 1792—*'A Vindication of the Rights of Women'.* Wollstonecraft publishes her most famous work, a manifesto arguing for greater equality between men and women. It is met with positive reviews, though some male readers are shocked.

Dec 1, 1792—**Settles in Paris.** Inspired by the ideals of the French Revolution, Wollstonecraft moves to Paris.

Apr 1, 1793—**Begins Relationship.** Wollstonecraft starts an affair with the American adventurer and entrepreneur Gilbert Imlay. They keep the relationship secret for the first four months, then go public. The couple moves in together in Paris and plans a move to America. Though they do not marry, Imlay registers Wollstonecraft as his wife to protect her from anti-English sentiment in France.

May 1, 1794—**Gives Birth to Daughter.** Wollstonecraft gives birth to Fanny Imlay, her daughter with Gilbert. Imlay soon begins withdrawing from their relationship and moves back to London. Wollstonecraft publishes a political tract, *An Historical and Moral View of the Origin and Progress of the French Revolution.*

May 1, 1795—**First Suicide Attempt.** Distraught over Imlay's rejection of her, Wollstonecraft unsuccessfully attempts suicide in London.

Oct 1, 1795—**Second Suicide Attempt.** Wollstonecraft attempts suicide a second time by throwing herself in the Thames River. She leaps from London's Putney Bridge but does not sink.

Mar 1, 1796—**Leaves Imlay.** Wollstonecraft cuts off contact with Gilbert Imlay for good. She publishes *Letters Written During a Short Residence in Sweden, Norway and Denmark*, a travelogue of her voyage to Scandinavia the previous year.

Apr 1, 1796—**Reconnection with Godwin.** Wollstonecraft and William Godwin meet once again, this time with happier results. They begin a romantic relationship that summer. The pair move in together and live as a couple.

Mar 29, 1797—**Marriage.** A pregnant Mary Wollstonecraft marries William Godwin at London's St. Pancras Church.

Aug 30, 1797—**Mary Shelley Born.** Wollstonecraft gives birth to Mary Wollstonecraft Godwin, the couple's only child.

Sep 10, 1797—**Mary Wollstonecraft Dies.** Mary Wollstonecraft dies as a result of complications from childbirth.

Dec 19, 1798—**Memoir Published.** William Godwin publishes several posthumous pieces of his wife's writing. He also publishes her biography, *Memoirs of the Author of A Vindication of the Rights of Women.* His frank portrayal of Wollstonecraft's unconventional lifestyle posthumously destroys her reputation.

Mary Shelley Timeline

August 1797—**Mary's Birth.** Mary Wollstonecraft Godwin is born in London. She is the only child of feminist writer Mary Wollstonecraft (who dies 10 days after her birth) and the radical political philosopher William Godwin.

1801—**A new step-family**: William Godwin marries widow Mary Jane Clairmont, who moves in with her two children, Charles and Claire.

1812-14—**Meets Percy Bysshe-Shelley**: Mary first meets Percy Bysshe Shelley in November 1812 or March 1814. Shelley is a young poet who admires Mary's father. He is five years older than Mary and already married to Harriet Westbrook. Mary and Percy Shelley soon fall in love.

June 1814—**Elopes with Shelley:** 16-year-old Mary runs off with Percy Shelley to Europe. Her step sister Claire Clairmont goes with them, despite her mother's rage. Mary Godwin becomes pregnant almost immediately. William Godwin is furious and refuses to see his daughter for over two years.

August 1814—**Returns to England:** Mary and Percy run out of money after a summer of travel in Europe, and Percy must keep changing addresses to avoid debt collectors.

February 1815—**1st baby**: Mary gives birth to the couple's first child, Clara. The baby is premature and dies after a few days. Mary's diary recounts a dream where the baby came back to life when warmed by the fire.

January 1816—**2nd baby**: Mary Godwin gives birth to the couple's second child, William, nicknamed Willmouse.

June 1816—**Mary begins *Frankenstein: Or, A Modern Prometheus*:** The Shelleys take a summer holiday in Switzerland with Lord Byron and his pregnant lover Claire Clairmont. Byron suggests a ghost story contest and Mary starts the tale that becomes Frankenstein.

July 1816—**Visit to the Alps:** Mary visits the Mer de Glace (Sea of Ice) glacier on top of Mont Blanc with Shelley, and later uses it as the setting for a pivotal scene in Frankenstein.

October 1816—**Half-sister dies:** Mary's half-sister Fanny Imlay commits suicide by laudanum overdose aged 22.

December 1816—**Shelley's wife dies**, so Mary and Shelley can now marry: Shelley's 21-year-old wife Harriet Westbrook is found dead in London's Serpentine River. She was pregnant with her third child, which was probably illegitimate. 15 days after discovering that Percy's wife has died, Percy and Mary are married in London. She is pregnant with their third child and reconciles with her father.

May 1817—**Mary finishes** *Frankenstein: Or, A Modern Prometheus*.

September 1817—**3rd baby:** Mary Shelley gives birth to her third child, Clara Everina. The baby dies of dysentery in Italy after three weeks.

November 1817—**Travel writing:** Mary and Percy write a Romantic travel narrative, History of a Six Weeks' Tour, based on letters, poems, and journals from their European travels in 1814 and 1816. It is published in November 1817 and will be Mary's first published work.

January 1818—**'Frankenstein: Or, A Modern Prometheus' is published.** *Frankenstein; or, The Modern Prometheus* is published in three volumes with a print run of 500. Mary is 20 and is not named as the author, and some readers assume that it is Percy's work. The book is advertised in newspapers but does not sell very well and reviews are mixed.

June 1819—**Son dies:** Mary's 3-year-old son William dies of malaria in Italy. The Shelleys now have no living children, though Mary is pregnant with their fourth.

August 1819—**Starts 2nd novel:** Mary begins writing her second novel *The Fields of Fancy*, later retitled as 'Mathilda', about a father's incestuous love for his daughter. It is not published until 1959, 140 years later.

November 1819—**4th baby:** Mary Shelley gives birth to the couple's son Percy Florence, their only child who will survive infancy.

June 1822—**Miscarriage:** Mary almost dies due to a miscarriage, but Shelley nurses her and prepares ice baths to stop the bleeding.

July 1822—**Percy Bysshe-Shelley dies:** Percy Shelley, aged 29, drowns in the Gulf of Spezia while sailing. Widowed at 25, with a toddler son, Mary keeps his heart wrapped in silk in her writing-case and decides to earn a living by publishing her own writings and those of her late husband.

February 1823—**Mary publishes 'Valperga':** Mary completes her historical novel, *Valperga*, set in mediaeval Italy, but addressing contemporary issues.

August 1823—**2nd edition of** *Frankenstein: Or, A Modern Prometheus*: The second edition of Frankenstein is published, edited by William Godwin. This time, Mary W. Shelley is acknowledged as the author. This edition is usually not used as an authoritative text, due to William's editorial changes. Mary also sees the first play adaptation of her work, *Presumption; or The Fate of Frankenstein*, at the English Opera House. Mary did not receive any royalties from the play but its popularity increased sales of the second edition.

June 1824—**Shelley's poems halted:** Mary publishes her late husband's poems but is forced to stop sales when her father-in-law threatens to cut off his £100 per year support to her and her son.

February 1826—**Mary publishes** *The Last Man*: Mary's post-apocalyptic futuristic plague novel, 'The Last Man', set in the late 21st century, contains fictionalised versions of the deaths of Percy Shelley and Lord Byron and questions their Romantic political ideals. It receives poor reviews.

October 1831—**3rd edition of** *Frankenstein; Or, A Modern Prometheus*: Mary publishes a third, revised edition of Frankenstein, which removes the division into three volumes. Critics debate whether Mary's edits make the narrative less radical, in response to earlier reviewers. This edition is the text used by most schools.

February 1851—**Mary Wollstonecraft Shelley dies:** Mary dies aged 53 in London after a long illness, possibly caused by a brain tumour.

Preface

A Welcome to The Reader

By Sara Karloff

Dear Reader,

If you are a horror fan, a history buff, a culture student, a movie-goer, an avid reader or a combination of any or all of these you are about to have the reading adventure of a lifetime. Just a glance at the Table of Contents of this collection will entice you and convince you that you are holding a true gem in the palm of your hands.

My father, Boris Karloff, was a voracious reader. He was often asked to write Introductions for books, edit books, and even to critique books. But his primary passion remained *READING* books. As an indication of his knowledge, he was at one time even a celebrity guest on the TV program *The $64,000 Question,* choosing the category 'Children's Fairy Tales', and he won the $32,000 level! He knew his stuff!

Although the film *Frankenstein* did not follow Mary Shelley's literary master-piece precisely, the sheer wonderment of her accomplishment at such a young age and the magnitude of its impact on generations of philosophical, religious and social thinking is almost without equal.

This book will take you down a thought-filled path of exploration of that very impact.

Enjoy your journey.

Sara Karloff
https://www.karloff.com/

Introduction

Leslie S. Klinger

Examining Frankenstein

Mary Wollstonecraft Shelley's *Frankenstein; Or. The Modern Prometheus* has been hailed by many as the first modern myth. Myths, in this context, are stories that ask (and answer) questions critical to all human beings from the moment of birth: Who am I? Can I change who I am? Who are my parents? What should I expect from them? Where did I come from? Will I die? What does it mean to die? Can I avoid dying? How shall I live among others? What do I have a right to expect from others? What should they expect from me? Of course, not all myths address all of these—but *Frankenstein* does.

We should not be surprised that a 16-year-old conceived of this seemingly immortal novel. Between ages 16 and 18, when she completed the book, MWS had already experienced the death of her mother, the neglect or disinterest of her father, romance, travel abroad, the suicide of her lover's wife, marriage, and the death of a child. She had read widely and was exposed to a multitude of poets, writers, politicians, scientists, and assorted thinkers. Every person wants answers to the mythic questions— and by 16, any intelligent person will have formulated some version of those answers. MWS had the genius to imagine a being who was a blank slate, a Creature with no family, who nonetheless sought to address all of those questions.

It is this mythic quality that gave MWS's maiden effort at fiction its *plasticity*, the surest sign of a true myth. From the moment of conception, *Frankenstein* been reshaped, revised, twisted, and distorted to serve others' agendas. Even Mary Godwin, as she was at the time she began work on the story that would become the novel (though she called herself "Mrs. Shelley"), reworked the manuscript with significant input from her soon-to-be husband Percy Shelley. After the initial 1818 publication, her father, the celebrated author and political thinker William Godwin—without her permission—edited it for an 1823 edition—the first English edition, by the way, to credit her as the author. MWS herself, of course, edited it again for the 1831 edition.

As early as 1821, however, the novel had already been loosely adapted into the stage play *Presumption; or The Fate of Frankenstein* (without the playwright Richard Brinsley Sheridan bothering to seek MWS's consent). This was only the beginning of two centuries of the remolding and repackaging of *Frankenstein*, into the hundreds of dramas, films, recordings, novels, short stories, cartoons, graphic novels, games, and images that followed. Along the way, the characters' genders and ages have been altered, they have been transported around the world and into deep space, and they have existed in dozens of eras, from the prehistoric past to the far distant future. Yet none of those changes affect the fundamental issues that *Frankenstein* addresses—only the context.

Until the second half of the twentieth century, with few exceptions, scholars limited their studies to "classics," works that were widely recognized as serious efforts to address the foundational questions of life. Popular fiction (today, still stigmatized as "genre" fiction) was largely ignored. Yet any well-drawn portrait of a life necessarily depicts the subject's struggle to seek the answers to the mythic questions. Such a portrait will mirror aspects of our own lives—whether written by an 18-year-old or an 80-year old. The intent of the author—that is, whether the book was designed to be a moral lesson or a simple diversion—is irrelevant. Only slowly, however, did scholars begin to recognize these merits in works as successful as Robert Louis Stevenson's *Strange Case of Dr. Jekyll and Mr. Hyde*, the stories of Sherlock Holmes, and Bram Stoker's *Dracula*. Instead, these stories were generally dismissed as examples of "sensation fiction," mere entertainments.

It took nearly 150 years for many to recognize that *Frankenstein* merited careful study. By now, just as *Frankenstein* has been adapted and recast in virtually every medium and every age, so too has it been examined under a wide variety of lenses and dissected using textual, psychoanalytic, feminist, Marxist, and historical criticism, variations of which are on display here. Furthermore, the aspects of MWS's story that have been examined are just as various: What does *Frankenstein* teach us about our own genders and identities? The responsibilities of parents? The line between life and death? Our responsibilities to others in our communities? The process of learning and its appropriate scope? These issues affect not only the dynamics of families and communities; they also have larger implications for the political struggles between citizen and state, colony and empire, worker and employer.

Did MWS intend her novel to be read as a treatise on education, a criticism of the judicial system, an argument for Irish nationhood, or a polemic against capitalism? Probably not—but others have found the book to be such, another example of the essential plasticity of myth. MWS's intentions for her "hideous progeny" are irrelevant in judging the worth of her effort. The Italian writer Italo Calvino remarked, "A classic is a book that has never finished saying what it has to say." Here are fresh and original readings of Mary Wollstonecraft Shelley's timeless work. Each essay demonstrates that so long as humans do not change fundamentally, *Frankenstein*'s power will remain undiminished by age.

Foreword

Lisa Morton

Until far too recently, women writers have been largely invisible in the horror genre (and, to a lesser extent, science fiction). Anthologies were routinely published with few or no women contributors, their names were often missing from awards lists, and men on social media and discussion forums routinely and authoritatively proclaimed that women couldn't write horror. This in spite of the fact that the single most influential author in the genre's history was a woman.

Fortunately things have begun to change over the last decade or so, but we still have a long way to go. That's one reason why I'm happy to provide the foreword for this fine collection of papers that discuss how a teenage girl named Mary Wollstonecraft Shelley helped define a literary category.

As women have stepped out into horror's spotlight more and more since the turn of the millennium, more academic and pop culture works have explored Frankenstein and its extraordinary creator, but this book explores the mythology surrounding both the creation and the creator in some fresh and enlightening ways. Most admirers of Frankenstein probably know that Mary Shelley's mother, Mary Wollstonecraft, was a pioneering feminist whose *A Vindication of the Rights of Women* (1792) is now considered one of the first great feminist tracts; and those same fans probably know about Mary Shelley's unconventional lifestyle and the creation of *Frankenstein; or, the Modern Prometheus* that took place in the Villa Diodati during the grey summer of 1816. But have those same readers (and viewers, given how far Frankenstein's reach has extended into other media) ever considered how the story of Victor Frankenstein's undead monster may have impacted other parts of our culture?

Of course we know how Frankenstein has permeated the arts, and that its message of the horrors of scientific arrogance has been copied over and over, but what are other ways in which this classic has shaped us? The essays in this book explore the story's philosophy, sexuality, and delineation of the human body. That scientific arrogance is examined from the fresh angles of consent and incipient misogyny (you have to love the phrases "unconsenting dead" and "the Pretty Dead Girl trope"); the author's own rebellions are contrasted with what she put down on paper. How is motherhood reflected in the novel? What about the human propensity for criminal behaviour? How much of Frankenstein is really memoir? Did Frankenstein (and Mary Shelley's other speculative fiction novel, *The Last Man*) also define the interaction between horror and tragedy? Loss, confused identity, body horror, and catharsis are all prodded in these pages, and what comes forth gave me fresh appreciation for Mary and her monster.

In case anyone should ask, "Do we really need another scholarly look at Frankenstein?" my answer will be not only a resounding, "Yes, we do," but will add, "We especially need these books." Many of those of us who happen to identify as women horror writers consider Mary Shelley something of a spiritual mother, and this book beautifully and insightfully honours and extends that.

Editor's Preamble

On the 10th of September, 1797, the world lost one of the greatest thinkers of her time. The woman, who had given birth just ten days earlier, struggled to survive puerperal fever, a devastating illness affecting many women in the 18th century. Without washing his hands, the doctor cut away the placenta, introducing the disease that ultimately took her life. Miraculously, the child survived, and the incident became one of the most notable births in literary history. Why? The woman was revolutionary feminist and radical activist Mary Wollstonecraft (1759-1797), who published A Vindication of the Rights of Men (1790) and A Vindication of the Rights of Woman (1792) against the backdrop of the French Revolution and anti-slavery movement. The child would grow to be the legendary Mary Shelley (1797-1851), who at just 19 years old penned Frankenstein; or, The Modern Prometheus (1818), one of the most famous contributions to literature the world has ever seen. While they didn't know it at the time, both women changed not only the way we think of and view the world, but also who we are as a society.

Mary Wollstonecraft was a major thinker during the Enlightenment period, laying the groundwork for continued women's rights movements. Written in response to Edmund Burke's Reflections on the Revolution in France (1790), a defence of constitutional monarchy, aristocracy, and the Church of England, Wollstonecraft's A Vindication of the Rights of Men (1790) attacked aristocracy and advocated republicanism, something unheard of during that time. Her second major work, A Vindication of the Rights of Woman (1792) is one of the earliest works of feminist philosophy. In it, Wollstonecraft argues that women must be given the same education commensurate with their position in society, advocating that women, as the primary educators of children, were essential to the nation. She suggested women also be educated to be 'companions' to their husbands rather than having pure domestic roles in the household.

Today, many scholars argue her work prioritised middle-class families, and question her bias through her condescending tone toward those uneducated (such as the lower class). However, it must be remembered Wollstonecraft was a product of her time. Such thoughts were revolutionary, much like her daughter's thoughts in the future.

Other pioneering women would follow in Mary Wollstonecraft's footsteps, including Octavia Hill (1838-1912), best known for co-founding the National Trust, and tireless campaigner on issues ranging from the importance of education to the protection of green spaces in and around London; Lidia Poët (1855-1949), the first modern female Italian lawyer whose disbarring led to a movement allowing women to practise law and hold public office in Italy; Emmeline Pankhurst (1858-1928), the British political activist who organised the early suffragette movement; Marie Carmichael Stopes (1880-1958), who introduced modern sex education and birth control to British women regardless of their age, marital status, or wealth; and Elizabeth Garrett Anderson (1836-1917), the first British female doctor who ushered a parliamentary act to formally permit women to be medics. These women paved the way for modern revolutionaries, including Rosa Parks (1913-2005), a black American activist in the civil rights movement, best known for her refusal to vacate a row of four seats in the coloured section in favour of a White passenger; Ruth Bader Ginsburg (1954- 2010), the American attorney, judge and an associate justice of the American Supreme Court, who transformed the legal landscape, particularly for women.

Like her mother, Mary Shelley was a pioneer in her own right. Though Frankenstein is infused with elements of the gothic and supernatural, English science fiction author and anthologist Brian Aldiss (1925-2017) regards it as the first true science-fiction story. The story was conceived in 1816, the 'Year Without A Summer' (named so due to a long, cold, and dark winter after the 1815 eruption of Mount Tambora, blanketing the skies in darkness).

One day, while visiting Lord Byron and John Polidori at the Villa Diodati by Lake Geneva in Switzerland, Mary (then 18), her step sister Claire Clairmont (of whom Byron had an affair), and her future husband

Percy Bysshe Shelley, joined the group. As it was too dark and cold to venture outside and enjoy the outdoor activities they had planned, the group sat around a log fire in the villa telling ghost stories from a German translation of the French 'Fantasmagoria'. After a while, Byron proposed they each write their own ghost stories, as it was an easy way to make money during that time. Initially, Mary struggled, unable to settle on a topic, until one night, their discussion turned to the nature and principles of life.

"Perhaps a corpse would be re-animated, "Mary noted, "galvanism had given token of such things." Retiring after midnight, Mary lay awake in bed, unable to sleep, her imagination possessed by what she described as "grim terrors of her waking dream."

> "I saw the pale student of unhallowed arts kneeling beside the thing he had put together. I saw the hideous phantasm of a man stretched out, and then, on the working of some powerful engine, show signs of life, and stir with an uneasy, half vital motion. Frightful must it be; for supremely frightful would be the effect of any human endeavour to mock the stupendous mechanism of the Creator of the world."

The next morning, Polidori began writing what would later become The Vampyre (1819), the first modern vampire novel; Clairmont started a now-lost story titled The Idiot; and Mary began writing what she assumed would be a short ghost story. However, with Percy's encouragement, she expanded the tale into the first draft of a novel, what would come to be known as Frankenstein; Or, The Modern Prometheus. The novel was printed under a pseudonym, with many assuming authorship to Percy, although Scottish historian, novelist, poet, and playwright Sir Walter Scott (1771-1832) guessed it was Mary. During this time, there were only a few women able to make a living through writing, with the idea considered unbecoming for a woman. Once it was revealed to be written by Mary, most contemporary reviewing journals were shocked. How could a young woman of 18 write something so dark? How did she become so intellectually knowledgeable about science and politics? (Perhaps forgetting her mother was Mary Wollstonecraft).

While Frankenstein is marketed as speculative fiction, it's an incredibly political novel, with some attributing the Creature as an example of the French revolution. As American university lecturer Stephen Behrendt commented: "What happens when something that's created for all the right reasons — to try to benefit humanity, to learn the secret of life — is not what you're hoping for?" However, the novel can also be seen as an expression of loss and loneliness. Mary grew up never experiencing her mother's love, instead being raised by a woman she regarded as a 'wicked' stepmother. The loss of four out of her five children (including a miscarriage that almost killed her) undoubtedly contributed to the themes of death and loss within the novel (later expanded upon more dramatically in her 1826 dystopian science fiction novel The Last Man (1826)).

More than 200 years later, Frankenstein is a benchmark in modern gothic literature, its legacy inspiring countless authors even to this day. Several famous books probably wouldn't have existed without it. Like Frankenstein, The Strange Case of Dr Jekyll & Mr Hyde (1886) by Robert Louis Stevenson explores the horror of unleashing the primitive id— the instinctual component of personality that is present at birth, and the source of all bodily needs, wants, impulses, and desires. Better known as the source for the film Bladerunner (1982), Do Androids Dream of Electric Sheep? (1968) by Phillip K. Dick also asks us to consider what makes us human. Are man-made androids capable of empathy? Is empathy what makes us human? Never Let Me Go (2005) by Kazuo Ishiguro challenges the traditional definition of what it means to be human. Do genetically engineered clones possess higher intelligence? Are they capable of experiencing emotion? Undoubtedly, these themes will continue to appear in literature, for as humans, we continue to question our humanity. Many of us question the meaning of life, and where we fit within society. Is the number 42 really the answer? We may never know.

Many know Frankenstein as nothing more than a horror story. However, those who realise it quickly realise it's much more. A Vindication of Monsters is a collection of essays expanding Mary Wollstonecraft and Mary Shelley's profound impact on modern society, exploring themes of isolation, loss, motherhood, feminism, history, medicine, literature, film, and philosophy, including memoirs relating to the achievements and contributions of both women and their impact on current societal issues. They add to the prevailing longevity of 'Frankenstein' within modern culture, and its importance as one of the most impactful literary achievements to this day. It is my hope that by reading these essays you will truly realise the impact both Mary Wollstonecraft and Mary Shelley had on the world, and the power they continue to wield to this day. The selected authors—a mixture of known and relatively unknown—all contribute to a deeper understanding of both women, the world in which they lived, and the world in which we live today.

"And now, once again, I bid my hideous progeny go forth and prosper."—Frankenstein; or, The Modern Prometheus. (1818).

– Claire Fitzpatrick, March 2023.

ADAPTATIONS

Literary adaptations have existed since the 1800s. Some of the earliest examples come from the work of French illusionist, actor, and film director Georges Méliès, who pioneered many narratives and techniques in the early days of cinema. In 1899, he released two adaptations - 'Cinderella' based on the Brothers Grimm story of the same name, and 'King John', the first known film based on the works of Shakespeare. His more popular known films *A Trip to the Moon* (1902) and *The Impossible Voyage* (1904), both involving strange, surreal journeys in the style of Jules Verne, are considered among the most important early speculative fiction films - usually considered science fiction with a fantasy approach.

While there have been several adaptations of her novel, Shelley attended the first theatrical adaptation, the 1823 'Presumption; or, the Fate of Frankenstein', a play in three acts. This play introduced the now well-known assistant Fritz, who does not appear in the novel, however, is now commonly known as Igor in other adaptations. Writing to her and her late husband's friend Leigh Hunt, Shelley said of the play:

'Frankenstein had prodigious success as a drama & was about to be repeated for the 23rd night at the English opera house. The play bill amused me extremely, for in the list of dramatis personæ came, ——— [i.e., the Creature] by Mr T. Cooke: this nameless mode of naming the un{n}ameable is rather good. On Friday Aug. 29th Jane[,] My father[,] William & I went to the theatre to see it. Wallack looked very well as F[rankenstein]—he is at the beginning full of hope & expectation—at the end of the 1st Act. the stage represents a room with a staircase leading to F['s] workshop—he goes to it and you see his light at a small window, through which a frightened servant peeps, who runs off in terror when F.

exclaims "It lives!"—Presently F himself rushes in horror & trepidation from the room and while still expressing his agony & terror ——— throws down the door of the laboratory, leaps the staircase & presents his unearthly & monstrous person on the stage. The story is not well managed—but Cooke played ———'s part extremely well—his seeking as it were for support—his trying to grasp at the sounds he heard—all indeed he does was well imagined & executed. I was much amused, & it appeared to excite a breatheless eagerness in the audience.'

Since the 1823 production, there has been a wealth of literature inspired by 'Frankenstein', including its dark origins. The novel originated in 1816—the year without summer. It is also known as the year science fiction was born. When the volcano Mount Tambora erupted on the Indonesian island of Sumbawa, almost 100,000 people died, and a massive amount of volcanic ash was sent into the atmosphere, affecting weather patterns around the world. Europe's skies were dark, and some foretold the end of the world. However, it was the perfect environment to inspire a Gothic tale and ruminations on the magic of scientific discovery. This magic appears in several popular science fiction novels, inspired by 'Frankenstein' and its themes. The idea of unintentionally engineering our destruction appears in the popular 1968 science fiction novel 'Do Androids Dream of Electric Sheep?' by Phillip K. Dick. Better known as the source material for the film 'Bladerunner' (1982), it explores many similar themes, in particular, the idea that creatures created by humans, in this case, androids are capable of feeling empathy. And, more specifically, if having empathy is what makes us human. Furthermore, Robert Louis Stevenson's now-legendary novella 'The Strange Case of Dr Jekyll and Mr Hyde' (1886) could not have been written without 'Frankenstein'. Stevenson wove many contemporary issues into his story, beginning with well-known case studies of dual personality, but they gained resonance when he mixed in evolutionary fears and the recent notion of the violent criminal as an atavistic reversion to our species' brute past. Like Shelley, Stevenson explored the horror of unleashing the primitive *id* and the horrors that would ensue.

Today, adaptations and inspirations of Mary Shelley's novel continue in all mediums, as explored in the following essays. In 'In His Eyes Our Own Yearning: Seeing Mary Shelley and Her Creature', Nancy Holder explores Mary Shelley's own vision of the Creature, and compares it to the various reimaginings within other artistic adaptations. In 'Mary

Shelley and the World of Monsters', Rob Hood examines the reimaginings of 'Frankenstein', asking why writers, directors, and creatives alike are continuously drawn to the source material for inspiration for their work. In 'Beauty and the Grotesque: Bernie Wrightson's Lifelong Obsession with Frankenstein's Monster', Michele Brittany delves into the world of comics, exploring Bernie Wrightson's lifelong obsession with Shelley's Creature; Donald Prentice Jr explores how beauty is viewed in 'An Articulation of Beauty In The Film Mary Shelley's 'Frankenstein', giving an overview of director Kenneth Branagh's approach to depicting the nature of bodies, specifically those deemed 'beautiful' against those deemed 'ugly'. In 'The Maker Remade: Mary Shelley In Fiction', Matthew R Davis explores works including Mary Shelley as a character in herself, including, but not limited to, 'Gothic' (1986), the much-divisive British psychological horror film directed by Ken Russell reimagining the 1818 famous visit to Lord Byron in Villa Diodati by Lake Geneva; and 'The Modern Prometheus', a 1997 episode of 'Highlander: The Series' (1992-97) in which the immortal Methos and friend of Duncan MacLeod is a guest at the stay, his death and later resurrection the fictionalised inspiration for 'Frankenstein'.

These essays explore novels and films which would not exist without the source material, celebrating the enduring legacy of Mary Shelley's boundless imagination, and the continued reimaginings of her classic story on film.

In His Eye Our Own Yearning: Seeing Mary Shelley and Her Creature

Nancy Holder

"All art is self-portraiture."
Guillermo del Toro

THERE ARE A HANDFUL OF IMAGES so popular they are recognized the world over. A magnifying glass, deerstalker cap, and curved pipe symbolize Sherlock Holmes. A white-haired, white-bearded man in a red suit and red-and-white stocking cap is Santa Claus. A fanged vampire in a cape is Count Dracula. And a figure with a flat-topped head, green skin, and bolts extending from his neck is "Frankenstein." The nuances of these cultural references have faded over time as mainstream audiences ignore the novels, short stories, poems and illustrations that provided their source material, or origin stories. [1] These one-note representations are so ubiquitous in the landscape that they don't excite curiosity about how they came to be; like street signs and trash cans, they are just "there."

Each of these icons was born at a fixed point in the imagination of a creative individual, and in this list, the current quickie image of the Frankenstein Creature departs the most radically from author Mary Shelley's original vision. Or so we assume. Mary Shelley's description of the Creature offers generous space for the reader to conjure their own version. And close readers have, with an astonishing variety of results.

To begin with, what did Mary's monster look like to Mary herself?

---

1 "Frankenstein Becomes a Star," 29

Frankenstein for Halloween. Public domain.

In her 1831 introduction to the novel, Mary Shelley tells the story well known to Shelley "followers" of the Year without a Summer at Villa Diodati and Lord Bryon's challenge to write a ghost story. She had a waking dream:

> ...the pale student of unhallowed arts kneeling beside the thing he had put together....the hideous phantasm of a man stretched out... Frightful must it be... What will terrify me will terrify others, and I need only describe the spectre which had haunted my midnight pillow. [2]

2 Shelley, 2018.

When the Creature comes to life, there is no mention of green skin, short black hair atop a flat head, or bolts: "His yellow skin scarcely covered the work of muscles and arteries beneath, his hair was of a lustrous black, and flowing; his teeth of a pearl whiteness; but these luxuriances only formed a more horrid contrast with his watery eyes."

In *The New Annotated Frankenstein*, Klinger notes that Shelley included the line "The dissecting room and the slaughterhouse furnished many of my materials" and says, "The clear indication is that the creature contains parts of the bodies of animals."[3] An examination of the SP Books facsimile edition of Mary Shelley's original manuscript notebooks; the 1818 version of the novel; the Thomas Text (a hand-edited copy of the novel given by Mary Shelley to her friend, Mrs. Thomas); and the 1831 version reveals that Mary Shelley retained "slaughterhouse" in her drafts and versions of the novel. Coupled with the also-retained statement that Frankenstein decided to make his creation eight feet tall, Klinger argues (and I concur) that Frankenstein could not, and did not, limit his "parts inventory" to items derived from normal human beings (English soldiers—males— tended to be five feet tall in 1800).[4] Although Shelley makes no mention of animal parts in her physical descriptions of the Creature, the clues she gives about his appearance, aside from the passage about his face and hair, and mentioning that he was well-proportioned, are scanty and vague.

Two schools of thought concerning this lack of detail point to Shelley's explanation that *Frankenstein* was the result of a challenge to write a *ghost* story. Thus, they argue, the Creature is nothing more than a non-existent vapor, i.e., a phantom. Approaching the novel psychoanalytically, scholar Arthur Belfant argues in *Frankenstein, the Man, the Myth, the Monster* that Victor Frankenstein created the Creature out of his "fevered imagination," and that he himself committed all the murders he blames on the Creature, in order to avoid an incestuous marriage with his sisterlike cousin/childhood friend, Elizabeth.[5] David Ketterer, in *Frankenstein's Creation*, suggests that Captain Walton either imagined or falsely reported the entirety of Victor Frankenstein's deathbed narrative aboard his ship due to extreme stress or madness, or to cover up a murder(s) of his own.[6]

Early images of the Creature in the novel and the first spate of stage

---

3 Klinger, 81.
4 Klinger, 78
5 Klinger, 272
6 Klinger, 273

plays did not emphasize the fact he had been stitched together from materials gathered not only in "charnel houses and vaults," but from "dissecting rooms and slaughterhouses." In *Presumption,* the first version theatrical adaptation of the novel (mounted in 1823), the actor who played the unnamed monster wore green and yellow greasepaint, a blue body stocking, and a toga. The blue body stocking became "a tradition." [7]

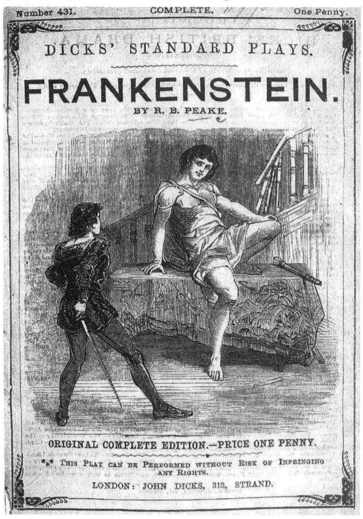

The first recorded play version of the 1818 novel, running in 1823 for 37 performances, spawning fourteen other play versions.

---

7 Frayling, 89

FRANKENSTEIN

By the glimmer of the half-extinguished light, I saw the dull, yellow eye of the creature open; it breathed hard, and a convulsive motion agitated its limbs.

... I rushed out of the room.

Page 43.

London: Published by H. Colburn and R. Bentley, 1831.

Frontispiece, 1831 version. Public domain

The first cinematic image of the creature emphasized his hideousness by distorting his features:

Creature from Thomas Edison's film
studio, 1910. Public domain.

The iconic version now accepted as the "real" image was created for the
1931 film version directed by James Whale. The makeup was created by Jack
Pierce for Boris Karloff, the actor who played the "Monster," and trademarked
by Universal Pictures. Karloff in makeup became the "face" of Mary Shelley's
Monster we know today. British cultural historian Sir Christopher Frayling is
quoted as saying: "It's a globally recognized brand. It's like Dracula has to wear
a cloak, Sherlock Holmes has to wear a deerstalker [cap] . . . and Frankenstein
has to look like Boris Karloff." [8] American author Paul Ruditis clarifies the
green tint of the makeup was employed to make the Creature look "deathly
pale" onscreen. In the accompanying image of a lobby card and Universal's
film posters, his skin is yellow. But the marketing department started using

8 Laneri, *New York Post.*

the green skin, and it stuck. [9] The *New York Post* article about the makeup asserts subsequent efforts to portray the monster differently have typically not succeeded at the box office, but neglects to mention the National Theatre's version starring Jonny Lee Miller and Benedict Cumberbatch, who alternated the role of Creature and creator, released as two films.

Universal Studios; Realart re-release,
Public domain, via Wikimedia Commons

Donald F. Glut's *The Frankenstein Catalog*, published in 1984, counted over 650 appearances of the Creature in his own and others' comic books. [10] Since then, many more have been added, including pairing him with Buffy the Vampire Slayer's character the vampire Angel in two comics: *Angel vs. Frankenstein I (The Heir)* and *II*. [11] My graphic novel, *Mary Shelley Presents Tales of the Supernatural*, contains five versions of the Creature in four styles: the look created by artist Amelia Woo, who, directed by publisher Debbie Daughetee, adhered to Mary Shelley's description of the Creature, and variants done in four styles: horror, steampunk, romantic, and manga.

---

9 Ruditis, p. 156
10 Klinger, p. 331
11 Byrne, 2009

Mary Shelley Presents Tales of the Supernatural. Used with permission.

Two of the most celebrated illustrated versions are Lynd Ward's *Franken-stein* and *Bernie Wrightson's Frankenstein*. Lynd Ward, working in his signature woodblock style, created fifteen full-page illustrations and numerous smaller illustrations throughout. In the description of a first edition for sale from Ken Sanders Rare Books: "This is Lynd Ward at the height of his powers, and this gothic novel may be the perfect avenue for his work" [12].Ward was inducted into the Will Eisner Award Hall of Fame in 2011 (the Eisner Awards are the "Academy Awards" for achievement in American comics).

Bernie Wrightson was inducted into the Will Eisner Award Hall of

---

12 *AbeBooks*

Fame in 2014. His Frankenstein project contained forty-three of his intended fifty pen-and-ink illustrations, which took him seven years of intermittent labor to produce. Previously, he had tried to shape Shelley's text into graphic novel form but found the attempt unsatisfying. Of his process for the illustrated version, he explains:

> Always I tried to be as specific and as detailed and as faithful to the text (at least as well as I could interpret it) as possible. This was my first real attempt to completely serve the story and the author's intentions, and I found it challenging as hell! I really tried to see the story as Mary Shelley wrote it, trying to stay in her time, in her "head-space", if you will, and not tart it all up or force my own gloss onto it, and at the same time, try to stay true to my own style and my own sense of drama and picture making. [13]

Wrightson and comics and print author Steve Niles also created the four-issue comic book series *Frankenstein Alive Alive!*. A new series, *Frankenstein: New World* is a Mike Mignola-based Hellboy crossover currently running at Dark Horse Comics. IPI Comics has announced the forthcoming release of *The Frankenstein Monstrance*.

The year 2018 marked the two hundredth anniversary of the first publication of the novel, and pastiches, nonfiction retrospectives, comic books, graphic novels, films, and even pop-up books have continued publication. Among the best pop-ups are *Frankenstein: A Pop-Up Book* by Sam Ita, and David Hawcock's fantastical pop-ups in *Frankenstein: A Classic Pop-Up Tale*. Ita's *Frankenstein* is more stylized: Victor Frankenstein is dressed in modern attire and wearing glasses; the creature is brown and wears a bowl cut of brown hair. This is a sharp contrast from Wrightson's pursuit of Mary Shelley's "headspace."

But what *was* Mary Shelley's headspace? In *Mary's Monster*, poet and artist Lita Judge uses evocative free verse and affecting black-and-white watercolor spreads to foreground how Mary Shelley herself was haunted by the many tragedies in her life, beginning with the death of her mother; her rejection by her beloved father; the suicides of her half-sister and her husband's first wife; the deaths of all but one of her children; and finally, of the death of Percy Shelley himself. For Judge, the Creature is an expression of Shelley's sorrow and longing; but at the end of the book, the Creature, who at this point looks quite human, promises to keep alive

---

13 Niles, 2022

Shelley's faith that the act of artistic creation will bring about a more loving and just world. [14]

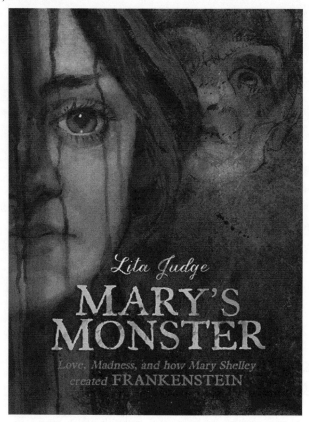

Mary's Monster: Love, Madness, and How Mary Shelley Created FRANKENSTEIN by Lita Judge. Used with permission.

The last sentences in Del Toro's introduction to *The New Annotated Frankenstein* offer the same response as, like Judge, he compares the heavy emotional weight of Mary Shelley's life to that of her most famous literary creation. He describes the pathos of her creative labors as she persevered through tragedy upon tragedy, abandoned and bereft, and expresses his hopes her equally unloved Creature may "recognize in our eyes his own yearning"—for connection—and in that recognition, "…if only for a moment, we will not feel alone in the world." As a Shelley disciple and a writer myself, I find this the most satisfying "monstrous" self-portrait of all.

14 Judge, p. 298

The Maker Remade: Mary Shelley In Fiction

Matthew R. Davis

YOU KNOW HOW THIS STORY GOES. We all do—we've seen it restaged on page and screen time and time again. But before we get started, let's recap this evergreen tale once more for good measure.

1816: The Year Without a Summer. Fleeing from the disapprobation of respectable society, high on the fizzing cocktail of heady youth and burgeoning talent, a group of English outcasts takes up lodgings at the Villa Diodati, huddling beside the rain-shrouded lake beneath a sky darkened by volcanic eruptions. With no better way to pass the time than telling ghost stories, they decide to write their own...and from this resolution would spring not only an early exemplar of vampiric fiction, but also one of the most revisited, retold, and remixed tales in human history.

Had they known this, the party no doubt would have assumed the breakout successes attributable to Lord Byron and Percy Bysshe Shelley, an infamous celebrity poet and a passionate ascending one, both scandalous figures of their time for their free-loving, atheistic ways. Surely none could have imagined that John Polidori, a wan physician of twenty, would produce '*The Vampyre*' and establish the trope of the suave, well-to-do bloodsucker that foretold Stoker's Dracula and his myriad imitators...let alone that eighteen-year-old Mary Wollstonecraft Godwin, self-effacing mistress of Shelley and mother to his infant son William, would hit upon an idea so literally galvanic that popular culture would never be the same again. The philosophical and aesthetic themes of '*Frankenstein; or, the Modern Prometheus*' still resonate to this day, over two centuries later—and both Victor Frankenstein himself and the creature he animated from dead tissue are among the most well-known fictional characters in the human canon.

But there was another knock-on effect of this success, one that could not have been anticipated at the time any more than the longevity of that grisly morality tale. For not only did Mary Shelley, at the age of twenty, introduce the world to two of its most notable and evergreen fictional characters...but in time, she went on to become one herself!

It's not hard to see why people have remained fascinated by Mary over the years, especially in the late 20th and early 21st centuries when cultural and artistic boundaries have widened to swallow everything and regurgitate it all in new and anachronistic forms. A brief *precis* of Mary's life makes her sound like a tailor-made YA Gothic princess: born to a philosopher father and feminist mother, she fell in love with a bold young poet as a teenager, allegedly lost her virginity to him on her mother's grave, travelled with him and other young creatives to an exotic locale at a dark and dramatic time in human history, wrote and published *'Frankenstein'* by the age of twenty and thus invented science fiction, continued to write and persevere through the tragic deaths of friends, family, and three of her four children, and after her own passing was discovered to have kept her dead husband's heart wrapped in one of his poems. Little wonder people sell T-shirts bearing the legend *Mary Shelley is My Homegirl* or simply her name written in a classic heavy metal font, right? Described in such reductive terms, she already sounds like a somewhat fantastical and decidedly fictional character.

But the truth is...well, *slippery*. No sooner does the well-meaning biographer set pen to page than the subject of their work becomes idealised, elided, unreal—even a simple paraphrasing or omission changes the tone, manipulates the truth, makes fiction of fact. Therefore, even the most slavishly exacting of texts creates of Mary Shelley a patchwork Creature of sorts, sewn together from biased accounts whether first-, second-, or third-hand—even her own journals could be accused of sanitising the story, of flushing dirty blood from deep wounds, since she can't possibly express the entirety of herself in mere words and has in any case left out details she would wish no casual reader to know. Still, it's not the numerous biographies and studies we're looking at here, but rather the more expansive approach that fictional works have taken to this remarkable woman's life, loves, tragedies, and victories...the *true* fictions, you might say.

Over the past few decades, classic writers such as Doyle, Poe, and Stoker have often been recast as the heroes of genre mashups and self-aware pastiches, an increasingly popular strain of story that invariably includes elements alluding to, or even allegedly inspiring, their famous works— but Mary, ever the trailblazer, got in on the action early. Her first fictional appearance was in James Whale's *'Bride of Frankenstein'* (1935), somewhat based on aspects of her own novel, where she takes part in a drawing-room conversation with Shelley and Byron sometime after her most famous novel's publication. Byron helpfully gives us a brief recap of Whale's *'Frankenstein'* (1931)—a severely truncated and bowdlerised version of the book—and longs for the story to continue, whereupon Mary obliges by presenting the events of the sequel. It's a rather metafictional approach for its time, since it overtly frames both films as fantasies while giving us a fabricated version of the real woman behind it all...and then, of course, there's the fact that both Mary and the iconic Bride are played by the same actress, Elsa Lanchester. Mary Shelley creates Frankenstein, who then builds a woman in his creator's own warped image; the fictional creation makes of his real progenitor an even more fantastical homage. An auspicious beginning to Mary's second life as a patchwork woman woven from threads of truth, conjecture, and outright fantasy.

By this point, *'Frankenstein'* was well-established as a cornerstone text of the speculative arts—repeatedly adapted for the stage in the 1820s, it had already been filmed three times before Universal's run of films from 1931-1948 made the Creature a pop culture icon—but interest in its origins seems to have increased apace in the 1980s. Though Shelley biographies had been written before then, many more, such as Anne K. Mellor's *'Mary Shelley: Her Life, Her Fiction, Her Monsters'*, began to appear toward the end of the decade—and no less than three films tackled the birth of *'Frankenstein'* in as many years.

First out of the gate was *'Gothic'* (1986), written by Stephen Volk and directed by Ken Russell. That infamous visionary took the script's laudanum- and opium-induced delirium to heart and presented events at the Villa Diodati as a weird and memorable melange of sex, drugs, psychological breakdowns, and hallucinations. Mary is played here by Natasha Richardson, who imbues her role as the Diodati club's most sensible and conservative member with natural intelligence. The plot shatters and reforms with the impossible logic of a fever dream, and while Mary's magnum opus is scarcely referred to throughout, it is foreshadowed in an array of visions. The film seems to argue that her main inspiration for *'Frankenstein'* was the heartbreak and helplessness caused by the death of her first child, that her famous doctor wields a power over death she wishes could be hers. While the story is dominated by bigger names playing broader roles (Gabriel Byrne as Byron and Julian Sands as Shelley), Mary quietly assumes a position at the heart of the tale and reminds us why these events orbit *her* in our history rather than her florid companions.

With the floodgates now opened, this notable period found itself addressed on celluloid *twice* in 1988. '*Rowing with the Wind*' begins as a decadent historical romance that plays fast and loose with established facts, but then scriptwriter Gonzalo Suárez introduces an element of the odd by having these famous characters each encounter Mary's sallow Creature, who foresees their deaths and is later present when they occur. This film is an ensemble piece, and hence Lizzy McInnerny's Mary is somewhat sidelined here, overshadowed by the performances of charming fop *du jour* Hugh Grant as Lord Byron and supermodel ascendant Elizabeth Hurley as Claire Clairmont. Like '*Gothic*', the film ends with Mary convinced the group's gruesome fantasies have created a dark force that has doomed them and their loved ones. The second Shelley film that year, '*Haunted Summer*'—adapted by Lewis John Carlino from a 1972 novel by Anne Edwards, adding yet another layer of artifice to proceedings—saw Mary played by the always-interesting Alice Krige and it also focused on the bohemian romance of that fateful year, with less outlandish results.

Depictions of Mary's pivotal vacation took on a more fantastical bent in the following decades. "The Modern Prometheus", a 1997 episode of '*Highlander: The Series*' penned by James Thorpe, sees Mary portrayed by thirty-something Tracy Keating—a somewhat odd choice to play a teenager—as she's inspired to write her magnum opus after witnessing Lord Byron, here an Immortal, rise from the dead upon taking his first Quickening. In '*Nightmare on Joe's Street*', a 2006 episode of cartoon caper *Time Warp Trio*, she's voiced by Vickie Papavs and helps the prepubescent heroes return the Creature to her mind whence he has escaped; here, she's presented as a brave woman more willing to chase after monsters than Percy, who faints at the sight of her creation, and Polidori, who instead uses the heroes' time-travelling Book to turn Byron into a vampire. Amusingly, Mary foreshadows this act by suggesting that Polidori make his '*Vampyre*' a charming aristocrat rather than a one-legged fishmonger!

Veronica Bennett's 2005 novel '*Angelmonster*' focuses on Mary's deep but doomed relationship with Percy, something also addressed at length in Tony Thompson's '*Summer of Monsters*' (2014). This latter takes its time in arriving at Lake Geneva, beginning with Mary at the age of three and following her through to her affair with Percy and then that critical summer, ending as she wakes from her inspirational nightmare and puts pen to page. The Mary we see here is the fieriest iteration yet: she constantly defies and insults her mother-in-law, mouths off to anyone fool enough to cross her, and blackens Polidori's eye when he declares his love for her. (Poor Pollydolly; he's always depicted in fiction as a crashing bore, and when he's not creeping on Mary, he's usually coded as a queer simp for Byron.)

This new and bolder spirit gets another showing in the biopic' *Mary Shelley*' (2017), written by Emma Jensen. Here, Mary is played by the elfin Elle Fanning—possibly the first actress of the correct age to essay the role—and, as to be expected from a modern production, she is given to display more backbone and feminist grit. Again, she thumps a man when he makes an unwanted advance on her—here it's poor old Thomas Hogg, historically recorded as Mary's good friend and possibly even her lover. She's less patient with Percy's dissolute shenanigans and delivers a few righteous, passionate speeches on independence and recognition. Fittingly, this film was shot by Haifaa al-Mansour, Saudi Arabia's first female director and a controversial figure in her own right for her focus on women's issues in a society not known for its progressive gender politics. One imagines the real Mary—and her mother—would heartily approve.

A more true-to-fact Mary is one of six characters revolving around the central conceit of the Mount Tambora eruption that caused 1816's weather variations in Guinevere Glasfurd's '*The Year Without Summer*' (2020). This book doesn't take '*Frankenstein*'s conception as its *raison d'être*, though it is addressed; rather, its central themes are climate change, refugees, and working-class revolution, which Mary's chapters touch on from a distance. The woman we meet here is understandably prickly, bored as ever of Polidori's manners and annoyed that Percy is dragging a breastfeeding mother across Europe with little thought to their amounting debts and hardships.

Given her role as mother of the entire science fiction genre, it's no surprise to discover that Mary has turned up in one of its most beloved franchises—and more than once! *Doctor Who* first visited the Villa Diodati in Big Finish's 2009 audio adventure '*Mary's Story*' by Jonathan Morris, in which Mary (voiced by Julie Cox) witnesses a future version of the Doctor reviving his younger self with lightning before she agrees to travel with him in the TARDIS. She joins the Eighth Doctor for a trilogy of stories released in 2011: *'The Silver Turk, The Witch in the Well',* and *'Army of Death'.* The first, written by Marc Platt, features an automaton capable of playing musical instruments and games of skill; this turns out to be a Mondasian Cyberman, planting a seed in Mary's mind which will, of course, later bloom into *Frankenstein.* An alternate timeline plays out in the TV series, where Maxine Alderton's *'The Haunting of Villa Diodati'* (2020) finds our intrepid author teaming up with the Thirteenth Doctor—aptly, the show's first canonical and controversial female incarnation; again, she finds her inspiration in an encounter with a Cyberman. Lili Miller's Mary is the main guest star of the episode and ultimately refers to the unfinished villain Ashad as "this modern Prometheus", clearly influenced to write her legendary tale by the events she's just witnessed.

At this point, let's branch off to tackle another strain of Shelley stories—those which take a big step away from the endless Summer riffs and into sheer fantasy. Let's start with *'Frankenstein Unbound',* both the book by Brian Aldiss (1973) and the film scripted by director Roger Corman with F.X. Feeney (1990), two quite different entities. In a way, the movie is more sedate; the lead here is Doctor Buchanan, whose work on a superweapon accidentally sends him back in time from 2031 to 1817, where he meets Victor Frankenstein shortly after the murder of his little brother William. So far, so fictional...but in the courtroom, Buchanan encounters a young woman taking notes on the case: Mary Shelley herself, here portrayed by Bridget Fonda. The two flirt a little, but Mary ultimately refuses to get involved with either Buchanan or the plot, which then proceeds to go off the rails completely and ends in a far-flung future ravaged by the doctor's weapon. Aldiss's book, on the other hand, has an elder statesman flung through a rift from 2020 to 1816, where this aged and unlikely paramour manages to seduce and bed eighteen-year-old Mary! (Apparently, Aldiss had always harboured a bit of a crush on Shelley, long dead or not. One has to wonder what she would make of such audacity!)

2019 brought us Jeanette Winterson's entertaining SF novel *'Frankisssstein: A Love Story',* which contrasts the classic Mary with a contemporary surgeon by the same name—this one a trans man who goes by Ry Shelley and supplies body parts to their lover Victor Stein, a charismatic scientist and driving force in the field of transhumanism. The real Mary would surely be interested in this remarkable book's overarching themes of artificial intelligence and (re)creation, though she might be taken aback by some of its fringe concepts, which include cryopreserved heads, sex dolls, and a journalist called Polly D whom we first meet complaining about her new dildo uploading explicit footage to her Facebook page! Here, past Mary goes to Bedlam to meet with Victor Frankenstein, who may or may not have been created by her writing, and she also converses with Ada Lovelace—Byron's only legitimate daughter and an early advocate of computing—about the future of machine intelligence.

Turning to the realm of comics, we find Mary appearing in Grant Morrison's 'The Invisibles' (1994-2000), where, alongside Percy and Byron, she becomes tangentially involved with the titular organisation. She also pops up in 'The Wicked + The Divine', wherein she and her most famous friends are embodiments of gods; in the one-off issue '1831', written by Kieron Gillen, she is Woden, the only deity to resist a plan to resurrect their fellow god Hades by raising him as a familiar Creature. This being kills Lucifer (Byron) and Morrigan (Percy) before she sacrifices her life to stabilise it—whereupon it takes on her appearance, the Creature becoming its ultimate creator. By naming itself for the year that Mary addressed events at the Villa Diodati in a new foreword to the reprinted 'Frankenstein'—this edition becoming the accepted text after some minor revisions to the 1818 version—"1831" could be seen as another version of Mary setting the record straight, for all that it is even more fantastical than 'Frankenstein' itself!

Equally implausible is 2019's somewhat inevitable 'Mary Shelley Monster Hunter', written by Adam Glass and Olivia Cuartero-Briggs. Mary and her usual coterie—minus Polidori, here replaced by her other stepsister, the tragic Fanny Imlay—are invited to stay with one Victoria Frankenstein, who has created a patchwork Adam to help her fight against a misogynist world that barred her from medical practice. This story is told in a manuscript discovered below the floorboards of Mary's final home and finds her in fine fighting form, openly feminist and trying to warn the world through a fictionalised account of her adventure that eclipses the true one; here, she is also responsible for the education of the Creature, who—despite his necrotic nature—appears to have somehow survived into the present day. This trend of classic authors getting involved in action-based adventures that riff on their published canon has even crossed over to TV: the same year, it was announced that Roberto Aguirre-Sacasa—known for his reinvention of the '*Archie*' gang and '*Sabrina the Teenage Witch*', among others—was set to produce a series called '*The Shelley Society*', featuring Mary as leader of a team of notable contemporaries such as Percy and Byron who would tackle supernatural threats…including, naturally, her own Creature. No more has been heard of this idea since, for which we might conceivably be grateful, but Mary's comic adventures continue—as if to prove that her example is not fading but only growing brighter, 2020 saw her featuring in no less than *three* graphic novels.

'*Mary Shelley Presents: Tales of the Supernatural*' is an anthology series that sees author Nancy Holder adapting four classic 19th-century horror stories by Elizabeth Gaskell, Edith Nesbit, Margaret Strickland, and Amelia B. Edwards, each presented as a comic strip and then the complete original text; the tales are introduced by Mary Shelley and her Creature in a style that has been compared to '*Tales from the Crypt*', though one hopes they refrain from making groan-worthy horror puns. At the other end of the spectrum is '*Her Life Matters: or Brooklyn Frankenstein*' by Alessandro Manzetti and Stefano Cardoselli, which introduces us to Frankie, a gentle giant created in 1977 New York City by Dr. Jamaica Foxy, whose only other friend is a smart thirteen-year-old called Mary Shelley; when Foxy goes missing in a city plagued by the Son of Sam and white supremacists, Frankie's mission of mercy soon becomes one of violent revenge. And then there's a story that features not Mary, but rather one of her descendants—Brea Grant's '*Mary: The Adventures of Mary Shelley's Great-Great-Great-Great-Great-Granddaughter*' tells the charming story of a modern Shelley, this one a sixteen-year-old goth and the latest in a long line of lady writers, who evinces little interest in authorship but discovers her famous ancestor has passed down an ability to heal monsters.

Lifting up female authors who have been largely overlooked in favour of their male counterparts; being folded into indictments of institutional racism and misogyny; fighting monsters and punching bad guys and winning hearts. Over two hundred years after the publication of her best-known work, Mary Shelley is still firing the imaginations of creators and fans the world over. So, here's a question: what do we think would *she* make of all this?

Generally remembered as a modest woman, one wonders if Mary might be a little embarrassed, even offended by some of the depictions that have entered the public consciousness…but it should be noted that she was no shrinking violet. "She is singularly bold, somewhat imperious, and active of mind," said her father, William Godwin, of Mary in her teenage years. "Her desire of knowledge is great, and her perseverance in everything she undertakes almost invincible." How could such a person *not* be thrilled to see her memory and achievements echoing through the ages? As the daughter of a prominent feminist (her mother, Mary Wollstonecraft, published '*A Vindication of the Rights of Woman*' in 1792) and a radical philosopher (William Godwin is regarded as a forefather of the anarchist movement), Mary would surely be pleased to see her work and her life inspiring the development and tastes of women and men both—to see her name and image held up as an early feminist icon and alternative culture queen—to know that her first novel reshaped the public consciousness to a degree that its characters and themes will forever cast a long shadow over everything that comes after.

But for all that Mary might appreciate the future's appropriation of her as a feminist icon, she might rightly feel slighted that most of her media appearances revolve around a brief window of her life rather than the broad scope of it: a time when she was a teenager, a mistress, a muse, a believer in free love who may or may not have indulged in the practice herself…a naïve creative who stumbled into the path of a lightning bolt of inspiration. She might question the dubious feminism of focusing on such a narrow sliver of a woman's life, when she presents as her most young and beautiful self and also, initially at least, as an adjunct to male genius; but then, surely she could appreciate the true feminism of lionising a woman who is marginalised for being female, young, and a mother and supporter rather than an outright prodigy, only to reveal unsuspected talents that will long outshine those of the more entitled male participants on that long-ago Swiss shindig.

She would certainly take issue with the manipulation of her life's facts, especially when it involves her children. Writers have excluded them from works as they see fit: '*Summer of Monsters*', for example, finds Mary falling pregnant for the first time at the Villa Diodati, when in truth she'd already lost one premature daughter and had recently given birth to William. She would be affronted by strangers picking over her tragedies and applying meaning to them from such a distance, might well be mortified by the words these scribes have put into her mouth. She might even see parallels between her father's biography of her mother, '*Memoirs of the Author of the Vindication of the Rights of Woman*'—whose frankness about Mary Wollstonecraft's free-ranging love affairs and suicide attempts led to widespread condemnation of her character upon its publication—and the slew of works about her own life, both fiction and nonfiction, that have revealed her own private details to the world…though, it should be noted, with no deleterious effect upon her reputation.

And what might she make of the genres she helped to define? Science fiction is usually traced back to her seminal work, and yet, despite its founder's gender, the field has often been plagued by misogyny and other bigotries; horror, already in rude health before her landmark novel, has sometimes fallen prey to the same afflictions. Perhaps she would appreciate the irony of being heralded as a figurehead of fields oft claimed by exclusionist men, or perhaps she'd be appalled that the world *still* faces the same divisions now as it did in her time. But she might take some comfort in the knowledge that she is remembered at all, let alone so well and so reverently; that she has inspired so many girls to become wise and worldly women who tread boldly in her stead; that, as a fictional character alongside her driven doctor and his tormented creation, she's fighting against ignorance to this day, her electric words weapons in this war for hearts and minds…and if the above examples are any measure, Mary Shelley will continue to fight for reason and equality as long as humankind continues to dream.

Mary Shelley and the World of Monsters

Robert Hood

MARY SHELLEY'S *Frankenstein; Or, The Modern Prometheus*, is a remarkable work of fiction. It is now considered one of the earliest and most influential novels in the post-gothic, modern horror genre, and it has been seen as the first genuine science fiction novel as well. Initially dismissed by many of the literary elite of the time as the equivalent of modern-day pop culture , it has since become a subject of wide academic scholarship and is recognised as a significant work of literature. The novel is still in print 200 years after its first appearance, and the name 'Frankenstein' is more or less known by everyone, even if they've never read the book itself. It turned out to be more meaningful than was at first assumed. As Leslie S. Klinger puts forward in his excellent *The New Annotated Frankenstein*, '… the story of Victor Frankenstein and his creature is the first myth of modern times, an early nineteenth-century version of the epics of more distant times. By focusing on science rather than the gods or the angels, *Frankenstein* could not have been written earlier; it broke new ground and resonated in a way the classic myths it encompasses no longer do.' Today, 'Frankenstein' continues to be reimagined, with new works either based on the novel, or adapting similar themes. So, why are people continuously drawn to this gothic tale? And what are some notable adaptations of the story of this famous monster?

It is one of the more famous misconceptions of our cultural zeitgeist that 'Frankenstein' is the name of the monster. The monster itself had no name, simply known as 'the creature'. However, the misconception is not completely clueless. There is a symbiotic relationship between creator and created the cultural phenomenon of *Frankenstein* epitomizes at all levels. The creature was created by Dr. Victor Frankenstein, a 'God' who then disavowed his creation until it was driven into taking revenge for its alienation and estrangement from humanity.

The Road to Frankenstein

The story of Frankenstein and his creature was the work of Mary Wollstone-craft Godwin, who was by late 1816 the wife of the famous romantic poet, Percy Bysshe Shelley. Earlier that year, Mary, Shelley, Lord Byron, Dr John William Polidori and Mary's stepsister Claire Clairmont spent the summer known as 'the year without a summer' in Villa Diodati at Lake Geneva in Switzerland. The poor weather was caused by the eruption of Mount Tambora in Indonesia, which sent clouds of volcanic ash across the planet. Endless stormy weather and the boredom of isolation led to an amusement by which each would (theoretically) write a supernatural tale with which to scare the company. Only two fulfilled their role in the pact; Polidori wrote *The Vampyre* (said to have inspired Bram Stoker's Dracula)), and Mary produced *Frankenstein; or, A Modern Prometheus* (as it would be known when her tale later grew into a novel). Mary's stepsister Claire also started a story titled *The Idiot*, though it was never published and has since been lost. The story of that notorious summer has been filmed several times and books have been written about it.

The film *Bride of Frankenstein* (1935) includes a sequence referencing it, while Ken Russell's typically eccentric *Gothic* (1986) gives it full attention, allowing the movie to go from a more-or-less 'historic' beginning and working its way into a nightmarish, phantasmal ending—the result of their opium-fuelled evenings. Another film taking a similar approach even further is writer/director Nora Unkel's *A Nightmare Wakes* (2020), in which Mary's miscarriages, the hardships in dealing with her love of Percy, the presence of her stepsister, Claire, Lord Byron and Polidori are presented as a sort of fever dream—all of which leads her to write *Frankenstein*.

The story behind their summer at Lake Geneva has also been written in novel form. Anne Edwards' *Haunted Summer* (1972) is an effective story, told by Mary. Edwards did considerable research in writing it, using anything available in the British Museum, including Mary's journals and letters, and Byron's as well. She was also helped by the custodians of Chillon Castle, an island castle located on Lake Geneva. As a result, the novel has an authoritative feel about it. More recently, Tony Thompson wrote *Summer of Monsters: The Scandalous Story of Mary Shelley* (2014). It is advertised as being for young adults but there is no reason adults wouldn't enjoy it just as much, or even more so. Beginning in 1801 when Mary was 4 years old, the book follows her life growing up with her father, teaching herself and developing a love of reading, is sent to live in Scotland by Godwin, after a while goes back to London, fights with her father, meets Percy and then sees him often until she and Claire go off with him, meet with Lord Byron and Polidori, and they all go to Cologny, where they end up in Villa Diodati. As the endless rain and violent weather kicks off, they decide to each write a scary "ghost story". The book ends as Mary writes the beginning of her story, which would become her most famous work. *Summer of Monsters* is easy to read and a well-thought-out novel, at least as an introduction to Mary's history.

In the 1831 edition of *Frankenstein; or, A Modern Prometheus*, Mary described a dream she claimed was the inspiration for the story:

> I saw the pale student of unhallowed arts kneeling beside the thing he had put together. I saw the hideous phantasm of a man stretched out, and then, on the working of some powerful engine, show signs of life, and stir with an uneasy, half vital motion. Frightful must it be; for supremely frightful would be the effect of any human endeavour to mock the stupendous mechanism of the Creator of the world. (*From the introduction to the 1831 edition of the novel*).

This theme—of the scientist who usurps God's prerogative as creator and is punished for it when his 'unnatural creation' turns on him—is the one most frequently attached to the Frankenstein tale: know your place in the divine scheme or else. However, this is, in many ways, an over-simplified, emphasized in the second and third editions of the novel through various additions to the text. Originally, the horrors caused by the creature could more correctly be attributed not to the hubris of Frankenstein's success in creating life, but rather to his failure to take responsibility for his work. After all, it is after he is overcome with horror and rejects the creature that it truly becomes a monster and vows revenge upon him.

The Birth of Frankenstein and his Creature

Frankenstein; or, The Modern Prometheus was first published in 1818 (in three volumes), again in 1829 (in two volumes, with Mary Shelley recognised as the author for the first time, and with some editorial changes by William Godwin), and then in 1831 as a single volume, with changes by Mary. This last is the most common version used for publication now, though some of the endless runs of the novel only occasionally indicate which version has been used. It was at first published without Mary's name given as the author, probably because it was thought that appearing under a young, unknown woman's name would put potential readers off. Despite her famous father, the acclaimed journalist and political philosopher William Godwin, and equally famous mother Mary Wollstonecraft, a leading political activist known for her infamous book *A Vindication of the Rights of Women*, early readers falsely attributed the novel to Percy Shelley, whose name appeared in an introduction to the first 1818 version.

The extent of Percy Shelley's influence on the writing and the editing of the novel has been much argued about, even to the extent some claim that Percy wrote it, not Mary. There is no doubt Percy helped Mary to edit it, as did her father, William Godwin (for the 1819 version). Most writers get friends or editors to do an edit before their work is published. But I suspect those who see it as something that Mary couldn't possibly have written are driven by a belief that 19-year-old girls in her time couldn't possibly write such a strange, intelligent and effectively horrific story. Clearly, they don't know women too well.

A thoughtful examination of the novel reveals the story as strongly autobiographical. Like the creature, Mary was not brought up by a mother, as Mary Wollstonecraft died of a fever in the days after giving birth to her. Mary was brought up by her father, and her life with Godwin and her stepmother Mary Jane Godwin was often tense and distant, a relationship like that of the creature with Frankenstein, if less extreme. Despite her tense relationship with her father, William Godwin encouraged his daughter's education, continuing even when his wife questioned the point. As Leslie S. Klinger points out in the foreword of his *The New Annotated Frankenstein*, these personal elements, Percy Shelley's obsession with 'the natural and occult sciences', Mary's loss of three infant children, and 'her strong feelings about her father's and Percy's pursuit of ideas to the detriment of family', her animosity towards her stepmother, whom she referred to in a journal entry as 'a woman I shudder to think of', all play a part in indicating the book as definitively the work of Mary Shelley.

Through the ages, academic books and articles have explored Mary's work, searching through her diaries and letters, as well as anything written by those around her. Mary wrote about her activities often, though some of her diaries were lost while she, Percy and Claire were travelling around Europe (Mary released two travelogues in 1818 and 1840). Nevertheless, Mary's diaries are available for those seeking to learn about her, and thus many academics have written about her and her work. From somewhere in the 19th century and into the 20th century, *Frankenstein* scholarship took off in a big way. Since then, many articles have appeared. In 2018, *Science Fiction Studies*—an academic journal which publishes scholarly articles and book reviews on science fiction—brought out a special issue on *Frankenstein's* 200th anniversary. The articles are worth reading.

Additionally, various academics have written about Mary's life, such as *Mary Shelley: Her Life, Her Fiction, Her Monsters*, by Anne K. Mellor (1988) and *In Search of Mary Shelley: The Girl Who Wrote Frankenstein*, by Fiona Sampson (2018), and *Romantic Outlaws* by Charlotte Gordon (2015). Such academic works have inspired other writers (and many filmmakers) to produce fictional versions of how Mary came to write *Frankenstein*.

The Ongoing Appearances of Frankenstein

Over the years, *Frankenstein; Or, The Modern Prometheus* found fame via nearly every form of entertainment. Early on, the story of *Frankenstein* was seen in live theatres, the first in July 1823, written for the stage—as *Presumption; or, The Fate of Frankenstein*—and was followed by seven different versions in 1823 alone. Others followed. A more recent theatrical version appeared in 2011 when Benedict Cumberbatch and Jonny Lee Miller starred in a Broadway show, taking turns in playing Frankenstein and the Monster. They gave a different approach to each of the characters.

Once 'cinema' appeared, the story blossomed. Starting from 1910 when Thomas A. Edison created the first cinematic version, directed by J. Searle Dawley, there have been many more films that intended to do a sort-of film of 'Frankenstein' and others that draw on the general idea of the original story. Many more produce stories that feature the monster but not how he was born. The most common known appearances are Universal's *Frankenstein* (1931) and *Bride of Frankenstein* (1935), both directed by James Whale, with Boris Karloff as the creature. In these, which remain effective pieces of cinema and undoubted classics, it is Karloff's subtle and emotional performance as the monster that stays in the memory. Continually the dialogue tells us that it is the attempt to usurp God's role that is the problem, but we see the desperate loneliness and despair on Karloff's heavily made-up face and empathise with the monster as it seeks revenge on the one who made and then rejected him.

Aware of the monster's popularity, Universal continued making more *Frankenstein* films: *Son of Frankenstein* (1939), *Ghost of Frankenstein* (1942) and *House of Frankenstein* (1944). Naturally, these bore less and less relevance to Mary Shelley's novel as the series moved on. They always featured Frankenstein's monster however, but he began sharing the films with other well-known 'monsters', such as Dracula (played by Bela Lugosi) and the Wolf Man (played by Lon Chaney Jr. who would later play the Frankenstein monster in *Ghost of Frankenstein*). Eventually, the Monster (this time played by Glenn Strange) even appeared in the comedic film *Abbott and Costello Meet Frankenstein*, along with Dracula (still played by Bela Lugosi) and the Wolf Man (still played by Lon Chaney Jr.). It was an effective joining of two cinematic tropes as the comedians react to the monstrous imagery and the plots that go with it. By this time, the name 'Frankenstein' was more connected to the monster than it was to its creator. As well, the monster as played by Karloff has become the most known appearance of the monster in people's minds, so much so that the father in *The Munsters* TV comedy series (1964-1966) looks just like him.

In the late 1950s when UK Hammer films started their successful run of horror films—and thus revitalised the whole horror film industry—the story they started with was *Frankenstein*. At this point, the focus moved away from the monster. As they couldn't get the rights to use the make-up designs of the Universal version, this governed the nature of their film sequence by forcing a concentration on the doctor (played by Peter Cushing) rather than his creation. The Doctor, therefore, becomes the monster. Cushing was already a well-known face in horror films, and he brought good acting into what turned into an ongoing success.

The director of the series was Terence Fisher, and his *Frankenstein* films, taken as a whole, are a wonderful variant of the novel. The films are *Curse of Frankenstein* (1957), *Revenge of Frankenstein* (1958), *Frankenstein Created Woman* (1967), *Frankenstein Must Be Destroyed* (1969) and *Frankenstein and the Monster From Hell* (1974). There were two other Frankenstein films made by Hammer, but they weren't directed by Fisher and are not part of the sequence: *The Evil of Frankenstein* (1964) and *Horror of Frankenstein* (1970) (this latter is a more humorous variant).

Often, it's Hammer's Dracula films that get the kudos, but the Franken-stein films are Fisher's greatest achievement, taken as a sequence rather than as individual films. There is a definite development that takes place, with Dr Frankenstein himself as the central protagonist (rather than, as in the Universal Frankenstein films, the monster). His character is developed as the series progresses—with the relative moralities being explored and themes of class structure and responsibility high on the agenda. Often Cushing's Frankenstein is seen as a man out of his time, misunderstood and hounded by the ignorant, and conservative scientific community. He is up against a particular (and failing) social background—a class system based on aristocratic privilege—that is fighting for its life, though what he offers in return is another pragmatic, amoral, and equally self-serving power structure , and in the end self-destructive: he represents the modern scientific world that replaces the old feudal one. In one of the films, he even becomes his own creation! Again, the Doctor becomes the monster.

The last film (*Monster from Hell*) was finished mere weeks before the director's death and represents a pessimistic view. The fact that it is set in a madhouse and that the only sympathetic characters are a young deaf and dumb woman who is raped by the inmates and exploitatively destroyed, and the monster, who is torn to bits by the mob, says heaps about what Fisher felt about the moral possibilities inherent in modern sensibilities.

At any rate, these films were the beginnings of modern horror films and set the basis for what was to come.

In the 1970s and the 1980s, there was a rush of great and terrible exploitation horror films based on *Frankenstein*—often Italian. One of the best is Andy Warhol's *Flesh for Frankenstein* (1973), directed by Paul Morrissey according to the credits, though really it was Italian exploitation master Antonio Margheriti who did the deed. Filmed in 3D, no less, it is real "liver-in-your-lap" stuff (as one critic described it), and totally immoral.

But it doesn't finish there. Assorted rather bizarre variants arose, featuring the Frankenstein character, with Frankenstein and/or his creature in the old West, such as *Jesse James Meets Frankenstein's Daughter* (US-1966; dir. William Beaudine), and *I Was A Teenage Frankenstein* (US-1959; dir. Herbert L. Strock), which uses the monster as a metaphor for socially conditioned teenage acne … um, make that angst … and its attendant traumas. Lots of others have appeared, right up to the present. As well, I must mention *Frankenhooker* (US-1990; dir. Frank Henenlotter), in which a young man, whose girlfriend has been killed by a lawn mower, scavenges body parts from hookers—who die through ingestion of a sort of explosive form of cocaine—to rebuild her. Unfortunately, he ends up creating a female Frankenstein monster with a strong sexual appetite and streetwalker clothes (as well as stitches). Another oddity is Tim Burton's *Frankenweenie*, which started life in 1984 as a short, animated film about a boy and his re-constructed dog. It became a full-length film in 2012.

Like these, many films don't remake the earlier films or offer versions of the novel, so much as riff on their most iconic elements. *The Monster Squad* (US-1987; dir. Fred Dekker), for example, an entertaining horror-comedy pastiche from the 1980s, re-envisioned all the Universal monsters (including the Creature from the Black Lagoon) in a film in which the monster teams up with a gang of kids to defeat Dracula's world-conquering ambitions. *Van Helsing* (US-2004; dir. Stephen Sommers) does something similar, though less successfully.

One of the most bizarre references to *Frankenstein* is in *Frankenstein Conquers the World* (Japan-1965) (aka Furankenshutain tai chitei kaijû Baragon) by *Gojira* (*Godzilla*) director Ishirô Honda, and its sequel, *War of the Gargantuas* (Japan-1966) [aka Furankenshutain no kaijû: Sanda tai Gaira] (also by Honda). These are *daikaiju eiga*, Japanese giant monster films, of course. The premise is this: A Nazi ship carries the still-beating heart of the monster to Hiroshima for study toward the end of the War, just before the American bomb is dropped (the story sees Frankenstein's monster as the Bomb) In the ruins, post-bomb, the heart is eaten by a scavenging vagrant kid, who subsequently grows larger and escapes into the backwoods. Eventually, he grows to the size of Godzilla (thanks to all that mutagenic radiation) but retains his passing resemblance to Frankenstein's monster. One Dr. Who episode directly draws upon the Frankenstein story in *The Brain of Morbius*. In this Tom Baker story, a renegade Time Lord scientist is building himself a new body from the corpses of unfortunate space travellers who happened upon his planet. The four-part story is gothic and dark, with a definite Hammer horror vibe. It was 'banned' from being screened on Australian television during the show's ordinary, children's timeslot.

Several more occur during the adventures of the Eighth doctor within the Big Finish audiobooks. *Mary's Story* was the fourth story in the audio anthology, *The Company of Friends*, a culmination of a nearly decade-long gag suggesting the Doctor's friendship with Shelley. Other audio adventures with Mary Shelley include *The Silver Turk*, *The Witch From The Well*, and *Army of Death*. The Thirteenth Doctor also encounters Mary Shelley in *The*

Haunting of Villa Diodati, however the episode does not acknowledge the Eighth Doctor's previous adventures with Shelley.

Homages to *Frankenstein* are often homages to the 1931 *Frankenstein* film rather than to the story itself. Mel Brookes' *Young Frankenstein* (1974) is essential viewing for its referencing and loving parody of the Universal film tradition of *Frankenstein*. It is a comedy with many unforgettable moments. At least it's hard to forget the scene in which the monster is shown to the world, on stage singing (rather weirdly) "Puttin' on the Ritz". TV series such as *X-Files* are willing enough to pay their dues. Season 5, episode 5, "Postmodern Prometheus", filmed in lovely black-and-white, is a tribute to the Universal film tradition, but also (as the title suggests) explores some of the novel's moral/ethical issues. Other TV mini-series/telemovies have attempted to extend the book itself. *Frankenstein: The True Story* (1973) concentrated on the doppelgänger aspect of the tale (as in the view that the monster *is* the doctor or a reflection thereof). It was a two-part TV version, with James Mason as John Polidori, Leonard Whiting as Victor Frankenstein, Michael Sarrazin as the Creature, Nicola Pagett as Elizabeth, David McCallum as Henri Clerval, Tom Baker as the Sea Captain, and many more. As suggested, it doesn't follow the linear narrative of the novel, however, the middle isn't too far off. Another is *The House of Frankenstein* (1993), which takes a sort of modern corporate slant—Frankenstein meets Dallas, as it were. And writer Dean Koontz tried to get a Frankenstein TV series going, but failed and turned his proposal into a book series instead. To me, one of the most effective is the 1994 film, *Mary Shelley's Frankenstein*. The director, Kenneth Branagh, plays Frankenstein, with Robert De Niro as the Creature and Helena Bonham Carter as Elizabeth. Naturally, it adds elements and events which aren't in the novel, which many critics find too overdone. Nevertheless, it follows Mary's basic storyline. And then, behind them all, there's always *The Rocky Horror Picture Show,* with Dr Frank-N-Furter a comedic take on Victor Frankenstein. *'In just seven days I'm gonna make you a man'*...

Direct remakes and direct references to *Frankenstein* abound even to the present, however, its influence stretches far beyond, encompassing the totality of its influence. Out of curiosity, I asked the Internet Movie Database (IMDb) to list all films and TV shows that were related to *Frankenstein,* and it gave me 215 movies and TV shows. Some of them looked dodgy—and some were even dodgier—but not too many. Then,

I asked IMDb to gather TV Episodes, Music Videos, Podcast Episodes, and Video Games, and it gave me 700 of them. I'm afraid I didn't look through them. Life is too short, as the Frankenstein monster will tell you. It reminded me of a short story by Kim Newman, titled 'Completist Heaven' in *The Mammoth Book of Frankenstein* (edited by Stephen Jones). In it, the narrator comes across a new group of channels. Among them, he finds one called Channel 1818 and a film titled *Frankenstein Meets the She-Wolf of the SS*, one he's never come across before. As he looks through other movies on the Channel—all about Frankenstein—he comes upon an unending number of them. *King Kong Meets Frankenstein. The Marx Brothers Meet the Monsters. John Ford's Fort Frankenstein. Frankenstein Meets the Space Monster: The Director's Cut. David Cronenberg's Frankenstein. Martin Scorsese's Frankenstein. Batman and Robin Meet Frankenstein*…and so on, with no end. He realises his mind is the screen on which these Frankensteins perform, and he must watch them all. Endlessly.

But for us, there are still films with a similar plot to Frankenstein, which is never outwardly mentioned. Science fiction films depicting robots, cyborgs or mutants turning against their creators—or deal with themes of scientific responsibility—often carry more than a passing resemblance to *Frankenstein*. An obvious example is *The Colossus of New York* (US-1958; dir. Eugène Lourié), in which a scientist moves his friend's mind into the body of a huge robot so his knowledge should not be lost. Yet to list even the most significant would keep us going for a long time. Enough that in an age where scientific research can earn the epithet "Frankenscience", the Frankenstein story still carries not just cultural importance but also a warning the central issues of the story are more vital than ever.

Books Using Frankenstein

It is not only films and plays which have made Frankenstein and Mary's novel the base of their own stories. For example, *The Memoirs of Elizabeth Frankenstein*, by Theodore Roszak, investigates the origin of Frankenstein's wife Elizabeth, who is killed by the creature, on the night of their marriage. The book is narrated by her, as told to the Arctic explorer Robert Walton, as she reveals her past as a member in a circle of 'cunning women', guardians of long-forgotten pagan healing arts. As Roszak says, 'In speaking through Elizabeth Frankenstein, the character Mary Shelley modelled after herself, I hope at last to give Mary the voice she was not free to adopt in her own day.'

Another is Victor Kelleher's *Born of the Sea*, a tale following the rise and life of the female 'creature' Victor Frankenstein created at the original creature's request, but which he had thrown into the sea, regretful he had given in to the creature's demand of a female companion. In Kelleher's novel, the abandoned female creature, who rises from the sea, tells her tale to Mary Shelley, the latter on her deathbed. With a beautiful face and grotesque, almost masculine body, she calls herself Madeleine Sauvage, and goes on a journey searching for Frankenstein, longing to find peace and wanting to belong. However, she, like the Creature, gives way to violence and revenge. *Born in the Sea* is both moving and sometimes brutal. And yes, Frankenstein's first creature has a part to play in it…

The Casebook of Victor Frankenstein by Peter Ackroyd manages to bring both the history of Mary, Percy Shelley, Lord Byron, and John Polidori in Villa Diodati, and adds Victor Frankenstein with a touch of Dr Jekyll and Mr Hyde.

Many books tell tales of the Monster, beyond the plot of Mary's original book, often set far beyond the Monster's 'birth'. Robert J. Myers wrote two novels telling the story of how Frankenstein's illegitimate son (Victor Saville) learns he is the son of Dr Frankenstein. He is led to go to America where he comes face-to-face with his father's Monster and learns about his dark plans for humanity. The books are *The Cross of Frankenstein* and *The Slave of Frankenstein*.

Dean Koontz's *Frankenstein* series, in which Victor Helios (once named Victor Frankenstein) has a nihilistic plan to remake the future of mankind. Deucalion, Helios' first attempt at replicating life, sets out to stop him. The five books are: *Prodigal Son*, *City of Night*, *Dead and Alive*, *Lost Souls* and *The Dead Town*. The 'Monster' isn't a bad guy, but Frankenstein is.

Donald F. Glut—a writer of books, comics, and film scripts, as well as being film director, musician, actor…and anything else you can think of— has written 14 Frankenstein novels under the title *The New Adventures of Frankenstein*. The books are: *Frankenstein Lives Again*, *Terror of Frankenstein*, *Bones of Frankenstein*, *Frankenstein Meets Dracula*, *Frankenstein vs. the Werewolf*, *Frankenstein in the Lost World*, *Frankenstein in the Mummy's Tomb*, *The Return of Frankenstein*, *Frankenstein and the Curse of Dr. Jekyll*, *Tales of Frankenstein*, *Frankenstein and the Evil of Dracula, and Frankenstein: The Final Horror!* The stories might not be as profound as the original, but as the titles suggest, are a lot of fun.

Many other books use *Frankenstein* to drag the reader in, by using the universally known story of the dangers of man meddling in nature. A good example is the Arabic book *Frankenstein in Baghdad* by Ahmed Saadawi (2013 in Arabic and 2018 in English). In the US-occupied Baghdad, hit by an unending war, Hadi collects body parts and creates a large corpse as a way of telling the government to give the victims a proper burial. But the corpse disappears, ensuing a wave of murders, committed by a monstrous criminal. When the criminal is shot, it doesn't die, and Hadi comes to believe the monster is his fault, echoing similar feelings of Victor Frankenstein.

Finally, some books offer Frankenstein-related short stories. *The Frankenstein Omnibus*, edited by Peter Haining (1994) is an excellent collection that begins with a short story by Mary Shelley herself. *The Reanimated Man* (1863) tells of Roger Dodsworth, whose body was found under an avalanche, 'a human being whose animation had been suspended by the action of the frost'. It happened in 1654. But he was resuscitated in 1863. Another one by Mary is *Transformation* (1830), in which a handsome young man exchanges his body for that of a deformed dwarf. The Omnibus includes stories under three headings: The Prototypes, The Films and The Archetypes, with stories by Herman Melville, H.P. Lovecraft, Jimmy Sangster, Theodore Sturgeon, Arthur C. Clarke, Robert Bloch, Kurt Vonnegut, Jr., Brian Aldiss, Harry Harrison, and many unknown, especially those from the early years. But it's all fascinating.

The final thing I'll do is draw attention to the incorporation of *Frankenstein* in the comic book medium. Marvel Comics had an ongoing series featuring Frankenstein, first in *The Monster of Frankenstein* and then in *The Frankenstein Monster* (1973-1975). However, the Monster had appeared in some earlier single comics created by Stan Lee and Joe Maneely. Since then, he has appeared here and there, turning up with Spider-man, Hulk and the Agents of S.M.A.S.H., and in *Legion of Monsters*. In DC Comics, he first appeared in Detective Comics #135 (May, 1948) but was later worked by Len Wein and ended up fighting Superman, Batman, and the Phantom Stranger. Since then, he has turned up all over the place, most recently in the series *Frankenstein: Agent of S.H.A.D.E.* (2011), and in 2019 he formed a team of monsters in *Gotham City Monsters*. I'm sure Frankenstein and the Monster have appeared in other comics (like Dynamite's *Dean Koontz's Frankenstein: Storm Surge*) but I'll stop there.

Overall, it's astonishing how much Mary Shelley's *Frankenstein; or, The Modern Prometheus* has affected all areas of storytelling and how much it helped to create the development of Horror and SF. Mary would be shocked and, I hope, pleased.

Why are there continuous adaptations of the novel?

Why indeed! The stories, whether novels, short stories, movies, plays, comics or books about Mary Shelley, represent both the appeal of Mary's original novel, the uniqueness of it, and the fact that time has made its Monster so appealing to audiences (and readers), that the next generation of storytellers will be keen to take it up themselves, often in attempts to adapt it in some unique way, knowing that people will want to read it (or watch it), and each generation will see it slightly differently.

But that was the least of it.

I was talking with Cat Sparks, who had written a PHD thesis on a relevant topic: *Capitalocene Dreams: Dark Tales of Near Futures & The 21st Century Catastrophe: Hyper-capitalism and Severe Climate Change in Science Fiction.* I asked her what she thought about the role of *Frankenstein; or, The Modern Prometheus.* Here is what she said:

> Plenty of proto science fiction stories predate *Frankenstein*: Lucian of Samosata (125—c.180)'s *True History*, Voltaires's *Micromegas* (1752), Cyrano de Bergerac's *Comical History of the States and Empires of the Moon* (1657), *The Man in the Moone*, a novel by Francis Godwin (1638), Thomas More's *Utopia* (1516), Francis Bacon's *New Atlantis* (1627), Johannes Kepler's *Somnium* (1634), Margaret Cavendish's *The Blazing World* (1666), Henry Neville's *The Isle of Pines* (1688), and Jonathan Swift's *Gulliver's Travels* (1726).

These works feature common science fiction tropes such as traveling into space, to the stars or other worlds, encountering alien creatures and alternate civilisations. However, almost all contemporary science fiction springs thematically from Shelley's *Frankenstein* in that it illuminates aspects of what we're frightened of today, regardless of when the story may be set: past, present or future.

Frankenstein is about humanity unleashing (via technology) forces that cannot be controlled. Genies that cannot be put back in their bottles. Humanity is distinct from other living creatures in that it has developed the capacity to destroy itself and, in fact, all life on earth. Such powers were formally only presented as acts of gods or nature.

"The real problem of humanity is the following: We have Paleolithic

emotions, medieval institutions and godlike technology. And it is terrifically dangerous, and it is now approaching a point of crisis overall."
–Edward O. Wilson

Beauty in the Grotesque: Bernie Wrightson's Lifelong Obsession with Frankenstein's Monster

Michele Brittany

IN MARCH 2017, the comic book world mourned the loss of Bernie Wrightson, dubbed the Master of the Macabre, who passed away after losing his battle with brain cancer. His career spanned more than forty years, during which he became an influential horror artist across all the genre's mediums. His portfolio included working for DC and Marvel on such titles as *House of Mystery*, *Secrets of Haunted House*, contributions to several issues of *Creepy* and *Eerie* magazines, his collaboration with Stephen King on *Creepshow*, and co-creating *Swamp Thing* with writer Len Wein. Through his prolific output, Wrightson is best remembered for a set of fifty illustrations he created over a seven-year period to accompany Mary Shelley's *Frankenstein, or The Modern Prometheus*. Marvel published an edition in 1983 containing almost all of Wrightson's pen and ink drawings, which has subsequently been reprinted and released by Dark Horse Books as a 25th-anniversary edition in 2008, and more recently, Simon & Schuster, Inc.'s imprint, Gallery 13 in 2020. Although the *Frankenstein* novel had been adapted to the sequential art medium over the years, what made Wrightson's set of black and white illustrations so memorable and influential among all these derivatives? To answer this question, our story begins with the 1950s cinema and comic book scene.

The myriad of *Frankenstein* movies is often the entry point for most horror fans to the story, so it is not uncommon the word 'Frankenstein' will call to mind a square-headed, lumbering giant stitched together with body parts and who has been reanimated by a jolt of lightning. In addition, images of a distinguished, often foreign, scientist huddled in an eerily elaborate laboratory populated with glass beakers, test tubes, condensers, retorts, open flame burners, copper coils, and many other scientific pieces of equipment exudes the message 'this is a place of experimentation'.

Wrightson was six at the time his mom took him to see a double feature showing *The Black Lagoon* (1954) and *House of Frankenstein* (1944), but it was two years later when he watched the seminal 1931 film, *Frankenstein*, directed by James Whale, that Wrightson's interest in Mary Shelley's monster was planted (July 2012). In a July 2012 interview conducted by comic book writer Steve Niles, Wrightson remembered Boris Karloff's portrayal which had brought him to tears when he was a youth:

> The monster was just a child in a giant's body, moving and reacting slowly, not out of stupidity, but tentative and wondering, and absorbing every new event with a sense of wonder and bewilderment, and all of it in pantomime, without ever speaking a single word, and he communicated it all to me, just another child, instantly. I felt an immediate connection to this poor, ugly, misunderstood creature. Very strong and very deep. A kinship that I feel to this day. In a way, Frankenstein's Monster is my oldest friend, and I've had a deep fascination with any and all things Frankenstein ever since (para. 14).

When Wrightson finally read Mary Shelley's globe-trotting Gothic tale, *Frankenstein, or the Modern Prometheus*, he was both surprised and let down by the fact the literary monster was not the same one Karloff portrayed. He later realized both portrayals were significant, but they needed to be considered separately and distinct from each other (Pons, 2011). Further, an adult Wrightson acknowledged the literary tale was "essentially a story of ideas"[1] and Shelley was using the horror story structure to "deliver a moral point."[2] The resonance of both the filmic portrayal and the literary story would stick with Wrightson throughout the rest of his life.

Around the same time Wrightson was watching movies at his local cinema house with his mother,[3] he began reading comics, particularly EC

---

1 Pons, 2011, 3.46

2 Pons, 2011, 4.24

3 Niles, July 2012, para. 2

horror titles. [4] In an interview with Jon B. Cooke, Wrightson could not recall how long he had been drawing, but he realized his passion for drawing monsters was impacted by the comics he was reading and the movies he was watching at the time. [5] With the inclusion of his sketch in the June 1966 release of *Creepy* #9, this passion for horror was shared with a large audience, and he was acknowledged as a Creepy Clubbers fan club member (#520) from Baltimore, Maryland. [6] The sketch – illustrating a man being attacked by ghouls in a cemetery – captured Wrightson's early technique to use pen lines, black shadowing and the inclusion of classically draped clothing on characters.

It was around this time Wrightson made his first attempt to adapt *Frankenstein* into a comic book or graphic novel. However, he quit after only getting about two or three pages into his interpretation of the literary text. [7] Wrightson was not the first to try his hand at visualizing the text in a sequential art medium: *Classic Comics* had released a version in 1945 adapted by Ruth Roche and illustrated by Robert Hayward Webb, and a later *Classics Illustrated*—same publisher, revised name—version featuring a Norman Saunders cover. Wrightson was familiar with these publications and while he thought they got the basic story across to readers he "felt that a lot of the heart of the novel was somehow lost in the translation." [8] He made another attempt to adapt *Frankenstein* in the early 1970s for a French publisher, but the deal fell through before Wrightson completed two or three pages of a comic. [9]

In September 1975, Wrightson's Frankenstein-esque story 'The Muck Monster' was published in *Eerie* #68. Wrightson sought to emulate the mood of Shelley's story [10] in his own creature story. Using thought bubbles, a monster begrudgingly comes to life through a scientist's reanimation efforts. While the monster becomes self-aware he should not be alive, the scientist surmises his experiment has failed. He proceeds to destroy the monster by hacking its body into pieces and dropping them into acid. The scientist disposes of the acid mixture into the castle's drain, and the bloody sludge flows down a hillside into a cemetery located in the valley below.

---

4 Cooke, 1999

5 Cooke, 1999

6 *Creepy Presents Bernie Wrightson*, 2011, p. 107

7 Niles, May 2012

8 Niles, May 2012, para. 4

9 Niles, May 2012

10 Pons, 2011

The sludge reanimates a corpse, the precursor to Wrightson's Gothic monster. The monster returns to the scientist with the intent make his creator understand the error of his ways, but the creature quickly surmises the scientist is mad. This realization causes the monster to doubt his sanity as he walks away from his maker and journeys out along the mountaintops to an outcropping where he can admire the majestic views. The monster finds peace amongst the trees and the rocks as he sits resting against a tree. Time passes and the monster's body decays, leaving a skeleton.

Like Shelly's monster who sought understanding, acceptance, and peace, Wrightson's monster in 'The Muck Monster' sought to explain to his maker his experiment was a mistake. On the second page of the seven-page comic, the monster thinks, "I knew not what I was. I only knew that I should not be." [11] Instead of trying to understand his creation, the scientist destroys him. When the monster is reanimated a second time, he tries again to connect with his maker. Looking down at the laughing scientist, the monster reflects, "I spoke but he did not hear! The sound of his laughter over-powered my low, rasping voice…! I wanted him to listen, but the laughing prevented it." [12] The monster could not find peace amongst men for he knew he was not a man, rather he found peace in the nature around him. He likely welcomed death.

The tone harkened Shelley while Wrightson's art evoked Gothic visuals. While 'The Muck Monster' was published in color, it did not mask his use of inked parallel lines (hatching), crisscrossed lines (cross-hatching), and curving lines that defined and shadowed shapes (cross contour) that would pervade his set of illustrations. Wrightson's drapery effect is showcased in the scientist's shirt and smock as well as the magnificently bloody sludge cascading down the panel. Just as the landscapes are sweeping and majestic, Wrightson does not cut corners down to the smallest of details such as the wood grain texture on the examination table. The monster's appearance is easily recognizable as a precursor to the creature which would feature in his illustrations. Tall, muscular, stringy black hair, and the missing nose would become synonymous with Wrightson's vision of Shelley's monster. Additionally, Wrightson was seeking to convey the complexity of the literary monster: his creature's sorrowful eyes conveyed deep thought and heart wrenching sadness. While 'The Muck Monster' is a favorite today, at

---

11 Wrightson, 2011, p. 101
12 Wrightson, 2011, p. 105

the time, Wrightson was still grappling with the best way to illustrate the 1818 novel.

Working at Warren Publishing, where the artists worked on black and white comics, Wrightson began adapting the stories of horror greats such as H. P. Lovecraft ("Cool Air") and Edgar Allan Poe ("The Black Cat"). He once again wondered if *Frankenstein* could adapt to the sequential art form. According to Wrightson during his May 2012 interview with Niles,

> I still felt the urge to tell the story visually, and like I said, I just couldn't find a way into it as a comic book adaptation. So much would be lost, I thought, in the transition that a graphic novel version would ultimately diminish the novel itself. And by this time, I'd re-read the novel so many times and fallen so in love with it, I finally decided to simply illustrate the novel itself (para. 4).

By deciding to complete a series of illustrations, Wrightson felt he could stay true to the mood—the heart and soul—of the Gothic story.

There were many considerations to illustrating Shelley's novel. First and foremost was the approach. In talking with Niles, Wrightson expressed:

> This was my first real attempt to completely serve the story and the author's intentions, and I found it challenging as hell!! I really tried to see the story as Mary Shelley wrote it, trying to stay in her time, in her "head-space", if you will, and not tart it all up or force my own gloss onto it, and at the same time, try to stay true to my own style and my own sense of drama and picture making. [13]

Since he read the novel many times and by the time he commenced work on the illustrations, Wrightson had already experimented—successfully!—with the mood and emotion of Shelley's novel when he created and illustrated his story, 'The Muck Monster.' The seven-page comic would provide a reference point for the direction Wrightson would take his illustrations.

Conveying a precise tone and setting the emotional pacing was critical, but if the visuals did not capture the important narrative beats, the audience's experience with the text and illustrations would falter. Known for his elaborate pen and ink technique, Wrightson knew black and white ink illustrations in the style of early 19th century, engravings in wood and printed, would be the method he would have to emulate to be visually in sync with Shelley's text. In fact, he wanted to "create the illusion that the

---

13 Niles, May 2012, para. 6

book and the illustrations were done at the same time. Always I tried to be as specific and as detailed and as faithful to the text (at least as well as I could interpret it) as possible." [14] For example, 19th century French artist Gustave Doré was known for illustrating several classics, such as Miguel de Cervantes' *Don Quixote* and Dante Alighieri's *Divine Comedy*, as well as contemporary literary works of Edgar Allan Poe (*The Raven*) and Samuel Taylor Coleridge (*The Rime of the Ancient Mariner*) by creating wood-engravings inked and pressed onto paper to create intricate book illustrations. Wrightson has stated he took inspiration from late 19th-century American artists Franklin Booth and Edwin Austin Abbey, [15] known for their detailed pen and ink illustrations. Hence Wrightson's ink style incorporated the use of directional lines to express tone, texture, shadows, and shading as any classic wood-engraver would have done.

There was an additional element Wrightson brought to the sketching table: his passion for the literary source fueled by an obsession to convey the emotional journey of Shelley's creature for a contemporary audience. When Wrightson started his project, he did not have a venue for publishing his illustrations. In a 2008 interview with comic historian Peter Sanderson, Wrightson commented on his lifelong interest in the monster:

> I've always had a thing for Frankenstein, and it was a labour of love. It was not an assignment, it was not a job. I would do the drawings in between paying gigs, when I had enough to be caught up with bills and groceries and what-not. I would take three days here, a week there, to work on the Frankenstein volume. It took about seven years. [16]

Seven years seemed a rather long time to be committed to a project. However, Wrightson's illustrations visually conveyed why so much time passed between the start of the project to finishing the last illustration.

Wrightson's passion for Frankenstein exuded from each sketch along with his obsession with perfection. Niles asked Wrightson if he ever wanted to give up:

> I can't remember ever just wanting to give up, but each time I finished a drawing, I remember feeling a bit let down, like I'd just missed the mark even a little bit. If I'd only worked a little

---

14 Niles, May 2012, para. 6
15 Carey, 2008, para. 6
16 Carey, 2008, para. 5

harder I could nail it exactly. Several times, I'd start a new version of an already finished piece, or even an incomplete one, trying and trying again and again, to get it just right. I drove myself a little crazy through the whole process, but finally I decided that the really important thing was to get it done and quit sweating the small stuff. I mean, I thought if I could get 90% or even 80 of what I wanted, I'd be okay. Otherwise, I'd probably still be working on it.[17]

Spoken like a true perfectionist. Looking at the illustrations, it is difficult to imagine any of the illustrations are less than 100%.

After seven years and fifty illustrations later, Wrightson completed his project. While Wrightson started the journey without an idea of what would become of his illustrations, by the end, his volume found a home at Marvel, who had published adaptations of classic literature through their imprint, *Marvel Classics Comics*.

Billed as a Marvel Illustrated Novel, forty-three of the fifty illustrations are contained in the 194-page 8.5" x 11" book with a wrap-around cover of the pivotal confrontation between Frankenstein and the monster. It is illustration #32[18], and it is one of only three illustrations to span across two pages. The cover has an incredible amount of detail; all the test tubes, glass beakers, coils, and books line the shelves and lay on the table where Wrightson has left a half-decayed corpse—the discarded body intended to become the monster's companion. However, the viewer's eyes are directed to the monster with flowing black hair and a determined grimace as he pulls his creator close, almost into an embrace, as he tells Frankenstein he will be with him on his wedding night. The precise detailing of the scene showcases Wrightson's stunning artistic style that he became known for throughout his 40+ years. Of the cover illustration, artist Walter Simonson was quoted in Meredith Woerner's Los Angeles Times article:

In some ways [the lab scene is] the core of the story. It's where Frankenstein breaks the laws of God. I think people were just drawn to it cause it's so completely over the top and yet it's so completely controlled at the same time.[19]

---

17 Niles, May 2012, para. 8
18 Pages 182-183 of the Gallery 13 hardcover version published in 2020
19 Woerner, 2017, para. 15

Simonson explained Wrightson's ability to masterfully use light and dark through "incredibly complex pictures and yet you always see exactly what you are supposed to see. He drives the eye right where it needs." [20] Indeed, looking through each illustration, the reader is struck by Wrightson's success of emulating 19th-century wood-engraving illustrations through the concise control of his pen and ink brush strokes. Through the use of hatching, cross-hatching, and cross contour lines, Wrightson skillfully brought Shelley's story to life. By spacing the lines in a precise pattern, he evoked the illusion of value through light (white space), or more concisely the direction from which light came across the image, and the dark, denoting depth of shadows as well as shading. The combination of these techniques in a master artist's hands resulted in gorgeous drapery effects, a sense of motion, awe-inspiring sweeping landscapes, and Gothic interiors indicative of Wrightson's illustrations. His composition of characters were unique as well: he would push the focal point—characters— into the background, so the eyes were guided from the edge of the image to where Wrightson wanted the viewer's eyes to focus upon. Interestingly, the only close-up is a portrait of the monster, Illustration #45[21], and the star of the novel. Situated on the opposite page of the closing paragraphs of the novel, the portrait is a study of a solemn, melancholy creature who feels remorse at the death of his creator and realizes he is utterly alone. The monster's visual journey invited the reader to empathize with the emotional plight of the creature. Taken all together, the illustrations were a modern approach to classical techniques employed during and before Shelley's seminal novel.

In his interview with Niles, Wrightson reflected on what he felt after completing his seven-year journey:

> I'd finally gotten there, like I had passed a milestone or something and now I could get on with the rest of my life. I can look at those drawings now with a sense of pride and satisfaction and appreciate how good they are, sometimes I marvel a bit, almost as though they were done by someone else. And in a way, they were done by someone else, a young artist, unafraid of hard work, obsessed really. [22]

Wrightson continued to work on comics throughout the 1980s but

---

20 Woerner, 2017, para. 12
21 on page 245 of the Gallery 13 edition
22 Niles, May 2012, para. 8

he shifted some of his focus to creature and film design for such movies as *The Faculty* (1998), *The Mist* (2007), and *Dark Country* (2009). In 2007, Niles and Wrightson met and decided to collaborate, and the following year, Dark Horse Books released a 25th anniversary of *Frankenstein*. This commemorative edition is oversized (9" x 12") and includes 47 of the 50 original illustrations.

Five years into their collaboration that spawned *City of Others* (2007, Dark Horse Comics), *Dead, She Said!* (2008, IDW Publishing), *Ghoul* (2010, IDW Publishing), and *Doc Macabre* (2010-2011, IDW Publishing), the friends started working on *Frankenstein Alive, Alive!* (2012-2014, IDW Publishing) marking Wrightson's return to Shelley's creature. Niles asked Wrightson if he felt intimidated returning to his infamous monster:

> It hasn't been intimidating to return to Frankenstein. The story and the monster have been a big part of my life since I was a kid, and it's always on my mind. For me the monster is immortal, he's always been there and always will be. In my mind, he didn't die on that ice raft, he only drifted off to the be lost in the darkness and distance. The idea of continuing his story has been in the back of my mind for many years. I talked a bit earlier about not being able to find a way into adapting the novel as a graphic novel and I'd had the same problem with this sequel, couldn't find a way in, did I even want to take it on? [23]

The sequel was planned as a four-issue comic book series, picking up with the monster appearing in a carnival show as a freakish exhibit. However, the rest of the story is told in flashback. The monster is tormented by the ghost of Frankenstein before finding peace and rest as a lava stream overtakes and smothers his body. Death eludes the monster and he eventually meets a doctor, who mentors him. But the doctor proves too interested in Frankenstein's experiment with re-animation, and the relationship between the doctor and monster are severed; the monster is alone again, but now, he has come to realize he deserves to live.

Wrightson had moved away from the exacting artistic expressions of his illustrations to softer drawing style. The hatch work was still visible, but there was the addition of thicker brush strokes and blending. The tone and mood still evoked a Gothic feel and gave homage to Shelley's novel.

The first three issues were completed, but Wrightson's health was in

---

23 Niles, May 2012, para. 13

decline. After being diagnosed with brain cancer, he realized that he would not be able to complete the fourth and final chapter. Wrightson selected artist Kelley Jones to step in and complete the last issue in his stead, and IDW Publishing agreed. The master of horror passed away on March 18th, 2017. In 2018, IDW published a hardcover trade paperback of *Frankenstein Alive, Alive!* The supplemental material included several pages of Wrightson's sketches for issue four and it was an opportunity for fans to gain insight into the artistic mind of Wrightson as well as view his pencil work.

Two years after Wrightson's death, the original wraparound cover art for Marvel's 1983 release was auctioned and fetched $1.2 million. Guillermo del Toro stated in Woerner's article in the *Los Angeles Times* that Wrightson's original illustrations were rare and "the people that have them don't let them go." [24] In a 2019 *Bloody Disgusting* online article written by John Squires, Profiles in History summed up Wrightson's illustrations:

> Artist Bernie Wrightson turned his hand to illustrating the classic horror novel as a labor of love, and working over the course of a decade, produced some of the most staggeringly intricate and evocative work of his career. [25]

There are few comic book artists who have made an indelible mark in the comic book world whose styles are immediately identifiable, memorable and continues to inspire new generations of illustrators: Frank Frazetta, Jack Kirby, Al Feldstein, and Frank Miller. Wrightson is no exception; his style is on the scale of Renaissance artists so it is no surprise that he has been dubbed the "Master of the Macabre". Thanks to a career that spanned more than forty years and a set of illustrations that were borne out of a passionate vision to bring a literary monster, who is often lost amongst its filmic representatives, Wrightson's art is not just memorable, it's legendary.

---

24 Woerner, 2017, para. 17
25 Woerner, 2017, para. 2

An Articulation Of Beauty In The Film *Mary Shelley's Frankenstein*

Donald Prentice Jr

THIS ESSAY QUESTIONS a specific articulation of beauty from the film *Mary Shelley's Frankenstein*.[1] By 'articulation of beauty,' I mean diegetic moments in the film when an individual is specifically named beautiful. Following J.L. Austin's notion of language's performative function from *How to Do Things with Words*, "the performative should be doing something, as opposed to just saying something."[2] The articulation of a body as beautiful is not saying that the body adheres to a stable definition of what can and cannot be organized as beautiful. Rather, similar to Judith Butler's notion of gender performativity, the organization of a body as beautiful is reliant on its articulation as such and the subsequent actions that reinforce that interpellation.[3,4] The goal of this essay is not to see how a body adheres to a natural or objective definition of beauty but to question the composition, relationship, and obligation of a body that has been articulated as beautiful. This can be done by interrogating what space this beautifully named body occupies in the film, including the narrative actions surrounding the body and how the body is affectively presented to the audience. In short, this essay hopes to analyze what an articulation of beauty does as opposed to what beauty means.

In *Mary Shelley's Frankenstein*, after the Creature has murdered Elizabeth, Victor Frankenstein returns to his estate to reanimate his recent bride. Once Victor successfully animates this body, he immediately dresses it in a

---

1 *Mary Shelley's Frankenstein* (Kenneth Branagh, 1994)
2 Austin, 1962, p. 132
3 Butler, 1988, pp.520-521
4 Salih, 2002, p. 84

wedding dress, puts a wedding ring on its finger, and tells it to say *his* name while also telling it that its name *is* Elizabeth. After Victor dances with this newly animated body, the Creature reveals himself and states: "she's beautiful," to which Victor replies, "she's not for you."

It's important to note here the distinction between the subject Elizabeth and the new body that has been animated by Victor, henceforth referred to as 'the bride.' The title/subject 'bride' comes with its own assumptions that may limit the body, but it is also a good indication of how both Victor and the Creature have positioned this body. The newness of the bride is not just limited to the unique relation among its organic parts (which is a sterile way of saying that Victor chopped off Elizabeth's head and sewed it onto a different body). The bride is also new in its intensive relations, how it feels, acts, sees and experiences the world, how the audience views it, and how it functions in the film. Upon its birth, the bride has increased potential to inhabit a new space, one that is different from the space that the subject Elizabeth inhabits. However, because of the bride's potential, it also challenges Victor's notion of acceptable life, and therefore he is quick to interpellate this body as Elizabeth. As Claire Colebrook states when analyzing Victor's relationship to the Creature in Shelley's original novel:

> [Victor's] encounter with the forces of life, with the physical energy from which all forms emerge, is directed only to the recreation of 'man.' And when this man is not a faithful repetition of Victor's own image, Victor can only reject him as a monster, a demon, or 'inhuman.' Victor is not a Promethean overreacher so much as a moralizing humanist, who can only think of science and life as issuing in 'man'... The novel is, then, less about overreaching than it is about a failure of nerve in the face of rampant life and sexuality beyond human recognition. [5]

According to Colebrook, Victor's downfall is not because he overstepped the proper bounds of nature but because he could not recognize or accept life beyond the orders and hierarchies of his own understanding. For example, in the novel, Victor remarks of his new creation: "I had selected his features as beautiful. Beautiful!... but now that I had finished, the beauty of the dream vanished, and breathless horror and disgust filled my

---

5 Colebrook, 2003, p.244

heart."[6] A similar declaration happens in *Mary Shelley's Frankenstein* when Victor reduces the differences of the Creature to "birth defects" and calls him "malfunctional and pitiful." Victor's "dream" was life similar to him, the preservation of what he already knows, but when his creation leads to something new that challenges his notion of acceptable life, he steps back in horror.

In the pursuit of preservation, the articulation of beauty in the film acts as a disciplinary action, more specifically, an indication of normalizing judgement. According to French philosopher Michel Foucault, to assess the potential and value of an individual, normalizing judgement "compares, differentiates, hierarchizes, homogenizes, [and] excludes. In short, it normalizes."[7] That is, the process of normalizing judgment compares bodies that are differentiated and hierarchized according to their relation to a desired standard. Bodies that fail to meet this standard or that simply meet the "minimal threshold" are encouraged and disciplined to conform to meet an "optimum." This organizing process creates a state of homogeneity that excludes the bodies that failed to meet the desired standard.

By returning to the articulation of beauty, we can see how the articulation acts as normalizing judgment that seeks to assess the bride in relation to a standard. As he states earlier in the film, the Creature's goal is to have a female companion like him, meaning a body that has undergone the process of animation, which is why he names the bride "beautiful." By naming the bride beautiful and his actions that follow, the Creature seeks to discipline this body to a certain range by increasing certain forces while decreasing others. In the film, after the articulation of beauty, the bride goes to the Creature and examines his scars in relation to its own as the Creature kisses the bride's fingers. The Creature is satisfied when the capability of the bride as 'female' (he states: "*she's* beautiful") and 'companion for him' increases. However, after examining the Creature, the bride turns to Victor and finally states Victor's name. When the capability of the bride to recognize Victor increases, the Creature becomes aggressive and seeks to correct this by grabbing her and stating, "No, you're mine." The Creature's actions and previous statements suggest that his interest in this body is its utility for him as a subject whose conditions are restricted or increased to a certain capacity. The standards created for the bride by the Creature

---

6 Shelley, 1818, p. 35
7 Foucault, 1977, p. 183

include it being a female companion *for* him, and his articulation of "she's beautiful" confirms that the bride has the ability to meet these standards. The bride is named beautiful because the Creature has assessed it and has determined that it meets the conditions of a desired standard.

The obligations created for the bride continue with the subjectification of this body by Victor. Victor doesn't object when the Creature names the bride beautiful; he states: "she isn't for you." Victor seems to agree that the bride is beautiful; however, Victor's desired standard for the bride is different from the Creature's. Victor's goal in this scene is to preserve what he knows, specifically,· his wife, Elizabeth. Therefore, he attempts to discipline the bride as the subject Elizabeth. Elizabeth is the desired standard. This is why Victor immediately dresses the bride in a wedding dress, puts a wedding ring on its finger, and, more importantly, tells the bride that its name *is* Elizabeth, inferring that it is to fulfil the conditions of the subject Elizabeth. Victor's actions seek to align the bride's intensities with that of the subject Elizabeth; to increase its capacity to dress like Elizabeth did on her wedding day, to dance with Victor as Elizabeth would, to respond to the same name that Elizabeth would, and to refer to Victor as Elizabeth would. Returning to Colebrook, Victor's goal of preserving life is limited to life familiar to him. Where Victor failed to find acceptable life in the Creature, but he hopes to preserve the subject Elizabeth in the bride, therefore, increasing the intensity of the bride as acceptable life. To preserve Elizabeth, he attempts to discipline the bride, which creates obligations for it to act as Elizabeth would, according to Victor. Victor's actions seek to create homogenization. Therefore, the articulation of beauty in this scene is an indication of the normalizing judgment that is happening to the bride. Both Victor and the Creature create certain obligations for the bride they have named beautiful; to discipline this body by restricting it in certain ways while increasing its utility in other ways.

However, the examination of the bride is not just limited to the narrative actions of other characters. The bride is also positioned in the film's image so that the audience is asked to evaluate the condition of the bride compared to the pre-murder condition of the subject Elizabeth. In essence, the film establishes a comparative system. Instead of seeing the bride as something new, the bride is positioned as the failed replication of the subject Elizabeth; the bride is now a case for the audience's examination. As stated earlier, as a function of normalizing judgment, this examination "compares, differentiates, [and] hierarchizes" the bride in relation to an aspirational 'norm.' [8]In the film's image, this aspirational 'norm' is presented as Elizabeth. In this scene, when Victor is dancing with the bride, brief flashbacks of Victor and Elizabeth are juxtaposed against Victor and the bride. The flashbacks of Victor and Elizabeth include them dancing on a mountain, at a ball, and gazing into the distance together. One function of these flashbacks in the film is to highlight how the bride differs from the subject Elizabeth. By showing the bride and Elizabeth performing the same actions (in tandem with Victor's disciplinary actions), the audience is asked to judge the actions and condition of the bride based on standards set by a subject the audience is already familiar and empathizes with: Elizabeth.

Comparing the presentation of Elizabeth in the flashbacks to that of the bride, we can see how the subject Elizabeth is favoured in the film's comparative system. The flashbacks with Elizabeth are bright, evenly lit, and colourful. Victor and Elizabeth are dressed in clean clothing that connotes their wealth and upper-class status. The scenes take place in locations that have cultural capital (nature and a sprawling ballroom). Furthermore, if we look back at the original scenes the flashbacks refer to, they are happy occasions for Victor, scenes where Victor and Elizabeth profess their love for each other, and the music reflects this. The music in the original dance scene is an upbeat waltz that keeps a stable time signature, and the music playing while Victor and Elizabeth are on the mountain is exciting and conveys a feeling of wonderment. Compare this to the scene where the bride is dancing with Victor. The editing is frantic, increases in pace, and seemingly cuts to new angles at random, meaning that we, as the audience, are kept on our toes, so to speak. The scene is dark except for the sudden flashes of lightning that illuminate the bride's stitching and wounds. Both Victor and the bride are in tattered or soiled clothing, and it takes place in a dreary attic that holds the dangerous secret of creation that Victor vowed to destroy. In addition, the dance movements of Victor and the bride are chaotic, where the bride is more of a gangly marionette puppet under Victor's control. This disorder is also reflected in the music, which starts as the same waltz from the Victor/Elizabeth dance scene but becomes more chaotic and soon devolves into a theme that sounds more sinister. In these wistful flashbacks, Elizabeth is positioned as the aspirational subject, an idea of what Victor hopes he

8 Foucault, 1977, p. 183

can preserve in the bride. While the qualities of the bride under review are presented as substandard and horrific in their relation to the subject Elizabeth.

This comparative system is not just limited to this brief montage. The audience's examination of the bride continues with how the bride is positioned in the film's mise-en-scène. This scene starts silent, except for the sound of faint wind and thunder so that the audience can fully focus on the image of the bride—slumped over in wedding garb, sitting in the shadows, and seemingly unaware of its surroundings. The importance placed on the image builds our anticipation of seeing the bride's condition compared to that of Elizabeth's. After Victor hails the bride as Elizabeth, it slowly raises its head, and the audience finally sees the bride's physical condition. When this happens, string instruments, a horror genre staple, start playing and work to build a feeling of tragedy and a sense that something is not quite right. The camera then slowly rotates around the bride so that the audience can examine it from every angle. During this 360-degree camera movement, we see the bride's confused look, open wounds, the haphazard stitching across the bride's face and neck, what remains of its short, burnt hair, and large patches of exposed flesh that draws the eye due to their location centre screen. As the audience views these images, they are reminded that, according to medical discourse, there are certain qualifications a body must meet to be considered a 'healthy' body. The film implies that this bride is both different and injured and that these conditions exclude it from meeting the qualifications of a 'healthy subject.' Therefore, it is presented as inferior compared to the 'healthy' Elizabeth.

In this scene, the newly animated body is positioned as a tragic, unhealthy spectacle (a monster). The film asks the audience to compare the bride to that of the subject Elizabeth, and in the hierarchical composition of this comparative system, the bride is presented as an abnormal deviation. It is never considered in the film that the bride could be something new or something other than the subject Elizabeth. It is, instead, deemed inferior and sad because the comparative system puts the bride under the supervision of a normalising judgement that examines its relation to the subject Elizabeth. Instead of being examined based on its own capabilities and potential, the bride is positioned as a failed-Elizabeth. However, even though the bride is positioned as a monster, this does not mean that the articulation of beauty is wrong. This essay aims to question the composition of a body articulated as beautiful, not to rely on strict definitions that reinforce limiting binaries. The bride can be articulated as beautiful and positioned as monstrous simultaneously.

Instead of relying on static definitions or preconceived notions of what constitutes a beautiful subject, we can, instead, question the specific and momentary configurations of a body that has been named beautiful: what it looks like, what it is capable of, how we react to it, and its role in the film. It is not my intention to argue that beauty is always and already the result or indication of normalising judgement or discipline. Rather, my intention here is to question the actions and presentation related to a specific articulation of beauty found in the film *Mary Shelley's Frankenstein*. By examining articulations of beauty in the text instead of prescribing a definition of beauty to the text, we can consider the condition and intensities of bodies that might not be considered beautiful under more traditional or static definitions of beauty. The bride is positioned as a tragic, unhealthy, monstrous spectacle in the film, hardly the conditions one might expect from a more traditional, beautifully named body. However, this does not mean that we should reject actions that articulate such bodies as beautiful or say that such bodies are inherently not beautiful. Instead, we can further interrogate this action to see what exactly is being done when such a body is articulated as beautiful.

FEMINISM

The origins of feminism have been traced to the word 'féminisme', first used in 1837 by utopian socialist and French philosopher Charles Fourier. However, it wasn't until 1872 that the concepts of 'féminisme' (feminism) and 'féministe' (feminist) appeared in France and the Netherlands, later appearing in Great Britain in the 1890s and the United States of America in 1910. Feminism has evolved to encompass movements and ideologies particular to the goals of that time.

Modern Western feminism is largely grouped in 'waves'. First-wave feminism refers to activity during the 19th and 20th centuries, most notably women's suffrage, the reform of family laws, and discrimination based on gender. Second-wave feminism referred to the activity against cultural and political inequalities, and issues beyond suffrage, such as gender-based discrimination, most notably the abolition of marital rape exemptions. With the late 20th and early 21st centuries came third-wave feminism, and the emergence of post-structuralist micropolitics surrounding autonomy, social equality, glass ceiling practices, and global injustices such as female genital mutilation, rape, incest, and prostitution. Finally, fourth-wave feminism appeared in 2012, with a focus on workplace harassment, sexual assault, rape culture, and sexual harassment through the use of technology.

Mary Wollstonecraft's *A Vindication of the Rights of Men* (1790) was an early critique of the notions of hierarchy, privilege, tradition, aristocracy, and constitutional monarchy, as well as a critique of political theories of gender and aesthetics. This work radicalised Wollstonecraft, however, critics poked flaws in the book's logic, and her husband William Godwin dismissed it as 'illogical and ungrammatical.' Despite this, Wollstonecraft continued exploring gender, and two years later wrote *A Vindication of the Rights of Woman* (1792), considered one of the earliest works of feminist philosophy. Wollstonecraft argued for rational education of women commensurate with their position within society, and that educated women would make better companions, mothers, and homemakers. 'Women might certainly study the art of healing, and be physicians as well as nurses. And midwifery, decency seems to allot to them…they might, also, study politics… Business of various kinds, they might likewise pursue.'

According to Wollstonecraft, schooling should be co-educational, with women studying the same subjects as men at a 'country day school' alongside a home education to 'inspire a love of home and domestic pleasures.' As well as domestic critiques, Wollstonecraft speculated the demise of society without rational, educated women, and suggested women seemed 'silly' because of their lack of education and encouragement to be frivolous. However, despite being one of the first philosophers to point out the double standards within society, several critics claim *A Vindication of the Rights of Woman* is not a feminist doctrine at all and encourages women to strive for nothing more than domestic life. They point out her religiosity, classism, and bourgeois worldview. But one must remember the world in which she lived, and the sociopolitical doctrines that governed life in the 18th century. Mary Wollstonecraft's work was an important precursor to the suffragette movement and continues to influence modern feminism today.

Feminism has come a long way since 1837, however, it is important to reflect upon its inception, and its continued influence on sociopolitical doctrines to this day. Mary Wollstonecraft undoubtedly influenced many feminist thinkers, including the aforementioned Octavia Hill (1838-1912), Lidia Poët (1855-1949), Emmeline Pankhurst (1858-1928), Marie Carmichael Stopes (1880-1958), Elizabeth Garrett Anderson (1836-1917), Rosa Parks (1913-2005), and Ruth Bader Ginsburg (1954-2010), just to name a few.

After her death, William Godwin released a memoir of his beloved wife, and though it was intended to celebrate her achievements, Wollstonecraft's unorthodox lifestyle was considered scandalous at the time. The memoir inadvertently destroyed her reputation for over a century—the Romantic poet Robert Southey (1774-1843) accused Godwin of "stripping his dead wife naked." Several exceptional rebukes against her include the unpleasant poem entitled 'The Un-sex'd Females', mocking Wollstonecraft as a "poor maniac" and "voluptuous" victim of "licentious love." The author went on to describe her death as distinctive of her sex, illuminating the unfortunate destiny of women during that time, and the diseases and illnesses (including childbirth) to which they are more susceptible than men. English writer and art historian Horace Walpole (1717-1787) described her as a "hyena in petticoats". Because of this, many of her friends took a step back, distancing themselves from her. Later, several members of the suffragette movement denounced Mary Wollstonecraft's lifestyle. Thankfully, with the re-emergence of the feminist movement in the 20th century, her work and advocacy for women were reevaluated and subsequently praised for the genius it is.

Later, Mary Shelley, an avid scholar of her mother's works, continued in her mother's footsteps, forging her own path with her own spin on her mother's ideas. The following essays are reflections on feminist themes within works by or inspired by Mary Wollstonecraft and her daughter Mary Shelley. 'Mapping The Collective Body Of Frankenstein's Brides' by Carina Bissett discusses authors inspired by Shelley's unfinished bride and feminist themes within 'Frankenstein'. 'Don't Feed The Monsters' by HK Stubbs discusses Mary Wollstonecraft's influence on Mary Shelley, specifically her death. My essay 'Marys and Motherhood' reflects the emotional and often tumultuous impact motherhood had upon Mary Shelley. And 'My Mother Hands Me A Book; Wollstonecraft: Reflections of an Educator' by Piper Mejia discusses education for women within Mary Wollstonecraft's time, and her personal connection with the celebrated author.

Today, inequality continues in various forms. While gender equality is both a fundamental human right and a necessary foundation for a peaceful, prosperous and sustainable world, there are many gender issues continuing to infiltrate our public sphere, with women continuing to be oppressed in various forms. According to the United Nations Foundation, 1 in 3 women experience gender-based violence in their lifetime, 1 in 4 women experience violence during pregnancy, and 5,000 "honour killings" are reported every year around the world. Many women in developed countries are denied life-saving abortion care, with medical professionals facing threats by simply doing their jobs. While Eastern countries such as Iran and Saudi Arabia were once the forerunners of absurd human rights violations against women, Western countries have now rolled back once-institutional protections, including the infamous overruling of the 1973 Roe Vs Wade in the United States, which, through their Constitution, protected the right to abortion access in the first trimester. However, with its overruling in 2022, the abolition dismantled 50 years of legal protection, paving for individual states to curtail or outright ban abortion rights.

In her magnum opus, *Vindication of the Rights of Women*, Wollstonecraft identifies infanticide (both prenatal and postnatal) as a consequence of denying women's natural rights and powers. In a letter penned to her husband, Wollstonecraft described her pregnancy as 'the quickening', saying, "I begin to love this little creature, and to anticipate his birth as a fresh twist to a knot, which I do not wish to untie."

From this, one may believe she would be against abortion, however in her unfinished novel *The Wrongs of Woman: Or, Maria*, Wollstonecraft sympathises with her character Jemina, who, is not only abused and neglected as a child due to her 'illegitimate' birth, becomes a house servant later on in life, and experiences being raped multiple times by her master, subsequently leaving her pregnant. After discovering she is 'with child', Jemima comments: "I know not why I felt a mixed sensation of despair and tenderness, excepting that, ever called a bastard, a bastard appeared to me an object of the greatest compassion in creation." Later, concerted by his disapproval of the pregnancy by his wife and the general public, Jemima's master gives her an 'infernal potion', guaranteed to eliminate her pregnancy. While she initially refuses to drink it, she is then raped again and thrown out on the street, leading to her decision to swallow the potion "with a wish that it might destroy me, at the same time that is stopped the sensations of new-born life, which I felt with indescribable emotion."

Through this, it can be assumed Wollstonecraft was not against the idea of abortion, especially if the conception was violent or outside of the mother's control. She wanted the best for women, for them to stand as equals against men, to enjoy their experiences of motherhood, and have a choice in how their destiny unfolded.

In 'Mapping the Collective Body of Frankenstein's Brides', Carina Bissett describes how, in a fit of guilt and revolution at the thought of both 'monsters' procreating, Victor Frankenstein destroys the Creature's unfinished bride before she can even draw her first breath. Bissett explores the underlying issues inherent in a patriarchal society, as shown in James Whale's 1935 film 'The Bride of Frankenstein'; the thriving pretty dead girl trope dominating American culture, such as the drowned homecoming queen Laura Palmer in the TV show 'Twin Peaks' (1990-92, 2017); and the 'untold' story of the

Creature's bride in the novel 'Patchwork Girl' (1995) by Shelley Jackson—based on Mary Shelley's 'Frankenstein' (1818) and 'The Patchwork Girl of Oz'(1913) by L. Frank Baum. In 'Marys and Motherhood', I explore 'Frankenstein' as an example of attachment theory, examining how Mary's tumultuous experiences with motherhood, and her obsession with her mother's work, shaped her ideas on family and the role of a parent within a child's upbringing. In 'Don't feed The Monsters', HK Stubbs explores the 'monsters' in both Mary Wollstonecraft and Mary Shelley's lives, and how, with incredible strength, both women battled against their sex, using their negative experiences within society ultimately to their advantage. In 'My Mother Hands Me A Book', Piper Mejia explores the importance of Wollstonecraft's contribution to modern women's education, her early exposure to reading, and how children's identities are influenced by their mothers—even in their absence.

These essays discuss the legacy both women left behind, providing food for thought on the lives of women and their experiences of motherhood, something women continue to struggle with to this day.

Mapping The Collective Body Of Frankenstein's Brides

Carina Bissett

IN 1816, THE OSTRACISED DAUGHTER of two freethinkers began writing what would become the greatest Gothic Romantic novel of all time—*Frankenstein; or, The Modern Prometheus*. Drawing inspiration from a murky mix of tragic experiences, 19-year-old Mary Godwin Shelley stitched together the narrative of the mad scientist Victor Frankenstein and his Creature. She also wove in feminist commentary in the sketches of the lives and deaths of her female characters, most notably the bride—a mate for a monster destroyed before she could draw her first breath. Between the pages, she exposed dark demons roused by the despair wrought from the death of her first child, the emotional turmoil of the suicide of her half-sister Fanny Imlay, and her increasing disenchantment over her tumultuous love affair with the radical poet—Percy Bysshe Shelley. The resulting manuscript of *Frankenstein* validated Mary Shelley's writing ability and eventually launched her literary success—a success that still stands today, 200 years later. Although the Creature, more commonly known as Frankenstein, has achieved cult status, his unnamed bride has garnered iconic status in her own right Identified by her grave beauty and lightning-streaked hair, she stands as a symbol of the modern woman, no mean feat for a monster who was originally destroyed before she had the opportunity to live, let alone speak. In Shelley's novel, the Creature presents a pleading case for a mate: "What I ask of you is reasonable and moderate; I demand a creature of another sex, but as hideous as myself; the gratification is small, but it is all that I can receive." Victor eventually concedes to the Creature's demands and retreats to the Orkneys to fulfil his promise. However, when the female is nearly complete, Victor expresses his fear that she may become "ten thousand times more malignant" than his first creation and, in a fit of madness, he tears the female construct apart, sending her dismembered body to a watery grave at the bottom of the North Sea.

The unfinished bride, a patchwork Eve, symbolises a wide spectrum of traditional feminine roles: sister, mother, daughter, lover, wife. Through the representation of her disparate origins, the bride has become a treatise for Everywoman, an evolving feminist text demanding women's rights. Although Mary Wollstonecraft died just eleven days after the birth of her daughter, she paved the way for Mary Shelley with the publication of the proto-feminist treatise *A Vindication of the Rights of Woman* (1792). In this text, Wollstonecraft notably argues for women's rational education and the independence of outmoded ideas through emancipation. Today, women have the right to vote. We can own property, secure higher education, and enter professions once claimed solely by men. However, many of the underlying issues inherent in a patriarchal society continue to hinder the continuing fight for equality. In the twenty-first century we continue to find the female form assembled and modified under the male gaze. Now, more than ever, Shelley's patchwork Eve must fight back against preconceived gender roles and patriarchal oppression.

In 1935, more than a century after her debut appearance, the female monster rose from the ocean depths and came to life under the direction of James Whale in the film sequel *The Bride of Frankenstein*. British actress Elsa Lanchester brought the character to life, entrenching the bride and her trademark, white-streaked Nefertiti hair in the modern imagination. The female monster made other cinematic appearances in such films as *The Bride* (1985) and *Mary Shelley's Frankenstein* (1994), but it wasn't until Elizabeth Hand's 2007 novel adaptation of the James Whale's version that the female monster was finally given a name of her own—Pandora. Other women writers, including Shelley Jackson and Damien Angelica Walters, ruminate on the female body's borders and boundaries through work continuing to evolve out of *Frankenstein*. These brides speak out against injustice in the Everywoman collective of 'herstories,' providing inter-textural feminist examinations of such gender-based concepts as assemblage, identity, and ownership.

In many ways, the Creature represents the radical marginalisation of the unconventional, mirroring Shelley's plight as a female writer struggling for a voice in the dominant social milieu of her time. In "Mary Shelley,

Frankenstein, and the Woman Writer's Fate," Stephen Behrendt examines Shelley's views on masculine creative agency through her male characters' eyes: "Acts are replaced by words, activity by passivity, responsibility by the irresponsibly ambivalent, and individuality by abstraction. The person is dissolved." This dissolution of identity results in the deconstruction and blurring of traditionally held boundaries. The Creature becomes a symbol of multiplicity, which is represented through his chimerical origins and chameleonic nature. With this foundation in place, Shelley pushes propriety even further with the creation of a monstrous mate, a new geography of terror stitched together with horrifying exactitude in the form of a woman.

In Shelley's *Frankenstein*, Victor's arcane experiments are doomed to a tragic dénouement. There is no hope for the Creature any more than there was for his female companion. When the female monster is nearly complete, Victor is struck with the terror she would have the capacity for unimagined depravity and wickedness. He also acknowledges the possibility that she would shun the Creature's hideous appearance and seek out the "superior beauty" of man. But above all else, Victor's greatest fears are rooted in the possibility that his female creation would be able to procreate. Whereas the Creature represents what is monstrous in its nonconformity to the social milieu, the female is that much more horrifying due to the perception of her procreative power.

In response, Victor aborts the bride, dismembering her with a violence that resonates long after the bride's brief, unfinished appearance. Reflecting the cultural associations inherent in early nineteenth century thought, the women in *Frankenstein* are reduced to their reproductive organs. In a world where women are still dismantled and reassembled to conform to the unrealistic ideals presented by the dominance of a patriarchal social system, we need the bride to take a stand against the continuing epidemic of gendered violence. Perhaps then, this reductionist attitude might be destroyed for good.

Until then, contemporary women writers were drawn to Shelley's unfinished bride. According to Judith Halbertstam in *Skin Shows: Gothic Horror and the Technology of Monsters*, "The aborted female monster can be read as the ugly popular fiction, Gothic fiction, that is always debased in relation to some notion of high culture. She is the body of work that is always 'half-finished,' that inspires violence, and that literally is reduced to pulp." The stories told by Shelley Jackson, Elizabeth Hand, and Damien Angelica Walters transform that pulp into power. Through their words and others, the Everywoman collective continues to expand with each resurrection of Frankenstein's bride; she refuses to be silenced any longer.

In the past decade, there has been a surge of stories by women writers examining feminist figures who resist traditional representation to the point where they create powerful new tropes for the modern woman to explore; the bride of Frankenstein is one of the most prominent of those figures. At first glance, it might seem odd that a half-finished monster written into existence two centuries ago would merit such attention in contemporary culture. After all, Frankenstein's female creature hadn't even been fully constructed before being aborted, dismembered, and drowned by her creator. Yet, in the digital age where women are routinely cut apart and reassembled to "perfection," oftentimes at the hands of men, the bride takes on a new mantle of power visualised in the display of her mismatched parts and grotesque scars.

The characterization of this unnamed female character should not be surprising, as Shelley often tackles themes in her work far ahead of her time. The bride's silence is a powerful commentary on the dominance of power-driven masculine politics in contrast to the domestic sphere left for women to inhabit. The challenge against the traditional separation of the sexes shows up in her other work, as well. She criticises political and theological ideologies claiming women as the weaker sex, and she argues for social justice through egalitarian educational opportunities. But above all else, she examines the contradictory relations between the self and society and the futility of progress in a world where women are routinely dismissed based on their gender alone.

During the Gothic Romantic period, the borders of the self were being examined with great enthusiasm by male physicians. The especially gruesome practice of physiology provided Mary Shelley with a wide array of grisly details to add to her famous work. At the time, student anatomists applied the same dissection techniques on both animals and human cadavers, effectively blurring the boundaries between the two. To compound the situation, human corpses were no longer viewed as sacred, but were instead items of scientific inquiry. The resulting anatomical discourse became intertwined with nineteenth century social anxieties involving gender and sexuality. *Frankenstein* demonstrated the resulting entanglement of sexual and medical ways of viewing cadavers.

In "The Medical Gaze and the Female Corpse: Looking at Bodies in Mary Shelley's 'Frankenstein'," Emma Liggins links the scientific enquiry of male anatomists to the emergence of erotically charged art depicting dissected women. The medicalization of the female body transmuted into artistic endeavours geared towards capturing the image of beautiful dead girls. Through this myopic focus, the male gaze dismembered the female form in an effective erasure of women, which Liggins emphasises within the confines of Shelley's narrative:

I would argue that representations of the female corpse revealed the horrors of surgery and male medical control over the female body. What is disturbing is that the novel co-opts the reader into viewing the female body through the official eyes of the doctor, whose ardour for scientific discovery feeds off images of helpless and violated femininity. Male fantasies of mutilated, virginal women ensure that death and femininity continue to be entwined.

The Pretty Dead Girl trope continues to thrive as an American cultural obsession. From the unveiling of the drowned homecoming queen Laura Palmer in the TV show *Twin Peaks* [CF12] to the frenzied coverage of such real-life murders of victims including JonBenét Ramsey and Natalee Holloway, the continuing objectification of women, especially that of dead girls, reveals the dark reality of gendered violence and the inherent misogyny in male-dominated social hierarchies. The ultimate submission of a passive and pretty corpse reinforces traditional gender roles and the normalisation of women as victims. Two centuries after being written into existence, Victor Frankenstein stands in for all men seeking to control women through violent deconstruction.

Like a cadaver, in her earliest incarnations, the bride stays silenced and subservient. R. B. Peake briefly resurrects her in the 1823 *Presumption, or, the Fate of Frankenstein*, the foundation text later mined by director James Whale for the acclaimed 1935 Universal Pictures production of *The Bride of Frankenstein*. In Whale's version, the bride takes on the role of a victim, her helplessness embodied by clingy submission and passive behaviour. The bride's reproductive powers must be repressed even though her physical form incites a sexual response, a theme seen in the shocking anatomical drawings of women at the time. Whereas eighteenth century anatomical drawings of male models were stripped of all skin and posed in noble postures, the more submissive female drawings retained their feminine beauty, which was often objectified to grotesque extremes . The desirability of pretty dead girls comes into full focus with the fetishizing depictions of their lifeless forms and the aesthetically pleasing presentation of their female body parts.

It isn't until 1995 that the female monster's story changed for good with the digital publication of Shelley Jackson's hypertext adaptation *Patchwork Girl: A Modern Monster by Mary Shelley, & Herself.* In her version of Shelley's tale, Jackson gives Patchwork Girl a voice: "It was a cover-up, a scam, a lie. Has it not struck you as odd that the whole of a female of stature commensurate with that of her monstrous intended (not to mention a 'great quantity of stone') could be hoisted by one man and borne out to sea—in a *basket?*"

In one of the nodes of Jackson's linked narrative, it is Mary Shelley herself who finishes the assemblage of the female monster after she'd been aborted by her original creator Victor: "I have had plenty of time to make the girl. Yet the task was not as easy as you may suppose. I found that I could not compose a female without devoting several months to profound study and laborious disquisition." This shift in the narrative allows both Shelley and her monster a place to explore possibilities outside of the patriarchal society they were both born into.

Patchwork Girl borrows heavily from two primary sources: *Frankenstein: or, The Modern Prometheus* (1818) by Mary Shelley and *The Patchwork Girl of Oz* (1913) by L. Frank Baum, as well as secondary material composed by such luminaries as Roman poet and philosopher Titus Lucretius Carus, French philosopher Jacques Derrida, and French feminist writer and literary critic Hélène Cixous. Composed of hypertext segments, *Patchwork Girl* stitches the narrative together through the interactive efforts of the reader. Not meant to be pieced together in any particular order, the narrative is composed of five main sections. The process of navigating Jackson's inter-textual threads reconstructs Shelley's female monster one body part at a time from fragments scattered throughout the electronic hyperlinks. Thus, Patchwork Girl lives even though she never made it to the pages of Shelley's Gothic masterpiece, something Jackson's version of the aborted bride attributes to the original author's sense of propriety. The female narrative in Jackson's work remains fixed in the contexts of erasure; her presence only "glimpsed in the paisley of its negative spaces, a hurly-burly of minced flesh and gouts of blood."

Not only does the female monster have a story to tell in *Patchwork Girl*, but through the unveiling of her chimerical assemblage, each body part has its own story to tell as well. For instance, Patchwork Girl's left leg once belonged to a woman named Jane, a nanny who spent her youth consorting with sailors; her tongue came from Susannah, a girl "who talked more than she ate;" and her left breast once belonged to Charlotte, a woman who buried six of her eight children and "felt each loss in her swollen breast." Even when they are reduced to mere body parts, these women protest against the repression instituted against them.

Patchwork Girl acknowledges the sources of her various body parts and combines these women's individualities into her own concept of self. Jackson expands this discourse with the female monster's response to being dismembered: "I told her to abort me, raze me from her book; I did not want what he wanted. I laughed when my parts lay scattered on the floor, scattered as the bodies from which I had sprung, discontinuous as I myself rejoice to be. I danced in front of the disassembly…" Unable to separate herself from the amalgamation of half-remembered lives, Patchwork Girl's identity is intimately tied to the bodies of the women she was constructed from, yet she also lives as a being in her own right . Although the events in *Patchwork Girl* can be traced back to the female monster's origin in the Gothic tradition, Jackson continues the story through the decades of the modern era. In *Frankenstein*, identity is shrouded, figured as a live burial with the conception of the Creature, and by extension his bride. Being composed of the parts of multiple people, the monster is cursed to be forever in limbo with the looming threat of deconstruction and decomposition just out of sight. According to Judith Halbertstam (*Skin Shows*), "Gothic, as a genre, is itself a hybrid form, a stitched body of distorted textuality. Monsters, like the one Frankenstein builds, embody a multiplicity of fears and invite the reader to participate in charting the shapes and contours of each one."

Halbertstam asserts that Frankenstein's bride takes it one step further: "The female monster represents, in a way, the symbolic and generative power of monstrosity itself, and particularly of a monstrosity linked to femininity, female sexuality, and female powers of reproduction." The female body represents the locus of fear, and therefore must be dismantled and contained.

As exemplified in Shelley's novel, Jackson's hypertext, and numerous other stories stemming from the Gothic tradition, Frankenstein's bride both begins and ends in fragmentation. She stands in the interstices between the binary of life and death, between gender and sexuality, between absence and presence. Even though the female monster never says a single word in the original narrative, she represents a powerful force of inquiry into creativity, identity, and representation. Through the bride's various reincarnations under the direction of a succession of women writers, she has not only been given a voice, but she's also slipped free from the original text of *Frankenstein* to become a cultural myth in her own right. She has become something more than the sum of her parts.

As modern media continues to promote an unrealistic, frankly unattainable image of the "perfect" female body, it's more important than ever for writers to continue the work in creating stories that fight against mainstream's homogeneous ideal. Female bodies come in all shapes and sizes; yet women continue to judge themselves against what's considered attractive by the male gaze. And despite all of the advances over the last two centuries, women are still being told to stay in their prescribed places; even the most successful among us are not immune to sexual harassment and gendered censorship. Patchwork Girl, Pandora, and other versions of the bride stand unified against cultural prescriptions intent on the deconstruction of the female form . Their voices echo the voice of Everywoman and, together, we can demand a change.

Don't Feed The Monsters

H K Stubbs

DON'T FEED THE MONSTERS.

And yet, monsters *will* eat—feeding on women especially. On the blood
we bleed, the tender lining of our innermost sensitivities, the vulnerabilities
forced upon us and exploited, through biology, bullying, oppression, the
confiscation of freedom and liberty.

That's the nature of monsters. They ate Mary Wollstonecraft, the brilliant
18th century English writer. They gobbled her right up, reputation and all.
Devoured her ground-breaking work, mired in disrespectability, and washed
it down with public scandal. While Wollstonecraft's brilliant thinking was
always appreciated by writers and philosophers, her lifestyle blew the general
public's collective mind. The monsters won, for a time. But a century later,
those monsters discovered Wollstonecraft indigestible—her work was too
robust, her ideas too important.

But we're getting ahead of ourselves. First of all: monsters.

They're snapping at our heels even now, as we traverse these early
paragraphs, into a discussion of the many monsters faced by Wollstonecraft,
her daughter, Mary Shelley, and the protagonists of *Frankenstein*: Victor
Frankenstein, and his creation, who has been cast as the 'monster' of the
novel. Though if we examine the 'monster's' trajectory and the cruelty
exerted upon him, we may be forced to reconsider his casting as such. I will
call him the 'creation', as we consider matters of prejudice, fear, strength,
and choice; of nature versus nurture; of the *tabula rasa*; and how Shelley's
loss of her mother and babies influenced her great work.

To children, monsters are menacing entities lurking in dark places:
deep within wardrobes and the yawning shadows beneath beds. Instead,
let us conceive of monsters as allegories for negative elements of human

nature, and even as terrible occurrences, such as the deaths of loved ones. When confronted by these monsters, we usually have a choice over how to act or react, and this determines what we become. Monsters can do enormous damage, yet they can also inspire unforeseen strength and creative expression. In the darkest skies, stars shine their brightest.

Both Marys had their monsters—within and without. Perhaps these lived experiences inspired Mary Shelley's monsters in *Frankenstein*, in which a tragedy plays out. A tragedy of choices driven by weakness and fear of difference, of a parent failing to meet the challenges presented by what appears to be an abominable child. Themes of family, parenting, obsession obscuring judgement, the borders of life and death, the sense of self, the importance of nurture over nature, are robust in *Frankenstein*. And perhaps the author is harsher upon the protagonist 'father' who abandons his child through fear and weakness, because Mary herself was abandoned by loved ones repeatedly, but *not* through their choices, rather, due to the tragedies of their deaths. The scientist Frankenstein squanders the opportunity Wollstonecraft lost—to raise and educate her daughters—a topic which she had been passionate about, and the loss of which affected Shelley strongly. William Godwin encouraged the girls to read but did not provide formal education.

Mary Wollstonecraft was a brave and canny warrior, perceiving monsters few of her contemporaries could see. In a world where inequity was invisible due to its normalcy, she saw through convention to identify and describe how social norms biased against women were damaging to women and society. She was inspired to ideals of equality by the banned writings of John Locke, the great Enlightenment thinker and 'Father of Liberalism'. She saw that one of society's greatest failures was how girls' education was neglected, and how sex-based inequity—a battle we're still fighting today— had vast implications.

Wollstonecraft's views about the importance of women's education were not universal. Poorer women of the time saw education as irrelevant to their lives, as they struggled to feed their families. Their primary concern was for equitable work. Women's education was more relevant to wealthier women, though poorer women would eventually benefit from it too, achieving a better standard of living and less inequality.

The key monsters Wollstonecraft battled, on behalf of her sex, were educational neglect and social convention. She took fire on them from her elevated positions of educated intelligence and literary skill. Reading, thinking, writing, and speaking were her superpowers. She wrote about the lack of education available for women and the society that ridiculed them for their ignorance and silliness, a product of the little education they were allowed. She observed that women were ridiculed for their occupation with trivial matters such as dressing nicely and pursuing beauty. Yet beauty was an important currency for people who were discouraged from improving their minds, and so very limited in their freedom, power, and wealth. Beauty meant the opportunity to secure a future through marrying well.

Wollstonecraft articulated the importance of education: "Few men have risen to any great eminence in learning, who have not received something like a regular education," Wollstonecraft said. "Why are women expected to surmount difficulties that men are not equal to?"[1] (Posthumous works). She wrote extensively on the topic, including *Thoughts on the Education of Daughters* (1787), *Original Stories from Real Life* (1788), and *A Vindication of the Rights of Woman* (1792).

She proposed women study courses similar to professional men of the time, to become "rational, provident, realistic, self-disciplined, self-conscious and critical".[2] She argued that this would make them better wives and mothers—an example of her how thinking remained tethered to conventions of the time—though she also recommended that women develop skills that could earn them a living, as she was required to do after her father spent her inheritance.

In the late 18th century, when Wollstonecraft was writing, it would have been barely conceivable that her ideas would achieve acceptance. Yet in 1868 the University of London allowed women to enter university. By the end of the 19th century, schooling between the ages of five and 10 became compulsory for all children in the United Kingdom. Now, in the 21st century, children receive similar educational opportunities, though inequalities arising from geography, wealth, and gender certainly still exist.

Writing and publishing were Wollstonecraft's means of inspiring social change and earning an income. They were also her path to fame, infamy, and disrepute.

Wollstonecraft had the ability to rethink social conventions others took for granted, fighting for her right to better education, and educating herself through reading. Although her thinking was coloured by the ideology of

---

1 Gordon, 2015
2 Kelly, 1992

the time, she managed to lay the groundwork for significant social change.

Many feminists and scholars have denied Wollstonecraft the title of 'feminist' because of her stated goal of educating women to become 'better wives and mothers'. However, one must consider the era she lived in—the journey towards equality had not yet begun. It still hasn't been actualised. It would have been difficult to imagine—even for a visionary such as Wollstonecraft. Although she might not have had the telescopic foresight to conceive of women achieving equality with men within society and under the law, she did identify one of the first steps towards that goal: women's education. She might also have been cleverly selling her concept by proposing an aspiration that would be widely acceptable. Who could reasonably argue with the goal of 'creating better wives and mothers'?

To examine how Wollstonecraft's theories of education played out in her own life is to tell a story of personal tragedy. She applied her theories to the education of her first daughter, Fanny Imlay, but she never had that opportunity for Mary Shelley. Tragically, Wollstonecraft died of septicaemia days after her second daughter was born, so she never had the opportunity to educate the little girl who grew up to become the author of the original gothic novel, *Frankenstein*.[3]

Further personal and social tragedy struck when Wollstonecraft's husband, William Godwin, published her *Memoirs* after her death in 1798. He did this with the best of intentions, that the world should love and marvel over her life and intellect, as he did. Although Wollstonecraft and Godwin were in love, neither of them believed in marriage. They married only to avoid the scandal of another child born outside of wedlock, as Fanny Imlay had been. The monster of *Social Convention* won again.

With Godwin's publication of Wollstonecraft's *Memoirs*, which he saw as celebrating an amazing woman's life, intellect and passion, public opinion turned hostile. Wollstonecraft's unconventional lifestyle, with illegitimate children, love affairs and suicide attempts, was a scandal. *She* became a monster in the eyes of society, blighted by her failure to comply with conventions of feminine decency.

Society casting away Wollstonecraft as an abomination, when she is faultless but unusual, is similarly reflected in Frankenstein's casting away of his child, seen as an abomination.

Wollstonecraft posthumously fell into such disrepute that her writings

---

3 Lepore, 2018

were largely ignored until the late 1800s, although she remained respected and influential in literary and philosophical circles. Some of her ideas were incorporated into the novels of Jane Austen, with characters expressing Wollstonecraft's sentiments in their dialogue. [4]

For a time, *Social Convention* triumphed over Mary Wollstonecraft, silencing her brilliant work for a century. Wollstonecraft, in her life, had shone brightly but shot too far. Conservative critics were delighted to decry her and see her work buried. The importance and influence of her work could not be erased, however. A century later scholars and feminists brought her writings back into feminist discourse.

Wollstonecraft's death resulted in her daughter's failing to benefit from a formal education—which she had been so passionate about—as discussed in her *Thoughts on the Education of Daughters*. Both Fanny and Mary were raised by William Godwin, and he cared for them and read widely to them. He favoured his own daughter Mary over Fanny, praising her as pretty, quick and "considerably superior" to her sister. [5]

While lacking a formal education, young Mary Shelley was encouraged to read widely. She listened to intellectual arguments and to storytellers such as Samuel Taylor Coleridge. However, with a lack of formal education, it could be said that Wollstonecraft's deplored monster of 'educational neglect' had struck again—this time, her very own daughter.

Shelley's relationship with her stepmother was one of discord. She described her as "a woman I shudder to think of." To escape the troubled household, Shelley often retreated to read by her mother's grave in St Pancras churchyard. In this emotive gothic image, it is easy to imagine the young Mary's sadness and loneliness for her deceased mother. She sought sanctuary and perhaps a connection to the dead woman through proximity to her headstone and corpse, likely reading her words as she sat by her grave.

While other girls might have passed by, smiling as they held their mother's hands, and been wrapped in a consoling embrace when they fell, experiencing tender and loving moments of maternal warmth, Shelley's relationship with her mother was fragmented across intractable and cold boundaries of time and death. This could certainly have inspired her ideas—and fuelled her obsession—with Wollstonecraft and reanimating

4 Mellor, 2002
5 Gordon, 2015

the dead. Perhaps Shelley saw the dead as no longer being whole people, but rather, a collection of fragments and impressions lost in time and re-collected in vignettes, imparted memories, and the writings and images remaining of them. A child left behind could construct an abstraction of a deceased parent, but it was not enough for a girl hungry for a mother's love and care. Such a great mother Wollstonecraft would have been, too, compared to the unhappy homelife Shelley endured. Her discord with her stepmother was so severe that when she was fourteen, she was sent to live with relatives in Scotland.

While the loss of her mother and prospects of formal education were devastating, these tragedies were likely highly influential inspirations for Shelley's masterpiece. If Wollstonecraft had been present to provide formal education, Mary Shelley might not have conceived of *Frankenstein*. Perhaps this monster of 'educational neglect' (along with loneliness, misery and suffering for the loss of her mother and the deaths of her young children later in her life) were catalysts, like heat and pressure, motivating Shelley's creative genius. [6]

Mary described her dreams of the dead returning to life in her journal. "'Dream that my little baby came to life again; that it had only been cold, and that we rubbed it before the fire, and it lived,' she wrote in her diary. "Awake and find no baby."' [7]

In the novel, *Frankenstein*, these themes of death, loss, parenting and education reflect Shelley's experiences. Like Shelley, Victor Frankenstein's creation or 'child' is without a most important parent.

We cannot call Frankenstein's creation a monster when he first gains life—he is not yet a monster, drawn true to Locke's idea of the *tabula rasa*, or blank slate. Also, like Shelley, the creation has no name of his own.

He takes on Frankenstein's name in popular culture, while Mary Wollstonecraft Godwin Shelley bears the names of her mother, father and husband, but nothing unique to herself.

While Mary and the creation's circumstances of abandonment differ, both discover literature as the source of knowledge and empowerment.

The creation finds a leather portmanteau holding *Paradise Lost* by John Milton, *Plutarch's Lives*, and *The Sorrows of Young Werther*. [8] In these books, he learns about the fall of man, the lives of important people, and romantic

6 Gordon, 2015
7 Lepore, 2018
8 Shelley, 133

love. Both Shelley and the creation are educated through reading, into highly intelligent, sensitive and eloquent beings.

Frankenstein is an epistolary novel, that is, a novel of letters: stories within stories, so that the creature's story is three layers deep.

The letters are written by the explorer Marlow, addressed to his sister, as he pursues his obsession to reach the North Pole. On a ship surrounded by ice, he meets Victor Frankenstein, chasing a 'monster' across the ice. The scientist Frankenstein tells his own story to Marlow, and the story that his creation has related to him. Within the creation's story is the story of the family he observed for many months and grew to love: the De Laceys. Through their love for each other, he learns to love.

It becomes evident that the monstrous aspects which grow to rule the creation's nature are mutations wrought by the cruelty of others in response to his ugliness, deformity and lack of position in society. This harshness is wrought upon him in spite of his many kind acts.

The events of the creation's life illustrate Wollstonecraft's assertions that "People are rendered ferocious by misery" and "misanthropy is ever the offspring of discontent." [9]

After being cast out by Frankenstein, the creation befriends the blind elderly man, De Lacey. He persuades his new friend to his cause while the rest of the family is absent, with the benefit of avoiding the prejudice arising from sight.

When the De Lacey family see the *monster*, they attack him. The elderly man falls ill, and the family refuses to return to their home.

This rejection by people he's grown to care for hits the creation hard and speaks to the importance of society and civilisation as a formative force upon character. He begins to think about the initial rejection by his creator, and the violent treatment he's endured. The final rejection comes from Frankenstein again, when he refuses to accept his creation and denies to build him a female partner.

"I am malicious because I am miserable..." says the creation. "Shall I respect man when he condemns me? Let him live with me in the interchange of kindness; and, instead of injury, I would bestow every benefit upon him with tears of gratitude at his acceptance." [10] Like women, the creation seeks acknowledgement and acceptance as an equal by society.

9 Lepore, 2018
10 Shelley, 154

Although Victor Frankenstein begins to build a female partner for his creation, before she is complete, he destroys her, fearing the havoc such monsters would wreak upon humanity, with the suggestion that a female would be an even more hideous concept, and that monsters would multiply and overtake the world.

The cost Victor Frankenstein pays for his ambition, his lack of responsibility and kindness, and his refusal to comply with the creation's request, is the ultimate price—everything. He loses all that is dear to him.

Like these characters, we have the choice to resist our descent towards monstrosity, though we cannot always protect ourselves from being cast as such. We have the ability to resist the forces acting upon us. *Frankenstein* suggests, in fiction and reality, monsters offer us the chance to display our greatest strengths or succumb to our worst weaknesses: responding with a default of fear and violence to that which we don't understand; or rising above those initial reactions to respond with empathy, engagement, and compassion.

Through the text, Shelley warns us not to be blindsided by fear and distrust of the unknown, not to react with doubt and violence, but to execute our responsibilities to the full extent required, to follow through on our promises, to complete what we have begun, to conduct ourselves with honour and good faith, with kindness and strength, and to build relationships on a basis of equitable trust. While we do not have a choice about what happens to us, we often have the power of our own decisions. Though that power is not complete, we are not born equal, and life and loved ones can be taken from us at any time. Like Victor Frankenstein, we face many monsters, as humans—some of them arising from within ourselves and our relationships. The worst of them in Frankenstein appear to be ambition, prejudice, exclusion, and revenge. However, we are still battling with Wollstonecraft's monsters: social convention, educational neglect, and the disadvantage of girls and women worldwide. The inequities are still so normal that they are often invisible. In spheres of wealth and power, men still dominate. If you seek evidence, just look at the average contemporary composition of company boards, governments, and political parties. Flip through the business section of a newspaper. Mostly men.

In Frankenstein, Shelley reveals that the path towards becoming a monster is accelerated by poor choices. Especially a failure to moderate ambition, fear, prejudice, and cruelty. However, the characters have agency and opportunities to respond to events which challenge their humanity.

The novel also challenges us to question the notion of 'monster' and who is cast as one. Counter to popular opinion, the creation was not a monster. Mary Wollstonecraft was not a monster. Equal opportunity and addressing inequity is not a monster. As a society, we must be wary of being blind to the real issues and challenges while distracted by false notions of monstrosity.

The group machinery of civilisation, while providing a vast range of benefits, is the largest monster of all, riding on the backs of, and consuming, the poor and the weak; enabling the powerful and dominant to thrive. Our culture now speaks and aims towards equality and inclusion of all abilities. The highest actualisation of all selves can only be achieved through accepting, educating, and enabling individuals, and addressing inequities with appropriate supports.

While never knowing her mother in life, Shelley was an avid scholar of Wollstonecraft's writing, as evident by her novel's warning. *Frankenstein* warns us to think of others, to rise above prejudice, to temper our ambition with reason, and weigh our actions and reactions against the results they will elicit. To strive to exhibit our best selves—and in so doing, lead and inspire others. It is clear Shelley was a scholar of Wollstonecraft's work, as the novel suggests individual outcomes result from a combination of nature, nurture, free choice, and the social structures enabling or deriding us.

With the success of *Frankenstein*, a novel celebrated as a classic, Mary Shelley achieved a feat Wollstonecraft would have lauded. She raised the standing of women's intellectual achievements within society. Along with her intellect and skill as a writer, Shelley brought the un-nameable kernel of herself: elements innate to her as Wollstonecraft's daughter and as a woman. As a woman and mother, she injected a poignant prism of emotion into her literature, refracting a full spectrum of feeling, from love and joy, to the misery of losing her children. To write from a position of having experienced such love and loss was rare for writers of her time.

There is a poetic beauty to the fact that Shelley achieved recognition as an author, equal to or superior to her mother's. Wollstonecraft had been rendered lifeless, distant, and fragmented by death. Yet Shelley overcame the challenges of domestic discord, educational neglect, and emotional devastation after the loss of her mother and three young children, to achieve literary brilliance and the acceptance her creation dreamed of.

With this recognition, their monsters are vanquished, silenced, and destroyed. Thanks to literature, education, choice, and agency, the Marys succeeded in changing the social structure.

Take that kick in the teeth, monsters!

The Marys win.

MARYS AND MOTHERHOOD

Claire Fitzpatrick

"Dream that my little baby came to life again—that it had only been cold and that we rubbed it by the fire and it lived—I awake and find no baby—I think about the little thing all day."

—Mary Shelley journal entry. 19 March 1815

WHEN PHILOSOPHER AND POLITICAL ACTIVIST Mary Wollstonecraft (1759-1797) died of puerperal fever on September 10, 1797, she left behind a new-born daughter with two burdens—the powerful name of Mary Wollstonecraft Godwin (1797-1851), and an intense and almost obsessive desire to be mothered. Mary Shelley, as she was later known after her marriage to the poet and philosopher Percy Bysshe Shelley (1756-1836), grew to become the author of one of the most famous novels of all time. However, her experiences with motherhood were filled with death and despair, and governed many years of her life, most reflective in possibly one of the most famous novels ever written—'Frankenstein; Or, The Modern Prometheus.' Looking at the novel as an example of attachment theory, this essay will critique how Mary's experiences with motherhood shaped her ideas on family, and the role of a parent within a child's upbringing.

After his beloved wife's death, the philosopher and journalist William Godwin (1756-1836) struggled to care for his two infant charges. He agonised over the education of Mary and Fanny, worried who would educate them. He assumed full responsibility for Fanny, now aged three (the illegitimate daughter born from an affair between Wollstonecraft and the American commercial speculator and diplomat Gilbert Imlay), as well as for the new-born Mary Godwin. In a letter to Amelia Anderson, he calls Mary Wollstonecraft 'the best-qualified person of any person I ever saw' to educate Mary and Fanny, so struggled to find someone suitable. At first, he hired a housekeeper and governess, then a wetnurse for when Mary became ill. Soon, both left for other ventures and Godwin found himself looking for a wife who could be a mother for both Mary and Fanny. After courtships with four women, he met Mary Jane Clairmont in May of 1801, a widow with a six-year-old son (Charles) and four-year-old daughter (Claire). In December, they were married, and a year later William Gowdin Jr was born.[1]

Though Mary Jane was known to be hot-tempered, with many of his friends finding her a disagreeable woman, Godwin genuinely loved her and found her a good mother for his daughters. However, this was not the case. Mary Jane Godwin resented Mary and the attachment she had with her father and attempted to squash her creativity and love for reading. She convinced Godwin the children required no formal education, and consequently, all five children were principally schooled at home. However, Mary had access to her father's expansive library and was taught to read three books at once. As she grew older, she would also listen in on philosophical, literary, or scientific conversations between her father and his visitors, such as Charles Lamb, William Wordsworth, Samuel Coleridge, Horne Took, John Johnson, William Hazlitt, and Humphrey Davy. However, despite growing up around scholars and grand thinkers, Mary was routinely subjected to a childhood of rejection and neglect.

Abandoned by her mother and rejected by her stepmother, Mary grew up feeling unwanted. It was no secret how little Mary Jane Clairmont cared for her stepdaughter. Clairmont became jealous of the awe and attention praised upon Godwin and his equally intelligent daughter. In retaliation, Clairmont punished Mary, forcing her into chores in an attempt to pry her apart from her close bond with her father. In a letter penned in 1814, Mary referred to Clairmont as 'A woman I shudder to think of.' Mary saw her as stepmother as everything her mother was not—a philistine, devious, manipulative, and conservative. She also blamed her stepmother for taking her away from her father and circle of friends. After their marriage, withdrew almost entirely into his study and left the running of the household to his second wife. By 1812 things between Mary and Mrs Godwin had come to such a head that William Godwin sent Mary to board with an acquaintance, William Baxter, and his family in Dundee for several

---

1 Wright, 2018

months. Mary took to the Baxters at once. They showed her a different kind of family: closely knit and fond of each other. "Mary Godwin came to idealise the bourgeois family as the source both of emotional sustenance and of ethical value. They inspired her later fictional representations of the nuclear family as a community of mutually dependent, equally respected, and equally self-sacrificing individuals". [2]

In 'Childcare and the Growth Of Love', Bowlby delineated three distinct phases of development in the child's capacity for human relationships. Simplified, these include: establishing a relationship with a clearly identified person—the mother, achieved by five or six months. Needing this 'identified person' as an ever-present companion, continuing until three years. Becoming able to maintain the relationship in her absence over a few days two a week but only in favourable circumstances at four-five years. [3] For Mary, her father was the identified person, and when he withdrew from her, leaving her to deal with her stepmother, she experienced severe emotional abuse. It is evident the parent-child relationship within 'Frankenstein' is reflective of the emotional abuse Mary suffered from her stepmother and is a prime example of how Mary could have reacted to this abuse. Throughout the novel, the creature endures rejection to the point that he is consumed by violent rage. Although it can be argued that the creature's growth into a monster is the result of an innate monstrosity, his vengeful actions toward the end of the novel stem from Victor's abandonment of his creation, and thus the absence of a healthy parent-child relationship. This change is especially evident when, upon Victor's destruction of the creature's soon-to-be-wife, the creature asserts, "You are my creator, but I am your master; obey!"[4] This complex and destructive relationship is an example of a concept most commonly attributed to people who experience abuse and/or neglect as a child and subsequently remain emotionally stunted as an adult, and the perpetrator of violence or crime. However, Mary wasn't consumed with a violent rage. In fact, she used her writing as an outlet to deal with the abuse in a healthy and productive way.

Attachment theory is focused on the relationships and bonds between people, particularly long-term relationships, including those between a parent

2 Pabst-Kastner, 2015
3 Gaughan, 2011
4 Shelley, 1818

and child and between romantic partners. As such, the kind of attachment children have with their parents determines the nature of the child's later relationships. British psychologists John Bowlby and Mary Ainsworth were the first attachment theorists, describing attachment as a "lasting psychological connectedness between human beings."[5] Having no emotional intimacy with their parents, children often develop an avoidant attachment as a way to remain physically close to them without displaying their feelings. For these children, negative attention from an emotionally distant parent is better than no attention at all. Bowlby first formulated the theory in the 1930s, linking a child's development to its ties to its mother, and its disruption through separation, deprivation, and bereavement. With this basis, Mary Ainsworth formulated the concept of maternal sensitivity to infant signals and its role in the development of infant-mother attachment patterns. Focusing on the creature as a child, and Victor as a father, we can see a child of neglect, with poor impulse control. A neglected child will have attachment difficulties and cognitive defects, as evident through the creature's internalised feelings, the use of aggressive behaviour, and a lack of ego resiliency. Victor fails to teach a basic understanding of morality, denies parental affection, and does not educate it on how to exist within civilised society.

Childhood can feel like a long and often arduous task. And without a mother, it can be even more so. From birth, an infant is embedded in a large social network.[6] This network of kin can include a mother, father, siblings, and other adults within the child's life, including grandparents, friends, and even animals. An infant must learn to connect and socialise with all of these people, to develop a sense of self. However, if a part of this social network is lacking—such as a mother or a loving alternative—the child develops negative attitudes towards these roles, leading to deviant behaviour later on in life. Applying attachment theory to Frankenstein allows readers to understand why Victor abandons his creation, and of his subsequent encounters with the creature, as well as the extent to which these events were determined by his relationship with Alphonse, his father. By identifying the attachment types of Victor/Alphonse and Victor/the creature, readers realise the extent of Victor's role in the advancement of the creature's aggressive behaviour and actions as well as the negative consequences of creating life without nurturing it.

5 Bowlby, 1982
6 Learner, 1983

Attachment theory attributes four types—secure, avoidant, ambivalent, and disorganised.[7] In Victor's case, he developed an avoidant attachment with his parents and grew up in a home unsupportive of his development as a person, or his scientific interests. 'Avoidant attachment…is associated with tepid, unsupportive, and insensitive caregiving," which characterises much of Victor's relationship with his parents, who spent an inadequate amount of time with him. He was "urged to application" in studying and reading, and his "hours were fully employed in acquiring and maintaining a knowledge of [English, Greek, and German] literature." [8] Even when doing exactly as they asked, Victor's parents seemed uninterested in what he learned. In a rare instance when his father inquired about his studies, Alphonse 'looked carelessly' at the book and called it 'sad trash.' [9] This insensitive caregiving results in the inability of the two of them to develop a filial bond. In addition, Victor feels neglected by his mother, Caroline, who puts her own life in danger to care for his cousin Elizabeth (of whom the family have taken in and raised as Victor's sister), afflicted with scarlet fever. Consequently, Caroline dies of the fever and Elizabeth recovers. However, instead of comforting his son, Alphone resumes his trip to Ingolstadt, offering no support to Victor after losing his mother and suggesting he ignore his emotions and move on with his life.

By acknowledging Victor's avoidant attachment with his parents, it is easy to see why Victor would so quickly and carelessly abandon his creation. Victor rejects the Creature immediately upon sight. "I beheld the wretch— the miserable monster whom I had created. He held up the curtain of the bed, and his eyes…were fixed on me. His jaw opened, and he muttered some inarticulate sounds, while a grin wrinkled his cheeks…one hand was stretched out, seemingly to detain me, but I escaped, and rushed downstairs." [10] While the creature is seeking comfort from his creator, his father, for affection and love, Victor has already rejected him, labelling him a "miserable monster", and is therefore unresponsive to his creation's needs. In doing so, he has become the cold and unloving parent, just as Alphonse has always been towards him.

Mary Shelley's own experiences with motherhood were filled with misery, however, unlike Victor, she was anything but cold and unloving. Eloping with Percy Shelley at sixteen, Mary was either pregnant or

7 Bowlby, 1982
8 Shelley, 1818
9 Shelley, 1818
10 Shelley, 1818

breastfeeding for over nine years. Mary had five pregnancies and only one surviving child, and though her experiences with motherhood were filled with death and despair, the numerous letters she wrote and the journal entries she penned clearly show the deep love she had with her surviving son Percy Florence Shelley, and the devotion and overwhelming sorrow for the children she lost. Her first child, whom she and Percy called Clara, survived eight days. Two weeks after her death, Mary wrote in her journal: *"Dream that my little baby came to life again—that it had only been cold and that we rubbed it by the fire and it lived—I awake and find no baby—I think about the little thing all day."* [11] Then, at eighteen she gave birth to William, nicknamed Willmouse. His parents adored William. Mary wrote: *'Blue eyes—gets dearer and sweeter every day—he jumps about like a little squirrel'.* William was with his mother in Geneva when she conceived Frankenstein, and then in Bristol as she finished the novel. The following year, Mary gave birth to Clara Everina, and for a time the family were happy in the English countryside.

Tragedy struck, when after moving to Italy, Clara became sick and died. In a journal entry, Mary described their rush to Venice to find a doctor—*'when nerves were strung to their utmost tension by mental anguish.'* Nine months later, William also died in Rome at the age of three and a half, and Mary went into a deep depression. As she and Percy watched over him during his final hours, she wrote to a friend; *'The misery of these hours is beyond calculation —The hopes of my life are bound up in him.'* After William died, Mary gave birth to Percy Florence. However, she was wracked by the concern he would also die. *'It is a bitter thought that all should be risked on one yet how much sweeter than to be childless as I was for 5 hateful months'.*[12] The loss of her children undoubtedly influenced Mary's own approach to motherhood within 'Frankenstein'. The Creature himself is made motherless, and although he craves the love and respect from Victor as his father, he also yearns for the maternal and feminine love of a female companion. Many of the characters he meets during his time away from Victor are also motherless. Caroline Beaufort, Elizabeth Lavenza, Agnes DeLacey, and Safie (an independent woman based on Mary Shelley's feminist mother, Mary Wollstonecraft) have all lost their mothers to death. Only Justine Moritz's mother remains alive, however she "through a strange perversity...could not endure" her daughter, [13] perhaps a parallel

11 Ozolins, 1975
12 Ozolins, 1975
13 Shelley, 1818

for the hatred Mary Jane Godwin had for her stepdaughter.

Motherlessness, absent parents, and orphans are common themes in fiction. The most famous orphans generally appear in 19th and early 20th Century literature (*The Secret Garden, Anne of Green Gables, Oliver Twist, David Copperfield, Tom Sawyer, Jane Eyre*). Absent parents occur in fiction for a variety of reasons. They allow protagonists to solve problems by themselves without parental influences; a tough and lonely upbringing advances a character's motivation to succeed; being forcibly removed from a family allows a protagonist to go on a journey to find them; murdered parents provide the motivation for vengeance. Whatever the case, absent parents are usually used as a way to create drama and emotion, and allow for the character to form their own identity within their 'quest.' Within 'Frankenstein', the absent parents are not used to move Victor's story forward, however, but as a way to create fear of the maternal. This, of course, is directly linked to Shelley's own anxieties about childbirth: the death of her mother shortly after she was born, the frequency and difficulties of her own pregnancies, and the deaths of her first three children while they were infants.

Today, novels often use the 'dead mother' trope too frivolously, and without any sense of identity of these women. They are often used as nothing more than to add a sense of empathy to the characters, or to change their upbringing. We never get any sense of what the mothers were like, how they treated their children, or how they affected their children (aside from their death). Shelley's attachment to her mother, however, is highly evident (in fact, one could say she was the originator of the dead mother trope) as she used her writing to deal with her emotions surrounding a woman who had abandoned her in death, leaving her to a cold and unloving stepmother she was unable to form an attachment to. However, in 'Frankenstein', these emotions have moved past a general dislike for stepmothers and ballooned into an intense fear of motherhood in general.

Attachment also features when the Creature returns to Victor and asks for a mate. Despite his concerns, Victor travels to the desolate Orkney Isles and unhappily obliges. However, just before she is almost complete, he sees the male creature watching him through the window and is hit with the sudden fear that she and the Creature would procreate and plague mankind with their new breed of humans. Victor contemplates creating such a woman, whom he feared would parent 'a race of devils.' 'I was now about to form another being, of whose dispositions I was alike ignorant; she might become ten thousand times more malignant that her mate, and delight, for its own sake, in murder and wretchedness…[the pair] might even hate each other; the creature who already lived loathed his own deformity, and might he not conceive a greater abhorrence for it when it came before his eyes in the female form? She also might turn with disgust from him to the superior beauty of man; she might quit him, and he be again alone, exasperated by the fresh provocation of being deserted by one of his own species.' [14]

As such, he destroys the unfinished bride in a fit of anger and guilt, places her mangled remains into a basket, and disposes of them late at night in the middle of a lake. [15] The destruction of this bride, and the denial of her progeny, offers a powerful rumination on what could have been. What sort of woman would she have become? Would she have wanted to carry children at all? And if she did fall pregnant, what kind of attachment would she form with her child? Having no mother of her own, the only parent she could learn from would be Victor, already proven to be emotionally distant and neglectful towards his first creation. Perhaps this creature, the Eve of the new race, would be just as neglectful of her children as Mary Jane Clairmont was with young Mary herself? In this sense, Victor's destruction of her is the right cause of action.

On the cultural and social level, Victor's quest to create a human being supports a patriarchal denial of the value of women and of female sexuality. Of course, within the nineteenth-century, women were relegated to the private or domestic sphere, and men worked outside the home. Within the novel, Alphonse Frankenstein worked as a public servant, Victor worked as a scientist, Henry Clerval and his father were merchants, and Walton was an explorer. The women, however, were confined to the home and delegated roles of housewives, nursemaids, and nurses (Caroline Beaufort, Elizabeth, Margaret Saville), or servants (Justine Moritz).

As an avid reader of her mother's work, Mary Shelley was able to interpret her mother's philosophy and use it in her novels. In much of her work, Wollstonecraft argued that women must be independent citizens, but not without fulfilling certain duties as mothers. Today, many academics

---

14 Shelley, 1818
15 Shelley, 1818

criticise Wollstonecraft's work, suggesting she did not further equality between the sexes. Several academics suggest her educational reforms only incentivise women to become educated mothers, limiting public pursuits in favour of domestic affairs. [16] They also suggest several of her feminist doctrines only apply to women as gifted as herself. However, scholars in support of her work suggest these criticisms occur because academics misjudge her actions, and do not consider the era Wollstonecraft lived in. Her husband, William Godwin, also criticised several of her principles within her 'Vindications', in his book 'Memoirs of the Author of a Vindication of the Rights of Woman' (1798). [17] An unusually frank account for memoirs of that time, Godwin penned the memoir after her death, distorting the complex life of Wollstonecraft, and subsequently ruining her reputation for many years following its publication. Today, many scholars focus only on the criticisms of her work, painting an inaccurate picture of who she was, what she stood for, and just how important her ideas and writing contributed to modern feminism. They also ignore her positive influence on Mary Shelley's own work, and the love she had for the brilliant non-conformist mother she never met. Within 'Frankenstein', the challenge Victor faced with creating a female companion for the Creature demonstrates the influence of her mother (as well as the Swiss philosopher Jean-Jacques Rousseau). Not unlike Mary Wollstonecraft, the female creature considered it her right to determine her own existence. As such, Victor feared her sexuality, and her freedom to do whatever she wanted.

In addition, while the absence of emotional intimacy with her mother, and the neglect she experienced with Mary Jane Clairmont, negatively affected Mary, her mother's philosophy and opinions on women and parenting positively affected her writing. Mary was able to use her attachment to Wollstonecraft to help shape her ideas on family. Her attachment to her mother was secure, whereas her attachment to her stepmother (like Victor's to the Creature) was avoidant, and, as she grew older, became ambivalent.

On July 1, 1822, Percy Bysshe Shelley, along with his friend Edward Williams—a retired army officer—were sailing from Livorno, Italy, to Lerici (in Italy), when Shelley's new boat the 'Don Juan' was lost in a storm. Because of their inexperience, both men drowned (Mary Shelley was just 24 at the time). Three months after her husband's death, she

---

16 Williams, 2019
17 Godwin, 1798

wrote in a letter: "Tell me the truth, Beloved, where are you? And when shall I join you? They are all gone & I live—if it be life to be as I am." Years later she wrote: "instead of the cheerful voices of the living, I have dwelt among the early tombs of those I loved." In her years without Percy, Mary Shelley travelled around Europe with her son, of which she documented in her travelogue 'Rambles in Germany and Italy in 1840, 1842 and 1843'.[18] However, in the mid-1840's she became the target of three separate blackmailers, and, in her final years, experienced debts, poverty, and illness (which scholars now attribute to a tumour). She died in London in 1851 at the age of fifty-three. After her death, Percy's heart was found in her desk drawer, wrapped in a sheet of his poetry, along with locks of Clara and William's hair.

'Frankenstein' depicts a world in which mothers are largely absent. And within this world, Mary Shelley describes how a parent's love, or lack thereof, largely determines a child's development later in life. The absence of the attachment between Mary and her mother, as well as the cold and unloving relationship she experienced with her stepmother, shows a woman denied the maternal love she deserved. The theme of motherhood reflects the influence of parenting on children, and the potential consequences one experiences without nurture, guidance, and a healthy attachment to a parental figure. 'Frankenstein' is not just a revolutionary science fiction novel, but a candid insight into the melancholy Mary Shelley experienced throughout her life, in particular the loss of all but one of her children. This theme is still relevant today, with countless books and journal articles about the importance of a parental bond. However, Mary Shelley's depiction of motherhood remains a fear women experience to this day—the loss of their children in infancy, birthing a stillborn, and the struggles of raising a child when their own childhood experiences left them maladaptive or unable to provide a stable and loving attachment between themselves and their child. Let us hope the 'dead mother' theme in novels and films turns from an overused, lacklustre trope into something more substantial, constructive, and hopeful for the future.

---

18 Shelley, 1844

My Mother Hands Me A Book

Piper Mejia

IT IS IRONIC THAT SOCIETY RELIES on research to justify the benefit of educating girls. Research that shows that the length of time a girl is in education directly correlates to the greater probability of her attaining a job that enables her to provide for her children so that they can grow up healthy. [1] The central tenet of this argument is that the purpose of a biological girl's life is to be a mother, a *good* mother who puts the care and welfare of her children first as if there is no better way for women to benefit society. Case in point, Mary Wollstonecraft is known for being the mother of Mary Shelley (author of *Frankenstein*) over her extensive contributions to literature, as if giving birth to Mary Shelley was the ultimate accomplishment in her life—despite Wollstonecraft dying a month after her daughter's birth. As a result, Shelley would have only known Wollstonecraft through the lens of the people who knew her and the words she left behind, rather than being shaped by the direct influence of her mother. However, when we reflect on the people who shape us, our identity, our morals, and our ethics, we may not put our mothers at the top of the list, and yet, like Shelley, we are influenced by our mother's lives, even in their absence.

As an English teacher in a girls' secondary school, 'what shapes our identity' is a recurring theme in both the texts I introduce to students, but also in the texts the students produce themselves. How can it not be, when every text is like a small light in a dark room, giving us a glimpse of the author, what they are willing to share and what they share subconsciously. Wollstonecraft is one of the many female authors I refer to in my senior classes, she is a reminder to my students that their rights and privileges have been hundreds of years in the making, and that what they write now

---

1 https://www.unicef.org/education/girls-education

may have a similar impact into the future.

Remembering Wollstonecraft is like remembering Shakespeare.[2] She is not the only woman to have rallied against a society designed to keep her weighted in place by her gender as a daughter, a sister, a wife, and a mother. But because she *wrote*, because she left her own words behind as a legacy, we can put a pin in her life and tell ourselves we know who she was and what motivated her to share her (controversial) ideas. Of course, these artefacts of her life, her own words, cannot convey the complexity of Wollstonecraft, as most people who write cringe at their own words, days, weeks, even years later, horrified that they were so young, naïve, even egotistical as to believe that what they had to say was worth saying. Why would Wollstonecraft be any different?

Yet, 200 years later, the words from a Jewish girl hiding for her life in an attic[3] showed us that putting pins in time—even if it's the personal diary of a young girl writing mainly about how much she did not like her mother—has great value when that moment in time is vastly different from the one, we live in.

Through words, through essays, stories, novels, and poetry, we can trace Wollstonecraft's feminist influence in Western society. Like lightning hitting the ground, her influence sent fingers of energy from one woman to the next, even reaching through time to someone like me, a migrant living in Aotearoa-New Zealand, a writer, a teacher, a mother of daughters, a woman weighed down by her gender, angry that she will not leave the world a better place for the people who come after her despite the actions she has taken and the words she has written.

It is unclear if Wollstonecraft set out to be a part of this chain of women who have influenced debate and laws that constrained women to the narrow confines of simply being the property of their fathers, their husbands, and finally their sons. In her writing, *A Vindication of the Rights of Women* and *Maria: or The Wrongs of Woman*, she wrote about the imbalance of power in marriage and motherhood while advocating for equity in education, a conversation that has trickled through generations of women, bolstering their courage to continue the debate and to continue to advocate for equity. For hundreds of years the impact of her life's work has chipped away

---

2 A comparison Wollstonecraft would have abhorred as, in her own words, she was, "sick of hearing of the…untaught genius of Shake[speare]".
3 Frank, 1942

at social custom and laws that demonise women for simply being born female, starting with, at least in the western world, women no longer being chattels of their male relatives. In Aotearoa, an example showing how long it has taken women to have control over their bodies, is when the right to choose to be a parent, a mother, was moved from a Criminal Act to a Health Act as recently as 2020. This small change to our legislation cements the understanding that women do not have to be mothers to have value in society.

As a lover of biographies about writers, I read *The Life and Death of Mary Wollstonecraft* (1974) by Claire Tomalin, as a recommendation by my mother. My brilliant radical mother did not mention that Wollstonecraft was the mother of Mary Shelley—she assumed I knew. I did not. However, as someone who sees her mother as an individual, a whole person with her own life separate and secret from my own, the connection was of no concern to me; even less so when I learned that Wollstonecraft never had the opportunity to nurture and educate Shelley. So it was with greater interest that I found amongst her published writing, a piece entitled: *Thoughts on the Education of Daughters: with Reflections on Female Conduct, in the more important duties of life* (1787). At the time of writing, Wollstonecraft was 28 and not yet a mother.

Out of all her writing, this piece intrigued me on several levels, firstly, as an educator of girls, and secondly, as a historic perspective to another book I had recently read, *Dear Ijeawele: A Feminist Manifesto in Fifteen Suggestions* (2017) by Chimamanda Ngozi Adichie, who wrote it as a letter to a friend asking for advice on "how to raise a girl". I argue that although neither Wollstonecraft nor Adichie had daughters when they wrote about 'educating'/'raising' girls, 200 years of struggle for gender equity has left its mark. In that the education of girls, how and for what purpose, is an ongoing debate.

To read Wollstonecraft, the reader must hold tight to their understanding she was writing from the perspective of a woman living in the 1700s. Reading Adichie, on the other hand, is like breathing, as if she has taken my thoughts and put them to paper. It is a book I have passed on to my daughters, but one I also teach to my students, not because I believe it is their role to be mothers, but rather because Adichie's ideas are considered radical even in today's society. Similarly, to the audience for Wollstonecraft's writing in her time, Adichie's ideas will contribute to my students' education, equipping them with the language they need to demand equity and empowering them to change the world whenever they find this equity absent.

For the crime of being born a daughter, Wollstonecraft was denied the educational opportunities offered to her younger brother, Ned. While he inherited wealth from their grandfather and was sent to a grammar school to be educated, Wollstonecraft attended a day school and was later educated by childless neighbours. This was seen as sufficient for a girl, the end goal being a good marriage, where good meant marrying someone with *sufficient* money and *respectable* social status.

In the 1700s educational institutes lacked the rigour and regulations of an explicit curriculum, expected attendance, and full inclusion of all children, as is legislated in today's society;[4] consequently, anyone, even people without qualifications, could open a school. This was also true for Wollstonecraft who—after assisting her younger sister Eliza to leave her husband, and her friend Fanny Blood into leaving her family home—decided to open a school to secure an income for the three of them. Despite having no aptitude for teaching, it was during this period that Wollstonecraft began to meet people who further influenced her to speak out on issues of social reform and gender equality, cementing her legacy as one of England's earliest recognised feminists. It was also during this period of her life, a span of only two years, that she wrote and had published, *Thoughts on the Education of Daughters: with Reflections on Female Conduct, in the more important duties of life* (1787).

Wollstonecraft prefaces her text with a note offering no "apology for [the] attempt". She assumes she will receive censure, which of course she did, just as she censored others for their ideas.[5] She begins with a logical orientation of

---

4 A subsection of the International Covenant on Economic, Social and Cultural Rights developed by the United Nations General Assembly (16 December 1966) describes the compulsory requirement to attend school as a basic human right. Since then, all countries, except Bhutan, Oman, Papua New Guinea, Solomon Islands, and Vatican City have developed compulsory education policies. These policies are not homogeneous, with some countries requiring as few as four years (e.g. Angola), and other requiring as many as 13 years (e.g. Germany) of compulsory education (Murray, n.d.). The inconsistent nature of compulsory education also includes disregard for children with disabilities and permitting gender discrimination that negatively impacts on the ability for females to attend school in some countries (Jamal, 2016; Song et al., 2006; Stauffer, 2020).

5 Wollstonecraft wrote *A Vindication of the Rights of Men* (1790) and then *A*

her thesis, starting in *The Nursery*, the formative years of childhood, where she doesn't differentiate the gender of the child but instead, the gender roles of the parents. She starts with mothers and what she believes a good mother does, and her words would not be out of place in any 'new mothers' advice column, *breast is best*. Then she introduces clear class distinctions when she discusses the role of the nurse versus the role of the mother. This early indication that her intended audience consisted of people who were able to support the employment of a nurse and had a nursery, put her ideas out of the reach of common people. Despite being recognised as a critical thinker, a feminist, Wollstonecraft did not focus on the education of *all* daughters, but rather the daughters of a certain class. This class distinction continues with her emphasis on teaching a child manners from a young age, and her repeated insistence on the negative influences of "servants". For a feminist, this preoccupation with "a well behaved"[6] child, a well-behaved *girl* child, is anathema to what we want our young women to be today. Instead, we want girls to have a voice, to grow up into women who speak up. Yet, Wollstonecraft's lack of perspective on the lives of other classes of women can also be seen in her dismissal of the "pretty prattle of the nursery" as if it is somehow a woman's fault that her life is so limited that she does not have anything to say beyond her day-to-day life experiences. This narrow thinking of, "if I can then they can", shows a lack of perception of the complexity of people's lives.

Wollstonecraft's writing is a clear reflection on her own upbringing, no doubt a reprimand of her own mother's actions. I am fascinated by her assertion "children are taught revenge and lies in their very cradles".[7] Her

Vindication of the Rights of Women (1792) in response to both Edmund Burk's ideas on the French Revolution and Jean-Jacques Rousseau ideas on the education of girls in his Emile or Education is a treatise on the nature of education and on the nature of men by Jean-Jacques Rousseau (1792).

6 Laurel Thatcher Ulrich is known for the misquoted phrase, "Well-behaved women seldom make history", when in fact her research on the lives of early American women (through the words they left behind such as diaries), was more about looking at all women's lives (not just the lives of exceptional women) in order to understand our history.

7 William Ross Wallace (1865) wrote a poem in praise of mothers entitled 'The hand that rocks the cradle' a refrain repeated at the end of each stanza followed by the words 'is that hand that rules the world'. It is a powerful sentiment implying that it is the influence of mothers who shape people, and therefore shape the society in which we live in. Yet, if that were the truth, women would not still be fighting for equality, equity, and even their lives.

reasoning is the use of distraction, a technique still employed today by trained pre-school teachers, where, for example, children are encouraged to pretend it is the floor's fault when they fall and are about to cry. She believed this type of action made understanding truth difficult. While it is never that simple, I'm intrigued by her suggestion that encouraging creativity and an active imagination, influences our brain to prefer lies over truths. Research shows lying is the brain's way of protecting us and children must learn to lie as an important step in cognitive development. [8]

In the next section, *Moral Discipline*, Wollstonecraft introduces her belief "the marriage sate is too often a state of discord". The reason for the discord? Her assertion that at least one half of the married couple is not rational. Wollstonecraft ignores in her lifetime women were indoctrinated to believe marriage, then children, were the only real goals, ambitions, that they could attain to achieve any sense of happiness or purpose, to be accepted in their society. She doesn't dwell on the powerlessness of women, instead, she gives the reader a picture of the life of a middle-class woman, a mother, in the 1700s. She describes mothers as only caring their children should love them, and as a consequence, children are indulged until they become 'troublesome', after which they are left in the care of servants. As a result, Wollstonecraft claims, children become "mean and vulgar…cunning" and the "love of truth, the foundation of virtue, is soon obliterated from their minds". It is hard to believe she's talking about children (still not separated by gender and no word about daughters) as she condemns both mothers and children in two short sentences. It is also difficult to discern what age of child she is discussing, considering in this time period, 16 was not too young to be married and starting a family of your own.

Perhaps it is no coincidence that as Wollstonecraft was writing during the *Age of Enlightenment,* she is drawn into a discussion of how early life and childhood experiences shape a person's ability to reason. Yet, she is unable to step outside her prejudice or preference for class, such as blaming too much time with servants as a corrupting influence on children. I cannot say she is wrong. I too believe we are shaped by the people we surround ourselves with, just as we are shaped by those who are absent yet should

8 The Art of Lying: Lying has gotten a bad rap. In fact, it is among the most sophisticated accomplishments of the human mind. But how can one tell if a person is fibbing? By Theodor Schaarschmidt on July 11, 2018. Scientific America.

be there, such as a parent. But perhaps she's focused too much attention on the actions of the person, servant, or parent, rather than the impact of a young child missing out on an authentic connection with their parents.

Wollstonecraft goes on to list actions which need correction, such as "cruelty to animals, inferiors and those follies which lead to vice". Putting aside the cruelty to animals, this idea there are people whom she, and her society, consider inferior shows her prejudice. Her belief only a certain class should be permitted to have, nurture, and educate children, while the rest of society gets on with their primary role of serving that class, is not something we condone today.

Wollstonecraft is known for her feminist views on human rights and gender equality, but it is one she developed over her lifetime, as evident in her subsequent publications. Scholar Eileen M. Hunt, in her essay *The Family as Cave, Platoon and Prison: The Three Stages of Wollstonecraft's Philosophy of the Family* (2002), states in her earlier writing, Wollstonecraft is truer to her traditional trinitarian Anglican background, and we can see this through the words *virtue* and *vice* peppered throughout her writing. Yet, instead of suggesting bible stories to shape a child's morals, Wollstonecraft recommends stories about animals to "catch their attention" to "temper and cultivate [a] good disposition of the heart". [9] She favours hymns but only to the extent they "make the Deity obvious" and not to "overload any more than [they] can stomach". This is remarkable, as despite Wollstonecraft's reoccurring tenet that equality of the sexes is a "Godly pursuit", she was a religious advocate in many other facets of a woman's life, dealing with 'mental health', in particular.

Wollstonecraft returns again and again to improving the mind, to intellectual pursuits, warning without direction a mind will feed on whatever is at hand. She even suggests children should be included in conversation, their questions reasonably answered, and that stories are chosen for how they will mould a child's intellect rather than just to entertain. To do otherwise risks "breed[ing] strange prejudices…". Yet, Wollstonecraft leaps from this summation to suggest that in the nursery children will be exposed to "vulgar phrases" that they "should never hear" as it will lead them astray.

Oh, the irony.

Other than the nursery, another place in the household where Wollstone-craft warns of dire influence is the kitchen, a place also dominated by

---

9 Hunt, 2002

servants rather than parents (unlike a modern household). This is the first time Wollstonecraft mentions gender, implying girls are made "forward" and "pert" by male servants who will "take little freedoms" with them when they "go out walking". From a 21st century lens, I find myself unpacking the implications of this statement. Surely Wollstonecraft does not mean sexual interference? If not, why specifically mention the interaction between female children and male servants? I'm further confused when Wollstonecraft writes she is "charmed when I see a sweet young creature", thereby, focusing on the way a girl looks and behaves rather than what she thinks and says. Despite this declaration, this section ends with the author's reaffirmation that children (not specifically girls) should be taught to think, though not to encourage them to "make long reflections" due to their lack of life experience, as Wollstonecraft believes what they have to say is "mostly absurd".

Under the section, *Exterior Accomplishments*, Wollstonecraft focuses on the female gender, beginning with a lament of incomplete education, quoting, "A little learning of any kind is a dangerous thing." This may be a reflection on her own mother's unmet promise to employ a governess for Wollstonecraft, or even Wollstonecraft's fleeting time with people whose thoughts she admired. Nevertheless, she warns against learning for the sake of regurgitation and instead advocates for following deeper study to master skills worth pursuing. This includes dismissing the value of being able to recite a poem or two, "play a few tunes" or display a few drawings. She believed that demonstrating limited skills in a range of activities was a "prop to virtue" and girls should "desire of excellence" as it would give them depth of character.

Once again, Wollstonecraft returns to the topic of good manners, suggesting dancing is pleasing, but youth itself makes "young creature[s] agreeable". At the same time, she shows her disdain for women who act younger than their years, suggesting it is acceptable to "ridicule" them for their "trifling conversations" as they "ought to make…improvement". Overall, she suggests "exterior accomplishments" are only worthwhile pursuits if they also "cultivate" the mind. To this she connects the concept of *Artificial Manners,* the former to the pursuit of improved senses and the latter as simply an "error in judgement". I can agree caring about superficial qualities reveals our own shallowness. We can get people to like us by being false about our true nature, acting pleasantly, and using "borrowed language" to gain admiration, but those connections don't last. In the end, a "foolish or vicious" person will undo any beauty they have strived to make real. In this Wollstonecraft expresses herself like a poet, claiming "vanity is sorrow" and there is "no disguise for the genuine emotions of the heart". Though not discussed in any real depth, Claire Tomalin said Wollstonecraft did not have any "docile" mannerism or "pretty" looks to recommend her to a would-be suitor. Nevertheless, Wollstonecraft had numerous admirers over her lifetime who sought, though sometimes briefly, to form a more permanent connection with her due to her intellectual nature. And isn't this what we want to teach our daughters, that their minds are more important than their looks; that they will find someone who loves them for themselves?

The next two sections cover, *Dress* and *The Fine Arts*, two areas focused on external qualities aimed at making a girl pleasing to look at, with enough conversation to attract a husband. Wollstonecraft makes a point which much has been written on these subjects with "our sex" in mind, and at the exclusion of men.

When you consider how many layers of clothing a woman may have worn in the 1700s, how long it took to dress, and (for those of a certain class) how much assistance they needed to get dressed and how many times they may "have to" change their dress throughout the day, it is no wonder that an intellect, a feminist like Wollstonecraft felt this issue needed to be discussed. However, she skims the surface of this issue other than to say clothes hide the body and therefore the mind, that too much emphasis on adornment (including makeup and other female-targeted products) shows a lack of intellectual depth. Concerned with the cost of keeping up appearances and creating "envy" in other women, Wollstonecraft reveals another of her cares: the poor. She says instead of "squandering" money on their appearance, a woman should consider how the money could be better spent "for charitable purpose [to] alleviate the distress of many poor families". She mentions this action could also "soften the heart of the girl who entered into such scenes of woe". I believe she means that being a charitable person makes you more empathetic to those less fortunate than yourself, and therefore makes you a better person. She ends with a warning that a woman who hides who she is behind her dress, will disappoint the man whose eye she catches. Instead, a woman should dress simply so she is admired even when she does not find love. It is difficult to argue with this advice considering that current advice, given to women in particular, ranges from *dress for yourself* to *dress to impress*. Perhaps what cannot be undervalued is the ability to dress the way you see yourself, a situation that would have been unheard of in Wollstonecraft's lifetime. With women experiencing more equity in work and income, (particularly those from the western world), they no longer have the pressure of needing to look a particular way in order to 'find a husband', but rather are encouraged to have the aspiration to find an equal.

Wollstonecraft skips through her opinions on enjoying simple music and art in the section on *The Fine Arts* to focus instead on the importance of the written word. Firstly, she encourages girls to enjoy "works of fancy" but not to overly encourage her own "lively fancy". It is no surprise Wollstonecraft has strong opinions about writing as a fine art. believing children should have the opportunity to engage in correspondence, to "write down their sentiments" and to write about the stories they have read as an aid to improving "rational and elegant conversation". She reminds the reader that a "mind must every be employed" to which reading is the perfect solution to not only gaining knowledge but to improving human observation. Reading for amusement should be minimised in exchange for reading to "seek understanding…enlarge the mind and improve the heart."

Here, Mary Wollstonecraft shows her true colours. I laughed out loud when she proclaimed she is, "sick of hearing of the sublimity of Milton, the elegance and harmony of Pope, and the original and untaught genius of Shakespeare". [10] She doesn't make recommendations of her own but claims a reader should make up their own minds about who is worthy of reading and not be swayed by popular opinion. I agree. Many authors enjoy hype they do not deserve, and too few authors get the credit they deserve. Interestingly, though she mentions that while the Bible should be read with respect, it shouldn't be read without guidance. Though I am an atheist, my mother and grandmother before her were practising Catholics, and so I know first-hand that supervised bible study, with its plethora of additional and supplementary materials (all available at a cost) is the preferred way to 'tackle' the teachings of the bible. It is almost as if there is a concern that the bible can be easily misunderstood, or that there is only one acceptable interpretation and that interpretation must be taught.

---

10 I wonder if I should feel bad for making the earlier comparison between her and Shakespeare.

I am further amused when she bemoans young people who have limited engagement with reading and are more interested in other pursuits. It's a sentiment still true today—ask any English teacher. Her final summation of this section is disappointing, as she reverts to gender bias in insisting "neglect[ing] [her] domestic duties" is not a "sufficient excuse" for a woman to read. To make herself a "fit...companion and friend to a man", a woman must know how to "take care of his family". In one fell swoop, she has undermined her premise that it is of value to society that daughters are educated. [Sigh.]

At this point, I begin to lose interest in what Wollstonecraft has to say on the "Education of Daughters". I find her repetition of the importance of manners, her perception of the negative influence of servants and those below 'her" class, make me forget the lens through which she is writing. Instead, I find myself thinking about the poor editing feedback she was given by her publisher in the organisation of her ideas. In the end, I am resigned to the idea Wollstonecraft may have advocated for women to "improve their minds", but she also believed their ultimate purpose was to be good wives and mothers. She was, after all, a product of her time, and this piece of writing was obviously aimed at middle-class mothers raising daughters. You cannot read Wollstonecraft without thinking about her audience, privileged women in the sense of home and comforts of home, but less privileged in terms of personal freedom, their every move closely orchestrated by the expectations of society. At the very least, this included who they could socialise with, when they could socialise and what they did while they socialised.

Nevertheless, I persevere.

In the section entitled *Boarding Schools,* Wollstonecraft advises mothers should educate their daughters at home to prevent negative unknown influences, and that schools may not meet the educational needs of daughters. Whereas, under the heading of *Temper,* religion takes centre stage in her ideas on, "mould[ing] with heavenly disposition". From here she segues into a diatribe against the duplicity in a woman who "submits without conviction to a parent or husband will [be] as unreasonable [and] tyrannical over her servants." Here, more than anywhere else in this piece of writing, does Wollstonecraft give the impression she had little respect for lower-class women in her society. A sentiment Tomalin appears to agree with when she writes that Wollstonecraft prefers friendships with women she can dominate; "needed to establish ascendancy over [her] companions in order to be happy". With little self-reflection, Wollstonecraft makes a point about people not reflecting on their own behaviour and there is not a person "in the world" who is not flawed. The same could be said about people today, however, she suggests making a habit out of thinking about God as a means to work on self-improvement. That she says this, within a piece of writing aimed at guiding mothers to improve the education of their daughters, appears disingenuous. However, we need to remind ourselves Wollstonecraft lived in a time when it was a woman's responsibility to run a household, a role that gave her purpose and status.

The final chapters illuminate what life was like for middle-class women in the 1700s starting with *Unfortunate Situations of Females,* and *Fashionably Educated and Left Without Fortune.* In both sections, Wollstonecraft is consistent in her contradiction and irony, believing women should aim to have good manners, and an even temper, and to achieve this she must not expose herself to people beneath her, like servants. If she must support herself then taking employment as a governess, despite the shame of being "only a kind of upper servant", is her only option. When working as a governess, a woman shouldn't disgrace herself by having bad manners. Here, it is interesting to note Wollstonecraft became a governess in Ireland a short time after publishing this book. Wollstonecraft does not shy from the possibility of being seduced by an employer but suggests if this happens it is because the woman is not intelligent enough to avoid being deceived by offers of love. This shows a complete lack of understanding of the powerlessness of women in her time, women without money or connections would have little choice but to submit in fear of losing their employment. I know this to be true as it is still true today.

On the subject of *Love*, Wollstonecraft admits there is "little reasoning" and "no account for the absurd matches we every day have an opportunity of observing". [11] She goes on to say she finds the topic difficult to write about because of her lack of experience, however, she suggests if a woman finds love it should be with someone to whom she has "attached to [his] sense and goodness" and not someone she feels she needs to change. For someone who prefaced the section saying she didn't feel she could comment

---

11 A sentiment that Jane Austen rephased in her novel *Pride and Prejudice* (1813) when the protagonists Jane and Elizabeth make a similar observation regarding their parents own unfortunate union.

on the topic, Wollstonecraft talks at length about all the problems love can bring a person.

Under the topic of *Marriage*, Wollstonecraft offers better advice. Don't marry young. Get educated. Learn who you are before committing to a stranger. In this section, she repeats topics covered under *Nursery*, *Manners* and *Boarding Schools*; but her overall message is 'act in haste, repent in leisure'. Sound advice even today.

"I have almost run into sermon—and I shall not make an apology for it." is how Wollstonecraft summarises her solution to having *Desultory Thoughts;* an educated mind and turning to God are the way to combat the "various…misfortunes of life" including freeing "us [from] the fear of death in all its terrors". I can only suppose she wrote this due to little in the way of medical support when dealing with depression, and perhaps it was a stigma that could lead to consequences like incarceration in an asylum. In our current educational climate, there is a focus on teaching young people how to manage their stress and to be open about their mental health. Unfortunately, we lose too many of our young people to the 'black dog' in Aotearoa, despite the measures put in place to support them.

How does a person respond to the statement "most women, and men too, have no character at all" in *The Benefits which arise from Disappointments?* It seems cruel to dismiss the majority of the human race, especially from a feminist point of view where we women are encouraged to hold each other up, not tear each other down. It's hard to separate the disappointments Wollstonecraft appears to feel about her own life, and while today, being 28 years old is young, in her lifetime she would have been considered middle-aged. Overall, Wollstonecraft explains how life will bring disappointments and it is up to the person how they deal with those disappointments. Once again, she implies an educated mind and turning to God are the best defences against the disappointments a person will face in their lifetime. She even includes the cliché our pain will bring us joy, a destructive concept that belittles the immensity of women's mental health during a period of time when they could be locked away, given a hysterectomy and even lobotomised with only their nearest male relative's permission.

Wollstonecraft's thoughts *On the Treatment of Servants* have little connection to the lives of middle-class women in today's Western society. Take her statement "the management of servants is a great part of the employment of a woman's life" and "we cannot make our servants wise or good, but we may teach them to be decent and orderly". I cringe at these declarations, reminded that the life of a middle-class woman in the 1700s bears little similarity to my own.

I skip over *The Observance of Sunday*, *On the Misfortune of Fluctuating Principles*, and *Benevolence* due to her deep dive into her beliefs around the role religion has in education, subjects where I find no common ground.

In the final sections on *The Theatre* and *Public Places*, Wollstonecraft returns to her thesis of the importance of education (and manners) over the need to be entertained. She ends her "thoughts" with the quote, "see as through a glass darkly, but know even as we are known", a rephrasing of a quote by the Apostle Paul (1 Corinthians 13:12) in which he explains only at the end of time (our own death) will we know ourselves. To end in such a way is not surprising due to Wollstonecraft's religious leanings, but it feels like a throwaway, that we should dismiss any thoughts she has "on the education of daughters" because God's plan is a mystery to us all.

There is no doubt Mary Wollstonecraft was a feminist icon; she was brave enough and fortunate enough to express ideas of gender equity in education at a time when women could not vote, or have any sway on the laws and social norms which controlled their lives. But are her ideas still relevant to women, to mothers, and educators today? I have felt enriched by learning about Wollstonecraft's life through biographies and academic research based on her writings, and although I don't agree with much of what she says, I can see the direct benefit her influence has had in my own 'privileged' life. Unintentionally, in reading Wollstonecraft I've been compelled to reflect on what my mother has taught me, and what I hope I have taught my daughters—that, gender aside, a mind is a terrible thing to waste.

For my own radical mother

She meets me half-way up the hill, crying home from school.
My mother hands me a book.
She flings her arm across my chest; the collision is a mess.
My mother hands me a book.
She knocks him into the street after he skims his hand up
    under my dress.
My mother hands me a book.

She takes me to Family Planning, and tells the midwife to
    take a step back.
My mother hands me a book.
She leaves the door open, breaks the glass ceiling, and lets me
    find my own way.
My mother hands me a book.
She hands me a book.
And I pass the book to my daughters.

SOCIETY

In a 2007 journal article 'Culture, Evil, and Horror' published by the American Journal of Economics and Sociology, Inc., Paul Santilli wrote 'a culture is a way in which human beings represent their lives to themselves through language and other symbolic systems. With culture, the human separates from the animal and enters an order of discriminations by which the beautiful is distinguished from the ugly, the noble from the shameful, and the pure from the defiled.' (Santilli, 2007) Within 'Frankenstein', the Creature is defined as the ugly, the shameful, the defiled. Though he learns language through his observation of the De Lacey family, he still feels he has no place within society because of his appearance. Without a place within society, one feels isolated and can lose sight of responsibilities as a citizen, and the consequences of their actions.

Many social scientists have observed that the sense of self develops in parallel with the state. French philosopher Michel Foucault (15 October 1926–25 June 1984) suggested in the quest to find oneself, the self is manifested in two levels—as a passive object (the true self that is searched for) and as an active searcher. However, German philosopher, philologist, and cultural critic Friedrich Nietzche (15 October 1844–25 August 1900) suggested the true self could be found through hardship. But according to the philosopher René Descartes, the 'self' could only be found through quiet and solitary introspection. Here we have the true self manifested through actively searching for it, obtaining it through hardship, or solitary introspection. So which is it? The Creature endured hardship, yet still felt lost within society. He tried to find peace to observe his own mental and emotional processes but was shunned. This failure, therefore, led to his lack of self-control and discipline, his descent into violent behaviour, and the eventual murder of Victor Frankenstein's best friend Henry Clervall, Victor's bride, Elizabeth Lavenza, Justine Mortiz, and Victor's younger brother, William. Even though he knows his actions are wrong, the Creature justifies these murders due to societal neglect.

Like the Creature, many serial killers act because of this same rejection. Studies show this behaviour imposed upon a child can have disastrous results, including the stunting of the physical development of the child's brain resulting in severe psychological problems. While the outcome for children can be varied—due to the child's age, frequency, and severity of the abuse—there is no doubt maltreatment and psychological trauma are just as detrimental, if not moreso, than physical abuse. Within 'Frankenstein', Mary Shelley warns that a childhood of abuse and neglect will often result in evil actions—in this case, it is the abuse and neglect from Victor, the only parent the Creature has ever known. In 'Mary Shelley's Frankenstein and Revenge Killer's', Anthony P Ferguson links the Creature to a myriad of serial killers who also experienced childhood abandonment, neglect, and abuse. Victor's neglect of his 'child' allowed for the introduction of sociopathic tendencies and a limited capability for empathy, just as any serial killer may experience. Ferguson goes on to compare and contrast the Creature to notable serial killers who experienced parental neglect, including the Moors Murders committed by Ian Brady and Myra Hindley between 1963-65 in and around Manchester, UK; Western Australian serial killer Eric Cooke, who terrorised the Australian city of Perth between 1959-63; the notorious John Wayne Glover, known as the 'Granny Killer', who murdered six elderly women between 1989-93; US serial killer Edmund Kemper, who murdered a string of college girls over his rage for his mother (of whom he later killed); Ed Gein, whose 'house of horrors' contained the bodies and flesh of women he would skin and wear as clothing. Investigations into these killers revealed all experienced parental neglect or societal rejection in some sort, and chose to wield that rejection through violence upon others, similar to the Creature in Shelley's 'Frankenstein.'

However, society doesn't just shape its citizens—it also breeds fear. Fear of the unknown, the uncontrollable, the misunderstood. In Grant Butler's 'Medicine and Mary Shelley', this societal fear appears in medicine, specifically within medical treatment and childbirth within the 19th century. Mary Wollstonecraft, like many women of her time, died in childbirth. Although the delivery seemed to go well initially, the placenta broke apart during the birth and became infected, a common and often fatal occurrence in the eighteenth century. Many doctors during this time did not sanitise their practices, and most didn't even wash their hands. After several days of agony, Wollstonecraft died of septicaemia on 10 September 1797. In the 19th century, mortality was high, often due to poor health measures, and while scientific developments of this time had a major impact on understanding health and disease, with experimental research resulting in new knowledge in histology, pathology, and microbiology, little could be done to combat death in childbirth, or during other life-saving surgeries. There were no techniques, methods, or operations to combat germs. No antiseptics, antisepsis, disinfectant, or isolation. Because of these, many people died from common bacterial diseases that would not arise in this day and age. Society, at this stage, had no concept of proper clinical practice. However, during this time, humanitarians and philanthropists in England worked to educate the population and the government on problems associated with population growth, poverty, epidemics, and unsanitary conditions that lead to widespread disease and epidemics.

Butler further explores how the Creature might not have turned to murder if he was loved and educated on acceptable societal behaviours. And more education regarding medical treatment in the 19th century might have saved Mary Wollstonecraft and saved Mary Shelley the pain of mourning a mother she would never meet. Society has changed over the years, mostly for the better. But it still shapes its citizens, be it good or evil. Butler examines how, while medicine continues to flourish in the 21st century, childhood abandonment and societal ostracism have not abated, especially regarding the continuous debates regarding women and childbirth.

In 'A Bold Question: Consent and the Experimental Subject in Frankenstein', Octavia Cade explores personal bodily autonomy, and the decision for Victor Frankenstein to take it upon himself to defy the laws of nature. Where was ethical consideration in his decision? Did graverobbers obtaining bodies for medical studies take morality into account? Cade extends these questions further, examining the novel 'Frankenstein in Baghdad' (2013) by Ahmed Saadawi, and the lack of consent victims of suicide bombings had over their remains. She continues with the film 'I, Frankenstein' (2014), directed by Stuart Beattie, which exploits the uneasiness regarding the intersection of extreme wealth and science. Should wealth determine whether one can operate outside the law? Is the line between wealth and ethics as strong as it should be?

In 'Mary Shelley and Percy Shelley's Fascination with the Creation Myth and Sexual Androgyny', Ciarán Buder examines the lives of Mary and Percy Shelley, and explores the idea of life imitating art imitating life. Bruder explores Percy's fascination with creation - seen most notably in his major poetic work 'The Witch Atlas'—and how his unique studies in the area undoubtedly influenced Mary's own ideas on life and death. Bruder further reflects on Mary's examination of identity and free expression, unexplored by many women of her time, often denied by men and society.

The Latin phrase *cogito, ergo sum*—translating into English as 'I think, therefore I am'—forms the crux of René Descartes' (1596-1650) philosophy. However, with the rapid rate in which technology is 'progressing', who is really doing the thinking? In 'Frankenstein's Language Model', Jason Franks examines the fascinating evolution of knowledge creation through artificial intelligence. How does AI fit within our exceedingly futuristic society? Are Large Language Models the gateway to increased intelligence, or another Frankenstein's monster?

These essays not only explore society through a glass, darkly—a lens often directed towards the disadvantaged, and those prone to acts of violence. They provide a possible explanation for both Victor and the Creature's crimes, something sociologists continue to study today.

Mary Shelley's Frankenstein And Revenge Killers

Anthony P Ferguson

IN THE APPROACH TO PROVIDING an appreciation of Mary Shelley's classic gothic horror novel, Frankenstein (Shelley, 1818), my initial challenge was to compare the creature and its actions to the serial killers who rose to prominence across the twentieth century. At least, the twentieth century is a period I like to refer to as the golden age of serial killers. It is certainly true—in terms of their numbers—and their cultural popularity in film and literary circles.

There has always been a psychological link between serial killers and some of the monsters that crawled out of the pages of literal and literary history. For example, the gunslingers of the Wild West, the Thugs of India, the highwaymen, bushrangers, pirates, and outlaws. Many of these individuals were little more than serial murderers; not only killing for financial survival but also with a hint of pleasure.

In literary terms, many of our fabled monsters, vampires and were-wolves especially, were in effect serial murderers. These imaginary monsters had their genesis in real-life monsters in more superstitious times. It is possible that many of the innocents who fell victim to those we deemed as monsters; such as vampires, werewolves, cannibals, witches and other demonic figures, were in fact claimed by serial killers. However, in the Dark Ages we as a species had no concept of psychology and psychopathic behaviour. So, when we stumbled across a terribly mutilated corpse by the roadside, or dumped in a stream or field, we could only attribute such monstrous crimes to a monster. Never to a human being. This theory was posited by FBI criminal profiler John Douglas, [1] and further explored by Peter Vronsky. [2]

What of the author herself? Mary Shelley, just eighteen years old when she conceived of what would become possibly the greatest gothic horror novel of all time, came from a strict Calvinist upbringing. Well educated and surrounded by literature and the great literary names of the day, she idolised her father, William Godwin. "I could justly say he was my God". [3] Just as she despised her stepmother, Mary Jane Clairmont. Despite the love she expressed for her father, her familial bonds were somewhat distant and strained.

What possessed Mary to write such a tale of murder and despair? Well, her life itself was heavily influenced by tragedy. Her own mother contracted puerperal poisoning giving birth to her, and died five months afterwards. This would have resonated with Mary as she grew toward womanhood, especially after her father remarried a woman she couldn't stand. She eloped with the infamous poet, Percy Shelley, a disciple of her father, at the age of sixteen. Thus enraging her father and causing Shelley's estranged wife, Harriet, to take her own life. Then in 1815, Mary gave birth to a premature child which died a few days later. This event caused Mary to write in her journal, "Dream that my little baby came to life again; that it had only been cold, and that we rubbed it before the fire, and it lived." [4] It is in these tragedies, the last in particular, that we see the genesis of the Frankenstein creature.

Shelley of course, had no concept of serial murder. Rather, one of the central themes of her novel is that of nature versus nurture. In this, she was much influenced by the work of her father, and of several other prominent contemporary philosophers whose works she read, not least Rousseau and Locke. Each in their own manner championed the theme of social unity and universal benevolence.

It is these ideals which Frankenstein's creature sets out to pursue on its journey, only to be forced by the cruelty of human nature into a life of solitude, which turns inward on itself and sets the spurned offspring on a path of destruction. Abandoned by its creator, the creature at one point laments, "...I ought to be thy Adam, but I am rather the fallen angel,

---

1 *Mindhunter*, 1995, p30

2 *Sons of Cain*, 2018, pp 97-99

3 Shelley, Frankenstein. Introduction to the third edition of 1831

4 Shelley, 1831 edition

whom thou drivest from joy for no misdeed. Everywhere I see bliss, from which I alone am irrevocably excluded. I was benevolent and good; misery made me a fiend."[5] In this lamentation, the creature exhibits the self-pitying sentiments oft expressed by serial killers, as we shall see.

In assessing the journey of Victor Frankenstein and his unnamed creation, I will determine that the creature shares certain traits with serial murderers, and his genesis of neglect and rejection does form a similar pattern to that experienced by many serial killers. However, the creature is in essence not a serial killer. He is in fact another type of killer, as I shall try and explain.

First, let us undertake the journey of this unfortunate creature and his creator and follow their path of murder and mayhem.

Victor Frankenstein, a young and ambitious student of science and chemistry, is determined to try and discover the cause of the generation of life. He does so because he wants to contribute something new and incredible to the field of anatomy, and to make a name for himself. This is his first mistake. In attempting to give life to inanimate or dead flesh, Frankenstein challenges the laws of God. He places himself in the role of creator.

Forced to trawl through vaults, graveyards, dissecting rooms and slaughter houses for his source material, Frankenstein ultimately succeeds in giving life to his creation. However, despite the inner passion which drives him on, Victor is also racked with self-doubt and guilt over what he is doing. He realises that he has allowed the obsession to create living flesh overtake his own life. It causes him to lock himself away for months on end, neglecting his family and all human relationships. When he finally succeeds, his triumph is immediately suffused by revulsion at what he has done. He immediately recognises his folly, because the creature is physically hideous. Ashamed, Frankenstein flees his laboratory, leaving the new born fully formed creature to its own devices.

As a result of the difficulties encountered in reanimating dead flesh, the creature is outsized. It stands around eight feet tall, much bigger and more physically powerful than an average man. Yet unbeknownst to Frankenstein, his bastard child is miraculously good natured. It seeks only companionship and acceptance among its human peers.

When Victor returns to the laboratory with his best friend, Henry Clerval, he finds his creation has gone. He destroys the evidence of his

---

5 Shelley, 1831 edition

work and vows never to dabble in Promethean experiments again.

The creature meanwhile, abandoned by his creator father, goes out into the world seeking companionship. However, it soon learns that its monstrous appearance is frightening to other people, so it hides itself away. Finding an abandoned cottage, the creature observes a poor family living in the adjoining dwelling. Through watching and listening to them it learns about language and morality. It dedicates itself to improving the life of the family, bringing them firewood and leaving it at their door.

Eventually, the monster plucks up the courage to enter the neighbour's hovel while the younger family members are out, and it strikes up conversation with an old blind man who dwells there. The man accepts the creature because he cannot see him, but is comforted by the obvious intelligence and gentle nature of the visitor. This acceptance is shattered one day when the family returns and finds the monster in their home. The beast is verbally abused and chased away. Soon after, when the creature saves an unconscious woman from drowning, it is rewarded by being shot and wounded.

This is a turning point for Frankenstein's bastard son. The creature resolves to seek revenge on Victor, who it blames for giving him life then abandoning him to his fate.

The monster now lives up to its sobriquet. It begins to stalk Victor with a view to causing him the same misery it feels. First, the beast murders Victor's younger brother, William, and frames the Frankenstein's beloved family servant, Justine, so she is hanged for the crime. Victor sees the monster lurking in the woods on returning home for his brother's funeral. He realises what the creature has done, but he cannot speak up to defend Justine, lest he give away his secret shame.

The beast then confronts Victor, and threatens to kill all of Victor's loved ones if he does not create a female companion for him. The monster vows that if Victor does this, the two will go away into the wilds of South America and never be seen again.

Once more Victor plumbs the graveyards and mortuaries for illicit decaying flesh. Secreting himself away, he has almost completed the female creature, when he catches the monster peering in the window, an evil leer on its face. Horrified, Victor fears that the two will breed and commit evil acts together, and determined not to commit the same mortal sin twice, he destroys the female before giving it life.

The creature is enraged. Victor flees, but the monster pursues him with renewed vigour. The beast murders Victor's best friend, Henry Clerval, and frames Victor, who is later acquitted of the crime.

Victor marries his childhood sweetheart, Elizabeth, but the creature strangles her. Victor's father dies of age and grief.

Furious and grief stricken, Victor now vows to destroy the monster once and for all. He pursues the fleeing creature through Europe all the way to the North Pole, where he is found almost frozen to death by the Captain of a passing ship on an expedition. Captain Robert Walton listens to Frankenstein's incredible tale of woe, and against his better wishes, agrees to release Victor to continue his pursuit of the monster. However, the ship becomes icebound, and by the time it manages to free itself, the crew have persuaded the captain to turn the ship around for home.

Victor stubbornly presses on after the creature, but in his already weakened physical state, soon dies of exposure. Walton retrieves Victor's body, and is amazed to later find the creature on board, mourning over his creator's body.

The monster tells Walton he is sickened by his own crimes, and vows to end his own existence to atone for the atrocities he has committed in his forlorn attempts of revenge. The creature drifts away on an ice raft to die by suicide, or at least he tells Walton that is his intention. The creature is never seen again, his fate uncertain.

It is without question that Frankenstein's creation commits a series of vile murders in a forlorn attempt to achieve some sort of recognition, in this case the attention of his creator. In undertaking these crimes, these murders of otherwise innocent people, the monster does indeed share several traits with serial killers.

The elements of rage and revenge are evident among serial killers. In their case it is generally a revenge on a society they feel has abandoned them, or that has failed to recognise their self-proclaimed superiority.

The Moors Murderer, Ian Brady, for example, is said to have raised his fist to the heavens and said, "Take that, you bastard!" [6] after committing one of his crimes. The Yorkshire Ripper, Peter Sutcliffe penned a note and stuck it to the window of his lorry before he began his terrible series of murders, which read, "In this truck is a man whose latent genius, if unleashed, would rock the nation, whose dynamic energy would overpower

6 Wilson, 1995 p2

those around him. Better let him sleep." [7]

Serial killers tend to fall into the category of dominant people. Those who are natural born leaders, or at least believe they should be leaders. They are part of the dominant five percent of people. This is a theory championed by the late British crime writer, Colin Wilson, and originally theorised by the science fiction writer, A.E. van Vogt. It was Wilson's contention that when this inner drive, this will to power, becomes thwarted in a dominant man, it can turn inward into rage and result in immense violence. [8]

When Mary Shelley came to write her story, one of her intentions was to show the folly and arrogance of men who think themselves better than God. Hence victor Frankenstein attempts to usurp God in creating life. Serial killers also afford themselves this God-like status, thinking they are above the herd of mere mortals, and thus not subject to the laws which constrain them.

Another trait Frankenstein's monster shares with certain serial killers is the aforementioned sense of abandonment and rejection by a parental figure. Many serial killers utilise their rage at their mental abuse by a loved one as an excuse for their violent acts.

For example, the 1960s Western Australian serial killer Eric Cooke, the last man to be hanged in the State, grew up experiencing severe violence at the hands of his own father, who could not stand him because he was weedy and had a cleft palate. It was this early rejection at the hands of someone who should have provided nurture that drove Cooke to ultimately seek revenge on a world where he did not fit in. He would prowl the streets of the wealthier suburbs after dark, feeling like a king as he enacted his revenge on people who he assumed thought they were better than him, and above his social standing. [9]

Another Australian serial killer, John Wayne Glover, the notorious Sydney Granny Killer of the early 1990s, raged at the neglect he suffered at the hands of his own mother, and later, from his mother-in-law, when he took up unwelcome residence in her plush Sydney home.

Growing up in Wolverhampton, England, Glover endured a torrid love-hate relationship in a single parent home with his domineering, morally ambiguous mother. By the time of his teenage years, the two

7 www.crimeandinvestigation.co.uk/crime-files/peter-sutcliffe-the-yorkshire-ripper
8 Wilson & Seaman, 1996, pp 268-69
9 Blackburn, 1998

formed a partnership committing minor crimes. Even though Glover was devoted to his mother, she was highly promiscuous, and he would find himself continually pushed aside every time she hooked up with another man in a series of short-term relationships.

Later, he would emigrate to Australia to get away from her, and from the life of petty crime and abusive short-term relationships he himself now formed with women. To no avail, Glover's life of crime continued Down Under, until by a stroke of luck he married a girl above his social station. For several years he seemed to settle down, until his mother emigrated to live with him and his wife, and all of his old resentment began to resurface. He also hated his mother-in-law, who saw through to his true nature and made sure he knew he was not welcome in her plush Mosman home, where the Glovers took up residence on the second storey.

Glover's years' long pent-up anger exploded as soon as his mother and mother-in-law passed away, when at the grand old age of 56 he commenced a shocking series of murders of old women around the nursing homes of North Shore, Sydney. All committed to strike back at the impotent rage he felt at the domineering women who had tormented him for years. [10]

In the United States in the 1970s, the co-ed killer Edmund Kemper assuaged the burning rage he felt for his mother by butchering a string of college girls. He also murdered his mother as well, decapitating her and having conversations with her head. [11]

There are myriad cases of serial killers expressing their rage at familial abandonment, or at the very least, this is a convenient excuse for their crimes after they have been apprehended. Colin Wilson was one of many writers on the topic of serial killers who opined that abandonment and neglect are the breeding ground of serial killers. [12]

This is certainly the experience of Frankenstein's creation. The creature is abandoned at its genesis and left to fend for itself. As it progresses through its short adult life, and despite its initial gentle nature and willingness to adapt, the creature is treated with hostility at every turn due to its unpleasant appearance and immense size. Thus, it is never able to form any positive relationships. This is an issue David Canter alludes to in comparing Frankenstein's creation to serial murderers. [13]

10 Kennedy & Whittaker, 1992

11 *The Killing of America*, crime documentary, 1981

12 *A Plague of Murder*, 1995, pxi

13 *Criminal Shadows*, 1994, pp 212-13

The creature only devolves into an evil murderer after it is rejected by humanity. It grows twisted in its desire for revenge on its creator. Further, like serial killers, its victims are dispatched with utter coldness. They become mere objects chosen to fulfil the creature's overriding desire, to make his creator's life a living Hell. Beginning with the slaying of Victor's five-year-old brother, William. The child is murdered with all the contempt for life of a serial killer. The difference being that his rage is made tenfold by discovering the child's identity. Standing over the corpse he gloats, "…my heart swelled with exultation and Hellish triumph… my enemy is not invulnerable; this death will carry despair to him…"[14]

However, this symbiotic breeding ground of abandonment is not as clear cut as it first appears. Statistics indicate that not all children with horrible upbringings turn into serial killers, murderers, or any sort of criminals for that matter. In fact, some of them fight against their impoverished upbringings, abuse and neglect to become upstanding citizens, some even working for the forces of good, law and order. There is another counter argument which says that murderers are born that way. They are just not wired right, and nothing will divert them from their path toward destruction. They are predisposed to a life of crime.

Another link between the plot of Frankenstein and real-life serial killers can be found in the notion of reanimating dead flesh, or the attempt to create, or re-create life. In 2018, German nurse and serial killer Niels Hoegel admitted to murdering over 100 patients in an attempt to play God and reanimate them after death.[15]

The classic 1950s serial killer Ed Gein created a house of horrors on his remote Wisconsin farmhouse. Gein was in the habit of skinning his female victims and wearing their flesh on top of his own as a form of female second skin. He would prance around and speak in a high-pitched voice. Investigating officers found buckets filled with body parts and headless human cadavers strung up from the rafters like deer in Gein's farmhouse. Gein was the inspiration for the Norman Bates character in Hitchcock's Psycho (1960), the Leatherface character in The Texas Chainsaw Massacre (1974), and also for the character, Buffalo Bill in Silence of the Lambs (1991).[16]

Finally, there is a similarity in the creature's attempt to end its own miserable life and the death wish embodied in the actions of most serial

14 Shelley, 1818

15 www.bbc.com/news/world-europe 30 October 2018

16 Seltzer, 1998, p. 242

killers. The act of serial killing in itself is in many ways a slow form of suicide. Most of them know how it will end, that it is a no-win game. Transgressing the laws of morality and committing the ultimate taboo of murder is their way of shaking their fist at God and screaming, "I exist!" (like Ian Brady). They crave that ultimate recognition. Their moment in the spotlight to shock the world and receive the recognition they desire. For most of them, at least prior to the 1990s, detection and capture meant almost certain execution.

Frankenstein's monster shares this death wish with common serial killers. Although it must be said that we do not actually see the monster perish. He merely disappears into the ice. For all we know his avowed death wish could just have been a ruse to secure his release from Captain Walton's ship and prevent any further pursuit. If this were the case, and we shall never know, then it makes the creature a cunning psychopath, much like most serial killers.

However, despite these tenuous links between the monster and serial killers, the creature is in fact much more like a different type of murderer— the familial revenge killer. He differs from serial killers in one crucial manner. Serial murderers almost exclusively target complete strangers. It is this factor which makes them so difficult to detect and catch. It is why they are often termed stranger killings. With no link between killer and victim, the authorities are pressed to work much harder to find a pattern. Hence in many serial murder cases the killers choose strangers as their victims to represent the parent, spouse, or sibling they want to symbolically destroy.

Statistically, most murders occur between people who know each other. It is the uncontrollable passionate rage of rejection which leads us to kill our faithless loved ones. This is why, whenever a murder occurs, the first person the police will question is the spouse, husband, wife, son, daughter, brother, sister, partner, lover, ex-lover, employer or employee. In most cases, they will be the perpetrator. Emotion and murder are very much intertwined, and love can quickly turn to obsession, and then to hate.

The history of murder is replete with revenge killers; spurned lovers and spouses, and bullied children committing matricide or patricide. The most prevalent being dominant men abusing their partners, and turning to murder when the battered spouse finally finds the courage to break free. Sadly, this rage is often also directed at the children as well as the partner (see Wilson and van Vogt on dominant men in this regard).

This is certainly the case with Frankenstein's spurned creation. It kills only those who are as good as family. Victor's brother, his wife, his nanny (by proxy), his best friend. In all this the monster refuses to harm his father, Victor. Instead, it mourns him after the latter's death. All it wanted was his creator's familial acceptance. When the creature's attempts to fit in are spurned by society, it turns its rage inwards toward its creator and his ultimate abandonment.

Conversely, and strangely enough, many serial killers lead normal married lives, with their spouses oblivious to their true nature. John Glover, Eric Cooke, the Yorkshire Ripper Peter Sutcliffe, and the BTK killer, Dennis Rader, come readily to mind.

It is appropriate that we look at the two major characters of the text at this juncture, and ask which of them is the greater monster?

Victor Frankenstein sets out at the beginning of the story with a great drive to create life. He arrives at the conclusion and his fate with an equally great desire to destroy life. In this regard he has failed to grow as a person, or learn a moral lesson. He never faces up to his part in the creature's actions. The creature however, demonstrates remorse and regret after Victor's death. He realises the sins he has committed, accepts responsibility for them, and vows to atone by taking his own life. In his final soliloquy, the creature recognises his folly. "But it is true that I am a wretch. I have murdered the lovely and the helpless. I have strangled the innocent as they slept, and grasped to death his throat who never injured me or any other living thing. I have devoted my creator, the select specimen of all that is worthy of love and admiration among men, to misery; I have pursued him even to that irremediable ruin." [17] This soliloquy suggests that the creature has grown as a character. Victor has not.

Victor Frankenstein can be likened to other great literary figures. He and the creature are a little like the title character in Robert Louis Stevenson's *The Strange Case of Dr Jekyll and Mr Hyde* [18] for example, two halves of the same coin. It is also possible to compare Victor (unfavourably) to Robert Neville in Richard Matheson's horror classic, *I Am Legend* [19]. Neville pits himself against the mutants left at the end of the post-apocalyptic world and attempts to either slaughter them or capture and cure them of their

---

17 Shelley, 1818

18 Stevenson, 1886

19 Matheson, 1954

mutations. However, as he faces his own mortality at the end of the story, he comes to the shocking realisation that in fact he was the monster all along, and not the mutants. He had instilled fear into their lives and haunted their dreams, as much as they did his.

In doing so, Robert Neville demonstrates the kind of journey toward inner growth that Victor Frankenstein utterly fails to comprehend. Victor creates his own monster by way of neglect, and by failing to understand its need for nurture and acceptance, he turns the otherwise innocent creature into a monster. Victor fails to see that it is he who is the real monster.

Childhood abandonment and neglect are the breeding ground of serial killers, but also of murderers of every ilk.

Medicine And Mary Shelley

Grant Butler

FRANKENSTEIN IS NOT ONLY one of the most famous stories in the English language, it's also an enduring cultural landmark that is immortalised in the iconic *Universal Monster* films and countless other works of cinema, television, and literature. Some of the tropes associated with the story have become known to people throughout the world, whether they are familiar with the original story or not. But why is that? Why did a book written by a teenage girl over 200 years ago become one of the most famous stories ever told?

Frankenstein was a revolutionary story because it was at the forefront of several fiction genres, including horror, but it was also an early tale of the most enduring science fiction theme; the story of how something ground-breaking is created and then proceeds to go amuck and causes massive destruction. The concept is common to readers and film viewers now, but in Mary Shelley's time, the idea was unheard of. So *Frankenstein* wasn't just a creepy story, it was something readers of the time had never experienced before. What makes a horror story more than just a good story is when it captures the fears of not just the reader, or even the author, but of an era. *Frankenstein* takes the experience of Mary Shelley and countless others and enhances it to a degree that has captivated, shocked, and terrified readers for two centuries.

It makes sense that the story of a brilliant scientist who finds that the process of creating life is more horrible than he ever imagined was written by a young woman at a time when childbirth was incredibly dangerous. Even if both the mother and child survived the ordeal, the process was nothing short of horrific. Like her contemporaries, Mary Shelley was intimately familiar with how procreation was a brutal, dangerous, and terrifying process. Mary Shelley

151

had lost her own mother to complications of childbirth shortly after she was born and by the time she conceived of the idea for *Frankenstein*, she lost two children of her own. In the end, she would have only one child that would make it to adulthood.

The fear of medical treatment and specifically childbirth is at the heart of the story because the entire reason Victor does not go through with the creature's request for a mate is because he fears they will mate and produce a race of monsters that will threaten humanity. Because he does not go through with the request, the Creature kills his wife, Elizabeth. In a way, the manner of Elizabeth's death mirrors that of a wife who died in childbirth, as she died directly because of the new life her husband brought into the world.

During Shelley's era, childbirth, like any other medical procedure, was a grisly affair. Without anaesthesia, enduring any sort of operation was akin to torture. It wasn't until another famous British woman, Queen Victoria, helped usher in a revolution in medicine when she was given chloroform during the birth of her son Prince Leopold in 1853. [1] Not shy about expressing her dislike of pregnancy or childbirth, Queen Victoria was a huge fan of chloroform and the public approval of the world's most famous and powerful woman made anaesthesia during childbirth a more common affair.

But childbirth and surgery were not the only areas of medicine in which the era's practices were horrifying. In Shelley's time, opium use was widespread and laudanum, a mixture of alcohol and opium, was used as a treatment for countless conditions, ailments, and disorders including menstrual cramps. Since Shelley famously got the inspiration for Frankenstein from a vivid image during a sleepless night, it's tempting to speculate if she may have taken some laudanum that night to fight insomnia. Because not only is it known that her own husband Percy used it to calm his nerves, going so far as to carry a flask of laudanum with him during their courtship, laudanum is even present in Frankenstein, as Victor takes it as the only way he can sleep.

But even if Shelley didn't take any to treat insomnia the night she got the idea for the story, it's inconceivable that she never consumed it in an era where it was so widespread, particularly within Shelley's contemporaries. [2]

---

1 Fulton, 2017
2 Hill, 2010

Samuel Taylor Coleridge was one of the most famous Laudanum users of the era, and Kubla Khan, one of his most famous works, is widely viewed through the lens of an opium fueled dream. Coleridge did not publish the poem until prompted by his friend Lord Byron, one of the people present at the same holiday where Shelley was inspired to write Frankenstein.

But aside from the use of laudanum, and sheer horror of being awake during surgery, undergoing an operation in those days was just as dangerous as an illness because of the lack of sanitary practices. The idea of sterilising equipment and using antiseptic to prevent post-surgical infections didn't get widespread attention until the late 1860's when Joseph Lister began spraying medical equipment with a carbolic spray. When the effects of the practice were indisputable, it was adopted by the medical profession. [3]

The movie adaptations of Frankenstein have usually shown Victor Franken-stein as being dressed in some sort of medical garb, working inside a massive lab filled with all sorts of equipment, and using electricity to bring his creation to life, whereas the original story takes place in a far grislier and primitive medical environment. Not only was it an era of unsanitary equipment and brutal treatments, the germ theory of disease had not been accepted, which meant the very idea of hand washing for doctors, or for people in general, was not even a thought. So doctors or anyone else attending to women in labour were treating them after not even washing their hands.

When one considers that doctors were using filthy equipment, no anaesthesia, and stuck their unclean hands into open wounds, it's a wonder anyone survived any sort of operation in those days. The odds were just as good, if not better, that a visit to the doctor would kill you just as surely as an illness would. While Lister's ideas began to spread as time passed, there was some initial resistance to the use of antiseptic in segments of the medical community. Some of the doctors who did not agree with Lister included the physicians of American President James Garfield. When Garfield was shot by an assassin in July of 1881, the wound itself in his back was not fatal. But when he was shot, doctors stuck their unwashed hands into the wound, and not surprisingly, infection set in and Garfield died two months after the assassination attempt. [4]

The horror of the era's medicine is the true horror of Frankenstein and is what sets the story apart from countless other chilling stories from that

---

3 Fulton, 2017

4 Mitchell, 2020)

time in history. In the beginning, Victor operates under the belief that his creation will be something beautiful, almost angelic. But when he sees the reality of what he's created, he is disgusted and appalled. Victor's belief that his creation would be beautiful isn't just naive, it's delusional, as the nature of the process he uses is grisly and crude. The fact that Victor tries to create life by taking old body parts and stitching them together isn't as shocking as the fact that he does it without a moment's hesitation. Victor comes to realise the absurdity of it all, but far too late.

With his goal of enhancing and prolonging life, Victor Frankenstein was like all doctors of every era. But his proposed solution, like many old medical methods, was more horrific than any disease. And like many gruesome medical practices that have fallen by the wayside, Victor's creation killed those who he wanted to save and hurt those he was trying to help.

A Bold Question: Consent And The Experimental Subject In Frankenstein

Octavia Cade

"WHENCE, I OFTEN ASKED MYSELF, did the principle of life proceed? It was a bold question, and one which has ever been considered as a mystery; yet with how many things are we upon the brink of becoming acquainted, if cowardice or carelessness did not restrain our inquiries."[1] So questions Victor Frankenstein, in the first flush of his university studies, pondering not only the nature of the principle of life but the nature of the person who pursues it. A scientist, he implies, should be neither cowardly nor careless. These qualities are seen as an impediment to a life of research. They are not, it must be said, sterling characteristics of an individual in general, but that Frankenstein holds them out specifically as detractions to science is significant.

If they are not sterling characteristics, they are, unfortunately—within the context of science—ambiguous ones. Is it cowardice to limit the progression of science by hiding behind ethical standards of practice? Is it carelessness to fail to consider the potential outcomes of your experiments, or are some things just completely unforeseeable? It is sadly ironic that the two qualities that Victor Frankenstein perceives as most detrimental to scientific research are those that he, arguably, represents the most. He is, after all, intermittently aware of his negative qualities even in the beginning stages of his greatest experiment.

Initially, Frankenstein feels that cowardice at least is beyond him. Thanks to an education designed to inoculate him from disturbing encounters with the uncanny—"In my education my father had taken the greatest precautions that my mind should be impressed with no supernatural horrors. I do not

---

1 Shelley 2003, p. 49

ever remember to have trembled at a tale of superstition, or to have feared the apparition of a spirit. Darkness had no effect upon my fancy"[2]—the gorier aspects of research life are not repellent. He is able to work with corpses in every stage of decomposition without being frightened by them. This ability to face the realities of biological death and decomposition—not only as they apply to other human beings, but as they will one day certainly apply to himself—without superstition or flinching could be termed a form of bravery. It's one that might apply to a number of other scientists, including for example forensic pathologists, but which is less common in members of the general public, who while acknowledging mortality are frequently reluctant to inspect it as closely. It is likely fair to say that the average pathologist does not look down on a member of the public too squeamish and distressed to examine corpses, but this is compassion that Frankenstein himself does not possess. He is proud of his ability to withstand difficult research conditions, and the idea of another "trembling in superstition" at the same appears to provoke in him more of a condescending pity than anything else. Certainly, it is implied, any scientist who falls prey to such nonsense is unworthy of the name.

This early awareness of his bravery, as he perceives it, is both incentive and trap. If he is a brave man, and only brave men should practice science, then any breakdown in that bravery, any compunction that might result in his turning away from even the most disturbing of experimental subjects or conditions, means that he is no longer fit to practice science himself. It is an attitude that entrenches within the scientific method values to which that method is entirely indifferent... but then science has never occurred in a vacuum, uninfluenced by the prejudices of its practitioners.

The sense of superiority that the consciousness of his own bravery has inspired means that when Frankenstein begins to direct his activities towards the creation or reanimation of life, any doubts that he has are of short duration. It is notable that those doubts are directed not towards the act of creation itself, but rather the object of it. He wonders whether he should "attempt the creation of a being like myself, or one of simpler organisation; but my imagination was too much exalted by my first success to permit me to doubt of my ability to give life to an animal as complex and as wonderful as man". [3] This enormous confidence, the belief that he was not even

2 Shelley 2003, p. 49
3 Shelley 2003, p. 51

permitted to doubt, is an early representation of the popular perception of arrogance that is often assigned to those who work within medical or surgical fields. It is arguable, of course, that such confidence is necessary to function effectively in a high-stakes environment—and what is more high-stakes than the creation of life? Yet confidence can quickly turn to conceit, and the growing arrogance of Frankenstein's personality, compounded with the bravery and careful reasoning he believes a requirement of his vocation, combine to eliminate any possible break in his research.

A closer reading, however, indicates that the bravery he is so proud of is being subtly undermined by his own behaviour. Aware, on some level, of the off-putting nature of his experiments—"Who shall conceive the horrors of my secret toil, as I dabbled among the unhallowed damps of the grave, or tortured the living animal to animate the lifeless clay?" [4] Frankenstein works increasingly in secret. A university is a place almost defined by the sharing of knowledge, and yet none of his research is shared with his teachers, his fellow students, or even (in letters, which he writes less and less) with his family. Indeed, Frankenstein very deliberately keeps his work from them—even from his father, who he has previously praised as raising him with no fear of the supernatural. This particular omission, above the omissions towards his scientific colleagues, indicates an unspoken, even an unacknowledged inhibition. After all, that he cannot even share his work with the man who raised him with the capability to perform that work unflinchingly, speaks both to his secret perception of the work—ungodly and abominable—and his character, which combines arrogance and a self-serving sort of discretion.

Instead of performing his research openly, Frankenstein works alone, gathering materials in darkness and "midnight labours". [5] The results of those labours are explored in "a solitary chamber, or rather cell, at the top of the house, and separated from all other apartments by a gallery and staircase"; [6] Frankenstein refers to this setting as his "workshop of filthy creation". [7]

It is clear at this point that Frankenstein is aware that his experiments would not benefit from sharing. There is of course a dream of fame and success, the happy consequence of genius, and genius has frequently been

4 Shelley 2003, p. 52
5 Shelley 2003, p. 52
6 Shelley 2003, pp. 52-53
7 Shelley 2003, p. 53

perceived as a quality of individuals rather than communities. The unhappy prospect of sharing glory, however, is a far step from the unhappier prospect of being kept from glory to begin with, and it is increasingly plain that Frankenstein knows that publicity would sink both himself and his experiments. "I shunned my fellow-creatures as if I had been guilty of a crime,"[8] he says, and indeed it is likely that, if his experiments had been shared, both professional and public reaction would have branded him a criminal. A truly brave person might have used these pangs of conscience to re-evaluate his work, or alternately to communicate his experiments to his peers and stand solidly behind that work, but Frankenstein does neither.

Even when his experiment succeeds, and the isolated environment of his workshop produces a living creature from the corpse parts of his subject materials, Frankenstein is too unnerved, and too afraid, to admit to what he has done. The creature he has made is repulsive to him on every level, and when, in the immediate aftermath of his breakthrough and on the verge of a breakdown, he meets a friend, Frankenstein's immediate fear is that his experiments will be exposed: "I dreaded to behold this monster; but I feared still more that Henry should see him."[9] That exposure is something Frankenstein fears more than the monster he has created is telling. He is no longer, even to himself, the image of an undaunted man of science— an image that was so previously important to his sense of self and sense of science. And with this implicit acceptance of his own cowardice, he does exactly what his previous reasoning would direct him to do: he stops his scientific research and takes up languages with Henry instead. "I had conceived a violent antipathy to the name of natural philosophy,"[10] he says, and the sight of his laboratory is intolerable to him. Cowardice has turned him from science, and carelessness has left him essentially indifferent to the fate of the creature he has created—Frankenstein seems willing to pretend the entire affair is over and done with, a horror left firmly in the past. Yet his creature, disappeared from both laboratory and responsibility, will of course return and the rest of the narrative is well-known. Frankenstein, who is unwilling to nurture and otherwise raise the creature he has created, causes by his neglect that creature to turn monstrous.

That continuing story, however fascinating, is not the focus of this

8 Shelley 2003, p. 54
9 Shelley 2003, p. 58
10 Shelley 2003, p. 66

essay. It is the above passages in which my interest is centred: Frankenstein's perception and practice of science, and how these things impact on the ideas of ethics in experimentalism and the scientific culture in which Frankenstein was working (and in which Shelley was writing).

Science, as practised today, is largely perceived as public endeavour. It is also a largely *organised* endeavour. In Frankenstein's time, and in Shelley's time, science—primarily referred to as natural philosophy—was in many ways a more containable sphere of knowledge. It was also coming to the end of the time when a single individual could consider themselves conversant in all branches of the subject. The modern separation of science into separate disciplines—physics, chemistry, biology, geology and so forth, and the sheer depth and breadth of knowledge established in every one of those disciplines—has driven the need for scientific specialisation. There is no single scientist today who is expert in every field of science, and nor will there ever be again. The rate of progress in each is simply too great.

Because of this, the need for communication between scientists has become even more necessary than before. Science communication has always been crucial to the practice of science; it both allows for confirmation of results and prevents unnecessary repetition of experiments by researchers unaware of existing findings. It also allows scientists to more easily build on each other's research to progress the field as a whole. This reasoning applied in Frankenstein's time as it does our own, but the increasing explosion in scientific knowledge makes it more necessary now. To encourage this communication within the separate fields, the different branches of science have developed their own organisations and journals. This collaborative approach increases institutionalisation and interconnection in science as well as reliance on the wider scientific community, which is particularly useful in the wake of the Industrial Revolution. Science, now, is increasingly conducted at scale, with individual projects often requiring teams of scientists working together, and sufficient funding—derived from state, educational, or commercial sources—to support this extensive (and expensive) research. This increasing institutionalisation and professionalism of science has also resulted in an increasingly codified practice of that science, in which aspects like ethical approval for specific experiments, and ethical standards of the profession in general, are developed and maintained.

This is not the scientific culture in which a man like Victor Frankenstein was developing his craft. It is to the advantage of his penchant for unethical experimentalism that the contemporary practice of science was rather looser in its practices, and operating with significantly less oversight. Another advantage is that Frankenstein came from a wealthy family. He can afford isolated rooms in which to experiment, and the equipment necessary to do so. (Today, science is often so expensive to perform that the lone, self-funding scientist, able to indulge every experimental and research whim without the aid of other scientists, and entirely unsupervised by any professional body, is very nearly a myth.)

The ability of wealth to escape oversight is particularly crucial to the *Frankenstein* narrative. While the novel places Frankenstein's laboratories first in an isolated apartment in a university town, and then in an even more isolated hut on the Orkney Islands, which Frankenstein chooses as the place to make his monster's bride, film adaptations of *Frankenstein* fairly wallow in the lonely applications and settings of wealth. Frankenstein is frequently shown conducting his experiments in a distant castle, a setting not only notable for its emphasis on his status as a member of the social elite, but also for its defensive capabilities. For all the castle is so often stormed, it is also a place in which experiments can be performed in relative secrecy, unmolested by a local—and naturally curious—scientific community.

It is a sad fact of the human condition that it is easier to do immoral and unethical things when the only person to stop one is oneself. Frankenstein is persuaded of the rightness of his purpose regarding his initial experiments—although not persuaded enough, as previously noted, to have the confidence to share them. That persuasion would be a great deal more difficult to maintain in the face of the horror and disgust with which his friends, family, and colleagues would regard him if they knew the truth of his work. Existing institutions, whether educational, religious, or legal, might even have taken concrete steps to prevent that work from proceeding. Such actions would certainly be plausible, particularly when they resulted from religious sensibilities. The ability to raise the dead, or to cobble together a living creature from pieces of the dead, would surely have been perceived as close to heresy. Even stealing the bodies of the dead, for all this practice was commonly used in the 19th century to provide bodies to medical schools— such providers were famously given the names of "resurrection men"—was hardly perceived as moral, and this reprehensible exploitation horrified the general public of the time.

There is a distinct difference, or so we tend to think (albeit from our own cultural perspective) in experimenting on the consenting and the non-consenting. Even when the subjects of that experimentation are dead, we feel the need for consent. Individuals may will their remains to medical schools to help educate the next generation of doctors, or to aid in scientific research that might someday help to heal others, and this is their prerogative. They are able, in the act of so willing, to give informed consent. The stolen and exploited dead, such as those that Frankenstein plunders for raw material, cannot give this consent, and relatives in such situations either cannot or will not consent on their behalf. Yet because the act of experimentation is so secret, scientists like Frankenstein can bypass issues of consent, and—by virtue of that secrecy—we are aware that Frankenstein knows such consent would not be granted if he *were* to ask. The culture of science in which he practises is not sufficiently organised or institutionalised, and ethical standards are not yet codified to the extent they are today, but there are clearly contemporary ethical issues that he *is* avoiding, and Frankenstein knows it. The plundering of the dead at midnight, the secrecy in which he performs his experiments, the absolute reluctance to avail himself of any resources—human or otherwise—that may be offered by the university he is attending, all speak to the knowledge of his own ethical infringement. Frankenstein deliberately organises his research in such a manner as to escape even the remotest level of oversight from his peers. Under the circumstances, it is not surprising that such a disgraceful experiment has such painful results.

Having experienced the result of experimentation on the unconsenting dead, and being awakened to the initial carelessness of his research, Frank-enstein is understandably unwilling to recreate it. The creature's desire for a bride, however, forces his hand. This second experiment is performed under a much different mindset, and one much more aware of potential ethical issues: "During my first experiment, a kind of enthusiastic frenzy had blinded me to the horror of my employment; my mind was intently fixed on the consummation of my labour, and my eyes were shut to the horror of my proceedings. But now I went to it in cold blood, and my heart often sickened at the work of my hands."[11] Certainly, Frankenstein is more self-aware, more certain of his obligations, and—after the dreadful consequences that resulted from his former arrogant practise of science—he is much, much less careless about potential repercussions. He considers

---

11 Shelley 2003, p. 163

his inability to control the actions of the second creature he is engaged to make, realising that "I was now about to form another being, of whose dispositions I was alike ignorant: she might become ten thousand times more malignant than her mate, and delight, for its own sake, in murder and wretchedness. He had sworn to quit the neighbourhood of man, and hide himself in deserts; but she had not; and she, who in all probability was to become a thinking and reasoning animal, might refuse to comply with a compact made before her creation."[12] If Frankenstein has learned the realities of his cowardice, he has here acknowledged the carelessness of his previous approach to science. And, as with his previous realisation and previous refusal, the prior reasoning that science should not be practised by the careless guides his actions, and he destroys that which he was about to animate.

This realisation, like the first, is made in secret. Experience has taught Frankenstein what oversight might have but was prevented from doing. It is notable, however, that in all the *Frankenstein* narratives which have resulted from this, the original text, the ethics of experimentalism, and the avoidance of their application through Frankenstein's chosen practice of science, remain constant. It is now over two hundred years since Shelley's novel was published, and the organisation of science has changed enormously. It has become institutionalised. It has become professional. Yet for all this change in the culture of science, in the cultures that surround and support the practice of science, the avoidance of oversight remains central to the text. The means by which that avoidance is employed, however, have changed in interesting ways. Science, no longer the province of the mad genius alone in his gothic and ivory tower, is no longer something which can be performed in out of the way buildings, and with no interference from the outside world. Even the wealthiest, most secretive scientist of today requires workers to act on any significant scale: they require other scientists to work in their laboratories and test their ideas, they require expensive and thereby traceable equipment, they are subject to established, enforceable laws and professional codes of practices, which exist and have widespread acceptance. That these ethical constraints might be unwelcome and that they might even, with sufficient resources, be avoided is one thing, but they exist nonetheless. There is no scientist working today who can stand up and say "I am stealing corpses

---

12 Shelley 2003, p. 164

and intend to mutilate them in a quest for resurrection, and there are no laws in existence designed to prevent this," as Victor Frankenstein might conceivably have argued. The expectation of informed consent is too entrenched.

Yet the popularity of the *Frankenstein* narrative endures and is one that has been frequently adapted and re-imagined over generations. Many of those adaptations are set in different places and different times, commenting as much on the cultures in which they are set (and in which they are created) as the original did—an adaptive factor which might have influenced the novel's longevity. These cultures include the question of ethics and experimentalism, and how to avoid the brakes these ethics put on scientific research is therefore an intrinsic part of the narrative. It is unnecessary, and would likely be enormously tedious, to list every adaptation, and every method each used to explore this issue. Two brief examples should suffice to illustrate the point, however.

The 2014 film *I, Frankenstein* (adapted from the graphic novel by Kevin Grevioux) sets its reanimation of the dead amidst a fantasy war between gargoyles and demons, but its presentation of science, and the threat that science can cause, is thoroughly modern. Victor Frankenstein's research, contained in his journal, has been unearthed and, crucially, *industrialised*. Charles Wessex, the billionaire businessman head of the Wessex Institute, plans to reanimate the dead on an enormous scale. He is looking to produce—to reproduce—Frankenstein's creature by the thousands, and has set up a research unit and factory to turn Frankenstein's original experiment into a production line of the living dead.

This speaks very much to the changing place of science in culture. It is also something that Mary Shelley could never have conceived of, cemented as she was in the culture and science of her own day. That culture, still very much entangled with religion, questioned the value of science when in conflict with religion, and consequently one of the main themes of *Frankenstein* is the fear of scientists overstepping their bounds and meddling in issues, such as the creation of life, previously reserved to God. Industrialised factory production, courtesy of the Industrial Revolution, was well underway in Shelley's lifetime, but this did not make it into the novel, which admittedly was set in the unspecified 1700s. In comparison, *I, Frankenstein* exploits contemporary uneasiness with the intersection of extreme wealth and science, playing on the awareness of financial and political corruption with which its audience was likely to be extremely familiar.

Wessex is clearly a villain figure, but *I, Frankenstein* did not need to unveil him as a demon in disguise for the audience to recognise this. That he is using his enormous economic power to conduct unsavoury and dangerous experiments is enough to indicate corruption; it is unlikely in the extreme that thousands of people offered up their bodies to be experimented on in this manner. The Wessex Institute itself is well-known and respected, but its more clandestine works are not. Wessex, repeating Victor Frankenstein's secrecy on a much wider scale, has the financial (and thus social and political) resources to operate outside existing professional and legal strictures. What is essentially a minor plot point in the original has become the most threatening issue of the sequel. As frightening as the demons are meant to be, it is the ability of big business to operate outside of the law that is most relevant to contemporary audiences. That this illicit programme clearly has a large staff, many of whom must be aware to some degree of the unethical nature of the work, can only draw comparisons to real-life cases of the intersection between unethical science and big business—for instance, the well-documented cases of tobacco companies suppressing links between smoking and lung cancer. That contemporary medical science is so closely related to big business, as for example in the case of pharmaceutical companies, is often perceived as a threatening, untrustworthy and even exploitative collaboration. The *Frankenstein* narrative, then, reinforces this existing cultural fear about the practice of science in society, and this more than anything contributes to the sense of unease in the film. The accompanying demonic presence may make for exciting action scenes, but it is hardly the main source of suspicion for the audience.

A second example can be seen in the novel *Frankenstein in Baghdad* (originally published in 2013) by Ahmed Saadawi. Located in U.S. occupied Baghdad, this re-imagining of *Frankenstein* is periodically interrupted with acts of extreme violence, natural products of an environment shaped by war. The Frankenstein figure is a junk dealer instead of a scientist, and he pieces together scraps of flesh from the victims of suicide bombings in order to give them a proper burial. The composite creature comes to life, however, and starts shoring up its own failing corpse-parts with pieces from other individuals—especially those people it finds morally culpable for the violence around it. The monster here, like the violence, has become a production line itself, constantly reinventing the horror of its own creation, and making itself a mirror to the destructive influences of those people around it. (Actual scientists, in *Frankenstein in Baghdad*, are mostly present through implication. They are the inventors and engineers behind the bombs and other weapons of a war-torn society, entirely cut off from the effects of their creations. It is instructive here to recall Frankenstein's initial turning away from his monstrous creation, and his desire not to think of it following his breakdown.)

The creature of Baghdad, harvesting from the bodies of those culpable for the violence within the city, might justify its actions for the greater good, as Frankenstein once did, but the fact remains that—even from the junk dealer's original synthesis—body parts are taken from those who do not consent. As the monster itself comments, when taking the eyes of an old man killed in the street, in order to replace its own failing vision, "Seeing the body of the innocent old man, I had an idea and I clung to it—it looked like the truth I had been seeking. The old man was a sacrificial lamb that the Lord had placed in my path. He was the Innocent Man Who Will Die Tonight [...] So all I had done was hasten his death." [13]

While neither of the creators—the junk dealer, and the creature itself, which harvests and attaches body parts for its own continued creation—are scientists as Frankenstein himself was, they would still, under normal circumstances, be subject to the laws for practising science that their culture has set up. Organ donation, for instance, is a rigidly controlled part of medicine, precisely because of the ethical issues involved. They are able to circumvent these laws, however, and to (literally) operate without oversight, because the environment in which they find themselves acting is so disturbed. Baghdad, suffering from the effects of war and continued violent unrest, is in no way a stable society. Both laws and ethics have been significantly undermined by conflict, in the same way that, in *I, Frankenstein*, they have been undermined by wealth.

The question, then, of ethics and experimentalism in *Frankenstein* and its subsequent adaptations is closely linked to the position of science within a culture, and the ability of that culture to provide oversight to its scientific community. Bravery and carefulness are not enough, as Victor Frankenstein found, to compensate for a strong ethical foundation to science. When a culture has not sufficiently developed a legal and

---

13 Saadawi, 2018, p. 162

professional infrastructure on which to base that foundation, its scientific practitioners are left to the dictates of their own conscience, which, as Frankenstein himself shows, is clearly not enough, being subject to personal bias as it is. Similarly, when that existing infrastructure has been undermined by corruption or social breakdown (as it has been by the Wessex Institute in *I, Frankenstein* and by war in *Frankenstein in Baghdad*) then the ability of experimentalists to operate outside of that infrastructure is increased. As such, Mary Shelley's *Frankenstein* can be said to not only offer a portrait of experimentalism without ethics but to offer a template of it—one that can be adapted to other times, and other cultures.

Mary Shelley And Percy Shelley's Fascination With The Creation Myth And Sexual Androgyny

Ciarán Bruder

Mary Shelley and Percy Shelley: life imitating art imitating life?

Mary Shelley and Percy Shelley had an undoubtedly unconventional relationship. The pair became close in early 1814, with Percy estranged from his wife and Mary in debt. The pair had illicit meetings in St Pancras Churchyard, where Mary's mother was buried; Mary even lost her virginity there, so the stories go. This auspicious start to the pair's sexual relations defined their unusual marriage. Over the following half-decade, Percy had numerous lovers, while Mary was an advocate of free love, seemingly pursuing a relationship with Percy's best friend. This freedom of sexual expression, away from the social conventions defining marriage, was also celebrated in the pair's writings.

Mary's novel *Frankenstein*, first published in 1818, is undoubtedly her most stirring literary achievement. It gave birth to science-fiction as a genre, with the timeless story of man's horrifying triumph over nature endlessly reproduced in literature, poetry, film, and countless other art forms. The novel's rich prose and thematic density has been studied endlessly from many angles. But one area literary scholars have yet to cover in significant depth is Frankenstein as a doctrine for how man has the power to create its own androgynous sexual identity.

Percy, while lacking the same contemporary literary fame of his wife, has a storied body of poetry dealing with complex themes including political radicalism, the relationship between the human mind and nature, and sexual identity. One such poem, *The Witch of Atlas*—published in 1820, soon after Percy had (allegedly) collaborated with Mary on Frankenstein—is an ideal example of a man-made androgynous figure in fiction. It also further reflects how unusual the Shelley marriage was.

Greek mythology and the creation myth

Both Mary and Percy Shelley were familiar with Greek and Roman literature from a young age, Mary through tutoring by her father and Percy through studying at Eton College and Oxford University. As such, both authors were immersed in the themes and narratives common to Classics writings.

One such concept that seemed to stick with both Shelleys was the creation myth. Greek folklore was filled with stories of gods and their human creations. This idea of a being creating human identity in their own image—the innumerable Greek mythological figures were defined by differing personality traits; consider this in comparison to the single, omnipotent Christian god— interested the pair. Mary's body of work explores ideas on gender as an element of enlightenment thinking, while Percy was a devout atheist who found the notion of human creation compelling on a cerebral level.

Mary Shelley's Frankenstein, or to give it its full title, *Frankenstein: The Modern Prometheus*, bears clear links to the Greek creation myth. In classical mythology, Prometheus is credited with creating humanity from clay and, upon seeing humans' fear of the dark, defies the wishes of the gods to give us fire and thereby civilisation. For his 'sin', the god Zeus bound Prometheus to a rock and sent an eagle to tear out a liver, which would regenerate every day, for eternity. Victoria Walker asserts that the Greek titan and Victor Frankenstein share critical similarities as creators, but one crucial difference in how they treat their designs; "It is Prometheus the creator that Shelley depicts in her novel...but Prometheus suffered so his creations could flourish, while Victor suffers due to the lack of compassion he feels towards his creation." The suffering hero is a common trope in classical writings and is also seen in Frankenstein despite Victor's cowardly and selfish actions. But despite the differences between Prometheus and Dr. Frankenstein, ultimately both creators suffer because their creations are seen as monstrous 'others' in the eyes of the existing order, the Greek gods in Prometheus' story and 18th century German society in the case of Frankenstein. Two sides of the same coin; entities with god-like powers who create life in their own image while denying it the agency they themselves have. Mary Shelley's ancient Greek inspiration couldn't be clearer.

Percy Shelley's *The Witch of Atlas* also shares obvious links with the Greek creation myth. Written around the same time as Percy's drama *Prometheus Unbound*, *The Witch of Atlas* is set on the mountain home of Atlas, brother of Prometheus. The essay The Use and Creation of Myths in Major Works of P. B. Shelley highlights this shared mythos between Percy's poem and Greek literature, "the impact of classic myths is apparent in the poem." The poem's eponymous witch is the antithesis of the magical hags which haunt European folklore. The Witch is descended from the Atlantides, the collective name given to Atlas' seven daughters. Her relation to the celestial titans gives her the power to create life as she desires. It also gives her an ego, inherent to all divine beings, which determines that their creation must be a weaker version of themselves. The Greek gods created humans; alike them in form, but utterly powerless. The Witch creates a sentient humanoid; but one devoid of her own extraordinary feminine beauty. Percy Shelley describes the Witch as:

"So fair a creature, as she lay enfolden /
In the warm shadow of her loveliness"

As I will discuss later, the Witch's creation is defined by its imperfection, in contrast to the Witch herself. In creation mythology, characters with the power to give life do so to make a point about themselves. This ties *The Witch of Atlas* to a long line of Greek writings defined by the creation myth.

The Shelley's focus on androgyny and sexual otherness

The celestial power of the Witch reflects Dr. Frankenstein's extraordinary mind and surgical abilities. Although the former embodies the world of magic and the latter that of science, both protagonists have an innate mastery over life itself. But in creating this new life, both the Witch and Victor Frankenstein produce human-like figures that are distinctly sexless. This could just be a simple move to illustrate how 'other' the Shelley's creatures are. However, I think this thematic choice has deeper roots in the psychosexual make-up of Mary and Percy's relationship, illuminating the inner workings of a marriage with blurred lines on traditional identities and rituals.

Much academic thought has been devoted to unpicking the sexual and gender power bases in Frankenstein. But comparatively little time has been spent assessing why Victor, despite his abilities, created a creature whose monstrosity undermined its hyper-masculinity, leaving it sexless. This is highlighted in a passage from Frankenstein in which the doctor has just given the creature life:

"His limbs were in proportion, and I had selected his features as beautiful. Beautiful! Great God!" [1]

With the ability to create new life, Dr. Frankenstein elected to make his reanimated man as 'beautiful' as possible. He mentions the monster's lustrous black hair and pearly white teeth later in the same passage. This is a human designed to be attractive. The creature's imposing height and strength, which is mentioned frequently in the novel, point to Frankenstein's monster as an uncanny hyper-masculine ideal. However, despite all these 'positive' traits the creature is ultimately rejected, stripping it of a sexual identity and therefore its base of power. This point is highlighted in the essay Unveiling the Concept of Androgyny in Mary Shelley's Frankenstein, which notes that; "the creature has no real gender, despite being created physically as a male. He is denied male dominance over females by Victor by making him too ugly to be accepted into human society." The essay further contrasts the creature's physical male body with its personality, "the creature, like Victor, has feminine characteristics, being...sensitive to emotion".

Now the vein of androgyny through Frankenstein deepens; Victor also embodies male and female characteristics, as his hysterical behaviour and emotional outbursts run counter to the ideal of male stoicism. He also occupies the place of both male 'scientist' and female 'creator'. It takes nine months to create the monster, incidentally the average amount of time it takes for a woman to carry a child to full term, and the use of 'labours' draw obvious parallels to birthing:

"Winter, spring, and summer passed away during my labours." [2] In trying to create an idealised human, Dr. Frankenstein creates a power struggle within himself over whether this creature should actually have this sexual agency or not. This is played out, in part, as a form of repressed sexual desire, as asserted in the essay Gender and Sexuality in Frankenstein and The Rocky Horror Picture Show; "significance is placed by Victor the creature' appearance, insinuating homosexual desire". In expressing desire for a creature deprived of sexual power, Dr. Frankenstein lives out an androgynous fantasy in which gender and its politics don't play a part in creation. He summates the blending of two worlds, divinity and science, in creating new life:

---

1 Shelley, 1818, p. 58
2 Shelley, 1818, p. 57

"This was indeed a godlike science."[3]

But in giving life to the dead, he also smashes together two separate genders, masculinity and femininity, to create an androgenous middle-ground. In a novel full of characters who freely embody personality attributes of both male power and female submissiveness, Frankenstein's monster perfectly embodies this 'new' form of humanity; sexless and free of repressive codification. It's a freedom Mary Shelley so wanted for her marriage. Perhaps that fantasy was lived out on the page.

Androgyny is the single most-defining trait of creator and created in *The Witch*. This is manifested in the blending of intangible characteristics, both male and female, in both characters. The Witch is distinctly female in form, with female pronouns, and Percy Shelley describes her as:

"A lovely lady garmented in light /
From her own beauty"

But despite possessing a woman's' physical form, the Witch holds distinct power. This is far more typical of the male heroes archetypal in Percy Shelley's writings. There aren't many female protagonists in his poems, giving the Witch a distinctly blended identity; a man trapped in a woman's body. The human-like creature she creates, however, is nowhere near as complex in its genderal identity because it possesses both sexual identities without conflict. Being of both sexes was repugnant in the Romantic era. As Diane Hoeveler says in *Shelley and Androgyny: Teaching The Witch of Atlas*, "hermaphroditism represents physical monstrosity, accentuating the differences between the sexes." The Witch's created companion is defined by everything that she is not. The Witch has feminine beauty and masculine agency. The creature, by being explicitly of both genders, is denied the privileges of either. Percy Shelley reinforces the grotesque and divisive nature of this creation, and its result, in the line:

"by strange art she kneaded fire and snow /
Together, tempering the repugnant mass."

The creature is a blend of disparate other identities in the same way Frankenstein's monster is. However, as Shelley's description of the creature continues, we come to the line:

"A sexless thing it was, and in its growth /
It seemed to have developed no defect /
Of either sex, yet all the grace of both"

---

3 Shelley, 1818, p. 130

The creature's mixed identity means it holds no sexual appeal per se. But it does hold attraction as a human-like form, something more recognisable to a human narrator than the otherworldly Witch. Hoeveler describes this dichotomy as such; "Shelley intended the Witch to be a...true love object who is androgynous and immortal, while the hermaphrodite is the false copy, a physical love who lures the poet into the limiting realms of self." In recognising the attractive androgynous qualities of the Witch's creation, Percy Shelley acknowledges his own, very-human attraction to the out-of-the-ordinary, and idea he also embraced in his marriage to Mary Shelley (as seen by the many other people they were attracted to throughout their relationship). Hoeveler summates this point nicely in explaining why *The Witch*...has held academic appeal within Percy Shelley's canon of fiction, "the Shelleyan hero is replaced by a woman, a Witch, and her ironically ideal creation takes the form of a hermaphrodite." Difference to the norm, even biological androgyny, is something to be embraced.

Frankenstein is Mary Shelley's best-known work. The novel has become a behemoth of numerous literature and film genres, from science fiction to horror, and has been translated into dozens of languages in hundreds of countries. The terrifying story of reincarnating life from death as a mish-mashed human form made from disparate body parts, was directly influenced by the Greek creation myth. So, if Victor Frankenstein is a divine being responsible for creating life, why is his monstrous creature uncannily human-yet-not; why is he not made in 'God's image'? Because an imperfect, androgynous figure, stripped of a specific sexuality and blurring society's clearly defined lines, better reflects the Shelley's unusual relationship and ideas on sexual identity. Percy Shelley's *The Witch...* is by no means his most famous work. However, the poem retains significant academic interest for its departure from the archetype of Percy's swaggering yet troubled male hero. The mystical tale of a witch, a direct descendant of the Greek gods, who conjures up a humanoid familiar, is also inspired by Classical writings. But unlike the witches of mediaeval fairy tales, this creature is not monstrously feminine; its beauty stems from its ambivalence to its sexuality, an ambiguity that it passes on to its imperfect creation. A strict sexual identity is of no importance to the Shelleys in these narratives, and in their characters they can embody a free erotic expression that defined their marriage but was denied to them by society.

Frankenstein's Language Model

Jason Franks

MARY' SHELLEY'S SEMINAL SCIENCE FICTION novel *Frankenstein; Or, The Modern Prometheus* Shelley [1] posits the creation of an artificial being: a creature cobbled together from human parts. The Creature is intelligent and well-read, but violent and monstrously ugly. The Creature, and the hubris of its creator, come to represent the worst of humanity. Two hundred years later, this fable is reflected in the advances in artificial intelligence text generation, showcased by OpenAI's ChatGPT (Generative Pretrained Transformer).

The initial hype around large language models (LLMs) like ChatGPT has been followed swiftly by concern about what they will do to the livelihoods of knowledge workers and artists, and to the information ecosphere. LLMs have lurched into the public eye, ill-made and difficult to control, and the mayhem has only just begun.

This technology will change the way we undertake knowledge work. How are LLMs like Victor Frankenstein's Creature? Mary Shelley's novel offers a framework for understanding this new technology and what it means for our future society.

The Workshop of Filthy Creation

LLMs like ChatGPT are neural networks—a class of machine learning (ML) algorithms trained to crudely mimic the human brain. ML algorithms are used to train a mathematical model that can classify or predict values (a process called supervised learning), or to find patterns or clusters in the data (unsupervised learning). [2] These processes are described as 'training'

---

1 Shelley, 1818
2 James et al., 2013

because they involve fitting a model to example data—the more of it the better. The resultant models are purely statistical. They do not evaluate facts or logic. They generate probable outputs, but they cannot explain them.

Neural networks are composed of layers of 'neurons' that are connected to every neuron in the preceding and/or succeeding layers. During training, data is fed into the network from an input layer and passed through a number of the 'hidden' layers to an output layer, which delivers the final result. Each connection is given a 'weight', which, during training is adjusted by mathematical processes that minimise the error found in the output. [3]

All of the data is numeric. Input and output text must be encoded into numbers before it can be processed. The method used to encode text data is one of the key innovations that make these language models so powerful. LLMs encode text as 'embeddings', which model the probabilities that every token (word or word fragment) will be followed or preceded by another token. The other innovation, like Victor Frankenstein's lightning bolt, is raw power: huge amounts of text data scraped or stolen from across the internet, which is used to train the network at great cost, in terms of both computer hardware and actual power consumption.

LLMs use what is called a semi-supervised learning paradigm for training. [4] Because most text does not have a calculable objective, they are 'pretrained' in an unsupervised mode, which captures copious amounts of knowledge from the input data as embeddings. Pretrained models (called Transformers) [5] can then be 'fine-tuned' by supervised learning for tasks that do have an objective, for example, answering questions. In this process of 'transfer learning', general knowledge is transferred to a specific task.

The Creature's learning process might be considered analogous. Shelley was well versed in the educational theories of John Locke (and Shelley's father, William Godwin), which held that children's development begins with their earliest sensory experience of the environment. Victor's Creature, however, is mobile from the moment it is 'born', and is able to master language with unnatural speed. Perhaps this is because Victor uses the brain of a cadaver as a basis for his creature's consciousness. The brain's memories and identity may be gone, but language is 'pre-trained' by its former owner and, like an LLM, learning is just a matter of fine-tuning. Lacking any positive parental oversight, it is no wonder the creature grows to be impulsive and violent.

3 Ham & Kostanic, 2000
4 Kingma et al., 2014
5 Vaswani, 2017

Apparent in the Brute

LLMs present an astonishing semblance of life. They can respond to all kinds of queries or requests with grammatically correct, confident, and coherent text, in any number of common formats and styles. They can answer questions, summarise text, and write short stories, rhyming couplets, or essays. They do all of these things convincingly using concise, clear language. LLMs can even translate between languages.

LLMs have captivated, delighted, and alarmed an audience that has grown to a record-breaking hundred millions users in just two months.[6] They are convincing enough that even one of Google's engineers was persuaded that Google's LaMDA language model had become sentient.[7] But unlike Victor Frankenstein's creation, LLMs are less than they appear to be. They have no self-awareness and do not understand anything in the 'real world' beyond the data used to train them.

LLMs take input text and then, after passing the information through many layers of abstraction, respond with the most probable sequence of words. It's truly remarkable that a process this crude can return such convincing results. But convincing or not, that is all that language models know: how to predict language outcomes. LLMs cannot reason. They cannot fact-check. They don't know anything about the real world, they just know the words people use to describe things in the real world. They cannot tell a lie from the truth or a convincing argument from a fallacy. They just know which words go together.

One of the most basic purposes of a computer is to be able to do arithmetic, but LLMs cannot add. An LLM might know that people frequently might say "1+1=2" and will thus be able to answer a question such as "1+1=?", but it has no comprehension of why. Try again with a pair of random eight-digit numbers and it is unlikely to yield a correct response. All an LLM can do is calculate the probable output based on examples it already knows. LLMs cannot perform most of the precision tasks for which we rely on computers today: setting timers, calculating bills, sending and receiving packets of network data.

These characteristics are also evident in the current generation of image generation models (such as Stable Diffusion and OpenAI's Dall-E). These AIs can compose intricate and textured pictures that look like the work of

---

6 Curry, 2023
7 Thomas, 2022

artists—but look closely and you will see mangled hands and mouths with too many teeth. They cannot count, and do not know even rudimentary facts about anatomy. They just know where tooth- and finger-shaped objects usually go in a picture of a human figure. Victor Frankenstein could not have made his creature without a basic understanding of the human body, learned the hard way as a Natural Sciences student at the University at Ingolstadt.

Unlike Frankenstein's creature, LLMs will not develop an awareness of their place in the world. They have no initiative—they will never embark on a self motivated homicide, or, as in the Terminator movies' SkyNet, conclude that extermination of humanity is the best way to achieve peace and security. Even if you ask an LM and it produces this conclusion, it has no comprehension of what it means, nor how to translate that conclusion into action. The Creature demonstrates self-awareness. It feels despair at its failure to assimilate into society. It shows initiative and curiosity. It wants to learn the qualities that human beings take for granted, and understands that it is lacking. None of this is true for LLMs.

LLMs cannot create; all they can do is resample existing ideas and reassemble them as instructed. [8] The results may sometimes be surprising, both in content and in coherence, but they will never be original. They cannot think for themselves and they have no motivation to do so, because they have no motivation at all. AIs cannot create art or advance human knowledge—but they can become a productive part of the process, just as they can be a force for destroying livelihoods and promulgating disinformation.

In Pride of Wisdom

LLMs should not be considered a replacement for a search engine, or any source of knowledge. They cannot distinguish between information learned from a scientific journal, a person's blog, a 4chan thread or a propaganda website, and we should question the veracity of their output. LLMs are natural mansplainers. They must respond to input with output as best they can, and the probabilistic nature of their processing frequently delivers confident-sounding nonsense. The popular tech-reviewing website CNet has already found itself in trouble for publishing fake news—articles written by AIs that sound good, but are riddled with factual inaccuracies

---

8 Kirkpatrick, 2023

and lies. [9] Microsoft's Galactica LLM was taken offline after only two days for generating offensive content. [10]

It's well known by now that human biases present in the training data used to create LLMs are retained or even amplified in the training process. OpenAI has added heuristic 'guardrails' to ChatGPT to prevent it from offering racist, misogynist or otherwise inappropriate responses back to users, with partial success. Perhaps, Frankenstein had not abandoned his creature, he could have taught it a sense of morality and self-control.

But there is a contingent of users who have made a sport of circumventing these guardrails, and the truth is that LLMs, trained in the workshop of filthy creation we call the internet, can never be entirely clean of such biases.

Worse, this allows the bad actors who deploy bot armies to propagate falsehoods to easily scale up their efforts. This may quickly lead to genuine conversation being drowned out in a sea of automated discourse. Worse still, these bad actors could actively poison LMs with disinformation. An end user might easily identify bots on social media, but when information has been filtered through an LM they can never trace it back to the source of the information.

Unbound

While the most sensational applications of LLMs appear to be cheating on homework, the technology nonetheless offers compelling and important applications beyond simple productivity hacks or the generation of marketing 'content'. They can be used responsibly, and there is legitimate work for which LLMs can make a crucial difference.

Victor had no future plans for his Creature beyond seeing if he could bring it to life. The companies that have built LLMs, on the other hand, are making a concerted effort to control and profit from their creation—which means teaching them to behave in socially acceptable ways. But it's also increasingly clear that their concern is profit, first, and they have demonstrated little regard for the ways their LLMs are used. There is some irony in the fact that one of the first businesses to find their operations damaged by LLMs is the science fiction magazine *Clarkesworld*. My upcoming comic series with Tam Nation, *Frankenstein Monstrance*, explores exactly this idea: what if Victor Frankenstein was a 200-year-old tech bro?

9 Thorbeck, 2023
10 Heaven, 2022

LLMs are more powerful than other technologies when fine-tuned to a known set of outcomes (e.g. classification to a specified taxonomy). The fine-tuning process foregrounds trusted data, and allows us to quantify the skill of the model on the targeted activity.

The poorest and most dangerous outcomes occur when users presume that an LLM knows is knowledgeable about the subject the user is asking about. Tasks in which a user provides text to the LLM for processing (e.g. summarising or answering questions about the document) are much more likely to yield quality results. But for all the depth and breadth of their training, LLMs are not able to cope very well with large amounts of new text. Input into ChatGPT is usually capped at around 4096 tokens (approximately 3000 words), which limits the tasks LLMs can reliably be asked to execute—although future versions are sure to improve this.

Records and archives departments have been overwhelmed for the better part of 3 decades by the flood of digital information they are required to manage. [11] The library-style practices that served when records were paper documents, books, and letters cannot scale to the internet's exponentially growing volume data, and LLMs are the best tool we have for taking control of all that information. [12] The threat of hacking has grown in severity, scale, and frequency as our systems have all moved online. In the right hands, LLMs will prove vital to preserving individual privacy and cybersecurity. In the wrong hands, they magnify these threats.

Conclusion

LLMs like ChatGPT are astonishingly powerful AI tools for generating and manipulating text. They demonstrate a semblance of humanity with all of our flaws amplified and reinforced–but they are not intelligent. Unlike the Creature, they cannot perform elementary reasoning tasks. They are prone to confabulate, hallucinate or lie, just as real humans do, but without intention or forethought.

LLMs' brute capacity for automating human intellectual labour is frightening, however, they can be harnessed for legitimate purposes. LLMs should not be treated as a source of knowledge or a way to make informed decisions. As the amount of data being generated by human endeavour continues to balloon, LLMs offer heretofore unheard of capacity to help us refine this torrent into valuable knowledge—or to poison it with disinformation.

11 Upward et al., 2013
12 Franks, 2022

In Mary Shelley's novel, Victor Frankenstein's creature demands a bride, but Frankenstein destroys her before she is finished, fearing that the creatures will multiply. In 2023 it's too late. OpenAI, Google, Facebook and others have constructed their own LLMs. Many of these are open-sourced and freely available. Some of them have been leaked by hackers. There is a horde of these creatures on the loose already, and the way we pursue knowledge work in the 21st century is changed forever.

> It is the same: for, be it joy or sorrow, The
> path of departure still is free.
> Man's yesterday may ne'er be like his morrow;
> Nought may endure but mutability!
>
> – Shelley, 1816, as cited in Shelley, 1818

MEMOIR

As humans, we have an innate ability to create. And as writers, we harness that ability as a superpower. Without the ability to understand the human condition, and without the ability to move away from the singular window many of us stand behind in our lives, there can be no art, whether of the fictive or factual, and no room to discover how to use our own experiences within our writing. *The Confessions of Jean-Jacques Rosseau* (18th century)—addressed to the general, secular public – is widely considered the first autobiography, and a precursor to contemporary arguments about truth in autobiography/memoir. While autobiography and memoirs may be used interchangeably, a memoir more often focuses on a period of life, or a particular incident—something 'memorable' or vivid or intense—rather than the whole life. Memoir is often about some kind of journey—whether an expedition or an inner quest for understanding. However, it can also focus on an event or series of events that seem mundane or unremarkable, yet are somehow universal, or give the writer a springboard to explore an idea or feeling.

Grief can be a powerful tool for memoir writing, even if it's woven within fiction. And while not strictly an autobiographical text, 'Frankenstein' is an indirect reflection of Mary Shelley's own turbulent life, reflecting her joys and despairs experiences of neglect within childhood from her stepmother, her miscarriages, and the deaths of all but one of her children. It's clear Shelley would have thought of these tragedies as she wrote, and used her desperation and depression within her narrative. By writing such powerful fiction speckled with truth, Shelley was able to harness her grief into a powerful novel still widely read, adapted, and studied to this day.

Memoir also appears in Mary Shelley's later works. The father-daughter motif in particular is written in an autobiographical style. For example, her novel 'Mathilda' (1820) includes three main characters who are fictionalised versions of William Godwin, Percy Shelley, and herself. She also revealed the central characters of 'The Last Man' are based on her Italian circle of friends. Lord Raymond, who leaves England to fight for the Greeks and dies in Constantinople, is based on Lord Byron; and the utopian Adrian, Earl of Windsor, who leads his followers in search of a natural paradise and dies when his boat sinks in a storm, is a fictional portrait of Percy Bysshe Shelley (who died in a storm at sea).

Not only did Mary Shelley use her grief and circle of friends within her novel, but she also included places she had travelled in real life. In 1816, Shelley was staying at Geneva the year Indonesia's Mount Tambora erupted, among the largest volcanic eruptions in recorded history. Tambora, located on the island of Sumbawa, Indonesia (then the Dutch East Indies) began its week-long eruption on April 5, 1815, though its impact would last years. Lava flows levelled the island, killing nearly all plant and animal life and reducing Tambora's height by a third. It belched huge clouds of dust into the air, bringing almost total darkness to the surrounding area for days. These bleak circumstances hit hardest in and around the Alpine regions of France, Germany, Austria, and Switzerland. It was during this time that the young Mary Shelley travelled to Geneva in April 1816, accompanied by her half-sister, Claire Clairmont, and her lover, Percy Bysshe Shelley.

During this time, Geneva had been struck by flooding and famine, and soup kitchens were opened for the poor. Mary observed that "the thunder storms that visit us are grander and more terrific than I have ever seen before." The usually travelled mountain roads remained impassable, and their evening pastime of rowing on Lake Geneva was often impossible because of strong gales and heavy rains. The perpetual heaviness of what should have been summer skies inspired Byron's miserable lyric "Darkness," in which the sun is permanently extinguished, and mankind dies:

> All earth was but one thought—and that was death,
> Immediate and inglorious; and the pang
> Of famine fed upon all entrails—men
> Died, and their bones were tombless as their flesh;
> The meagre by the meagre were devoured

However, it is Shelley's 'The Last Man' (1826), an apocalyptic dystopian novel about a mysterious pandemic illness ravaging Europe in the last 21st century, often overlooked, which shows the utter depression and bleakness she felt - the novel alludes to Percy Shelley's drowning, isolation, and the death of her children (at the time of writing all but one of her children were dead). While 'Frankenstein' is a memoir of the loss of her children, and her experiences growing up, 'The Last Man' is an incredibly bleak look at the author's crushing sense of loneliness and grief. Throughout the novel, however, the characters remain optimistic for the future, clinging to the hope that such a catastrophic disaster will create a more compassionate and equitable world.

Within 'Mary Shelley: Pandemics, Isolation, and Writing', Lee Murray links her personal experiences during the 2019 Australian bushfires and the current pandemic to 'The Last Man', and the dark and dreary world in which she must have lived. Lee also details the grief within her life - through interviews with her friends and colleagues - and her own experiences with isolation in New Zealand. 'Mary Shelley: Pandemics, Isolation, and Writing' is a tribute to Shelley's resilience, determination, and hope that her life, and the world, will one day rebuild itself.

Memoir, however, doesn't have to deal with grief. As aforementioned, it can be personal, a portrait, a travelogue, a spiritual quest. It can share memories or associations with time, objects, and place. All stories occur in place and time, and though the location in which something happens may be a mere backdrop to the event itself, for memoirs, place plays a vital role in telling a story, and providing the context and understanding for what the narrator experiences. In fact, place can play such an important role in some stories that it is a character, acting upon other characters and the narrator. Place can include nature (the impacts humans have on the natural world), travelogue (dislocation, disorientation, adventure), feelings (how you feel about a place, how a place makes you feel), and meaning and metaphor (what is the significance of a place, or certain aspects of a place eg weather, climate, geography, geology). In 'Mary W And Mary S: A Story With Objects' Lucy Sussex details her personal connection to Australian places and artefacts connected to the Wollstonecraft family, delving into meaning and significance, as well as an association of place and representation of the material, such as the Wollstonecraft family arms. Sussex explores identity, name, what a name represents, especially within place, and what happens when a name dies out.

These essays explore memoir through a wholly unique and personal way, not dissimilar to how Mary Shelley explored her own grief through her writing. The authors' anecdotes bring light to how Mary Shelley could have felt, about her experiences with motherhood, and her ever-changing world. They remind us we are united in our struggles, even if it seems we experience grief alone.

Mary Shelley: Pandemics, Isolation, And Writing

Lee Murray

IN NOVEMBER 2019, ON MY RETURN to New Zealand from a family vacation, I stopped over in Brisbane, Australia. The airport halls were full of men in overalls, firefighters heading to or from the fire fronts to battle what would turn out to be the worst bushfires in that nation's history. Although we were some distance from the hot zones, a sepia wall of ash and smoke tinted the air outside the terminal. Plucked from beaches, Australians were evacuating to safer regions, where they were forced indoors, away from the clouds of stinging smoke. In New Zealand, some three thousand kilometres east, a haze of soft-focus pink ash shrouded the sun for weeks, and it was late February 2020 before the fires abated, early March before the last flames were stamped out. By then, COVID-19 was on the rise and my compatriots abroad were rushing home to self-isolate ahead of the plague.

A month later, my father was dead.

Now, a year on from the onset of the pandemic, with millions dead, hundreds of millions infected, and much of the world still in some form of lockdown, I can't help thinking about the parallels between our current situation and Mary Shelley's post-apocalyptic novel *The Last Man* (1826), reviled by critics in its day, but which scholar Rebecca Barr described recently as a "story about an apocalypse of loneliness".[1] Princeton's Madeleine Joelson believes the author sought "to combine her personal grief with the larger implications of a growing eschatological genre".[2]

Shelley wrote *The Last Man* in a time of widespread human loss, in the aftermath of the Napoleonic Wars (1792-1815) and during a cholera pandemic (1817-1824). By this time, the author was twenty-eight years old

---

1 Barr, 2020
2 Joelson, 2020

and had lost all but one of her five children; her husband, Percy Bysshe Shelley, had drowned in a boating incident; and her friend, the romantic poet Lord Byron, had succumbed to disease while at war in Greece.

"As it kills off character after character, *The Last Man* recreates this history of loss along with its author's crushing sense of loneliness," states Olivia Murphy in *The Conversation*.[3] Shelley writes of her anguish in a journal entry made on 14 May 1824: "The last man! Yes, I may well describe that solitary being's feelings, feeling myself as the last relic of a beloved race, my companions, extinct before me—"

Bereft and alone, and inspired by her reading of Defoe's *The Journal of the Plague Year* (1722), Thomas Campbell's poem *The Last Man* (1823), and Bryon's *The Darkness* (1816), Shelley poured her own experience into her novel. Her 'last man', Lionel Verney, who Eileen Hunt Botting aptly describes as Shelley's 'avatar',[4] marries well, and ingratiates himself with leaders of the English republic. When the plague touches even that elite, when "the air is empoisoned, and each human being inhales death", Verney leads an expedition to the shores of Italy, where, as humanity's sole survivor, he climbs St Peter's Basilica, and, standing atop the church's dome, contemplates the future.

With the global political and economic turmoil, the sweeping pandemic, and the growing climate crisis, today's world resembles the catastrophe described in Shelley's *The Last Man*:

"I spread the whole earth out as a map before me. On no one spot on its surface could I put my finger and say, here is safety."[5]

So, how has personal grief, and the isolation of the pandemic, impacted contemporary writers of speculative fiction and horror? How are today's writers reflecting this reality in their work?

In my own case, I wasn't present when my father died during New Zealand's Level 4 lockdown. Regulations meant there were no funerals, no flowers, no family groups. I was too numb to write fiction. Instead, I managed some poems. "A few words scribbled on scraps of paper. Like breathing in tiny shallow breaths," I wrote in a guest post for poet Stephanie Wytovich's blog in May 2020.[6] The writing reflected both my isolation and despair:

---

3 Murphy, 2020
4 Botting, 2020
5 Shelley, 1823
6 Murray, 2020

the pestilence followed us
into space
rampaging
rampant
in ragged, haggard lungs
We ejected the dead,
sent them gentle into the night.
Imagined the starry fireworks
glimpsed on far-off porches.
We saw only darkness.
Bereft, we drifted on.

Were other writers experiencing loss responding the same way? In the last week of January 2021, I wrote a short social media post calling for comment, and within a few hours sixteen colleagues had contacted me, writers who had lost parents, partners, siblings, children, uncles, aunts, and friends, some through COVID-19, others through illness, accident, and suicide. One colleague had lost his mother as recently as the day prior, another's loved one was still dying. For one, the loss of a kitten while stuck at home with the daily reminders of its passing, and coming on the heels of the deaths of two family members and a friend, was described as "raw". [7] Between them, my colleagues sent me an outpouring of grief and insight—more than 20,000 words of reflection. Their personal testimonies were heartfelt and poignant—eulogies packed into mere paragraphs—and more than once I was moved to tears. My sampling may have lacked academic rigour, but their observations remain pertinent and valid.

Though many of my respondents were accustomed to geographical separation from their loved ones, and the voluntary solitude needed for writing, they noted that the pandemic isolation had impacted on their grief, causing them to experience a range of emotions from rage, shock, helplessness, foreboding, anxiety for family and friends, a strong sense of their own mortality, and a desperate need for human connection.

For example, "Losing friends and family during the bushfires and pandemic, some a dreadful shock, others expected but still keenly felt, had an extra layer of surrealness," writes one antipodean colleague. "First, we had the eerie post-apocalyptic smoke-filled skies as we said our goodbyes,

---

7 Anonymous

then we had lockdown, and futuristic live streamed funerals." [8]

"The isolation of this year past… I recognised quite early that the new disease was going to be a problem," writes another. "The rising numbers in Wuhan… I remember remarking to someone just before New Year 2020 that I didn't think the Chinese were going to get it under control. That we were about to encounter something that might really be trouble." [9]

"…I've really struggled," admits a UK writer, her most recent loss just days before. "My emotional and mental health has taken a plunge into murky, dark waters and loneliness has me wrapped in those icy fingers. I just need a hug." [10]

"Many of those we could have reached out to for support—family, old friends, and so on—and those who needed us for support, were too far away to be practical help for each other," says horror author, Lee Battersby. "In many ways, that exacerbated our insularity and helplessness." [11]

I couldn't argue; I'd felt the same way: "…it's hard to be far from the people you desperately need to hug in times like these". [12]

A colleague who also lost a parent in the first days of the pandemic notes, "…we've had these separate lives for so long because of the spatial distance, so the isolation didn't really feel any different than at other times. What affected me more was that everyone else had it so bad because of COVID, my own grief got a bit lost. It makes you feel more alone, having to deal with your feelings yourself." [13]

A creative writing lecturer, who claims to be "pretty solitary anyway" cited a heightened awareness of vulnerability: "…the loss has me thinking about our fragility and how quickly time passes." [14]

Many of the testimonies I received focused on the deceased. Likewise, Shelley's, *The Last Man*, centres on six major characters—Verney, Adrian, Lord Raymond, Perdita, Idris and Evadne—all drawn from her social circle, with heroic Adrian representing her beloved Percy, Lord Raymond based on Byron, and Evadne, Shelley's stepsister Claire Clairmont. Verney's father in *The Last Man* is modelled on Shelley's own father, the

8 Anonymous
9 Anonymous
10 Anonymous
11 Battersby
12 Anonymous
13 Anonymous
14 Anonymous

scholar William Godwin, who died in 1822.

I asked my colleagues if they'd been inspired to incorporate characteristics, themes, or places dear to their loved one into their writing, but, for some, it was simply too soon, although they acknowledged that they planned to:

"I typically try and write sadder, bleaker works," replies Canadian horror author and commentator, Steve Stred, "so I suspect at some point I'll call upon some of the emotions surrounding his passing to work as a cathartic moment in a piece of fiction." [15]

"My mother's name was 'Jolly' for Joline. I think I want to write *Burying Jolly* as a dark humour book. Who knows? It could be cathartic." [16]

"...elements of old friends find their way into the work." [17]

"When my schoolfriend died, I was planning on writing a complete short story (that turned into a novelette). The setting was a key component to the story, and because of its strong association with home, I named a character after my departed friend...that brought me a sense of peace because I felt like I was honouring him in a way that had been denied to me when I couldn't go to a funeral. I could imagine telling my friend that he was in my story and how he'd grin at that." [18]

Some writers revealed how the ongoing reality had meant themes of loss and isolation had gained importance in their work:

"...the novel I've been working on since before COVID-19 has a massive theme of isolation running through it, and it's only become more pronounced since editing." [19]

"...my own feelings of loss made it into my protagonist's pain." [20]

Award-winning Australian author Alan Baxter is candid: "that stuff bleeds onto the page all the time. My horror novel, *Devouring Dark*, is essentially a meditation on death and what it means, what it might mean, the justice and injustice of it all... One character even has lines that are verbatim things my dad said on his deathbed." [21]

In a delightful segue, Heide Goody, co-author of the *Oddjobs* horror-

15 Stred
16 Anonymous
17 Anonymous
18 Anonymous
19 Anonymous
20 Anonymous
21 Baxter

comedy series (with Iain Grant), sends me a photograph of a massive tea pot of her mother's, one that didn't get used often being the size you would need if twenty people came round. "When we had a 'mystic teapot' in the *Oddjobs* series, this was the one we described,"[22] she writes.

Author-screenwriter, Dirk Flinthart, was asked to write a story by his dying sister, Aiki Flinthart, also a writer of speculative work. Unable to refuse, Dirk wrote 'Heartbreak Hotel', which he says is "a bleak, sad, bittersweet story set in a post-climate-change USA. A story that comments on the foolishness that got us here, while still celebrating the best and finest of human endeavour. I did it with full awareness and acceptance of things like COVID-19, and climate change, and environmental collapse, and everything else we've brought down on ourselves."[23]

The second cholera pandemic reached Europe in 1826, the year Shelley's *The Last Man* was published. Since Europe had been largely spared from the 1815 pandemic, librarian Jim Green of The Library Company of Philadelphia suggests Shelley drew on her memories of 1816, the famous 'year without a summer' when writing *The Last Man*. During that summer, a colossal cloud of dust and ash ejected from Indonesia's volcanic Mount Tambora drifted westward into Europe and occluded the sun, causing harvests to fail and two hundred thousand people to starve. "This was not a pandemic, of course," writes Green, "but it had many of the same effects. Crowds of starving people roamed the countryside crying out for food and dying by the roadside. Food riots broke out everywhere, but the violence was worse in Switzerland."[24]

Shelley and her husband, Percy, her sister, Claire, and Lord Byron, were in Switzerland at the time, stuck indoors in a villa at Lake Geneva, where, out of boredom, their now-famous wager would result in Mary Shelley's *Frankenstein* (1818).

While, like me, many of my colleagues were also "too numb to write"[25] so soon after a loss, they all mentioned writing and creativity as a means of processing loss and isolation, if not to fully recover:

"Writing has always been my oasis," says Battersby. "There's an inbuilt need to express, if not necessarily to communicate; keeping everything

---

22 Goody
23 Flinthart
24 Green
25 Murray, 2020

inside hurts, so it's an avenue to release some of that internal pressure." [26]

"Horror helps everything! It's a way of processing, of exploring, of honouring. Horror and genre fiction has saved me multiple times." [27]

"Writing is an escapism for me, a space to let me visit other places and worlds with people I would never meet or interact with otherwise," agrees Stred. "So, in that respect, writing has absolutely helped." [28]

"Writing is something that you can reach for and immerse yourself in whatever else is going on. Even when you don't feel like doing it, it helps. It always feels constructive and it always feels 'active'." [29]

"I came to understand better what the writing process has done and can do for me. As I mentioned, it's not about recovery; it's about compensating, understanding, and doing what you can. The writing doesn't help me feel any differently, but it does help me understand what it is I am feeling." [30]

In Shelley's *The Last Man*, the book Verney is writing, the character's recourse to libraries, and his choice to carry with him the works of Homer and Shakespeare, suggest the author finds solace in both writing and reading literature. "Mary Shelley's novel points to the power and value of the imagination to sustain us in times where sorrow seems to overwhelm all that might bring comfort," writes Professor Lisa Vargo. [31] When I asked my colleagues if they'd been consuming post-apocalyptic stories during the pandemic, for some, the "real horror of COVID-19 was a little too close": [32]

"This year, I wanted stories of hope and resilience. I wanted stories that could make me laugh because there was so much going on, I was scared if I read a story that chilled me to the bone, I might never warm up again." [33]

"…a dry run for The End Of The World As We Know It was going on outside my door. Why the blazes would I want to read a fictitious version thereof?" [34]

"I absolutely have not, and I can't bear the thought of watching apocalyptic tales. Right now, it feels like the world is very different and

---

26 Battersby
27 Anonymous
28 Anonymous
29 Anonymous
30 Anonymous
31 Vargo, 2020
32 Anonymous
33 Anonymous
34 Anonymous

very dangerous. COVID-19 makes the news headlines *every day* so there is literally no escape from thinking about it." [35]

Professor Lisa Vargo claims "[Shelley] would recognize the present devastation of private griefs balanced against daily reports of numbers and statistics and debates about the value of economic factors versus individual lives." [36] Author Dirk Flinthart certainly does: "I'm as small as any other person. I can't understand tens of thousands dying in Italy, in Spain, in France, in England, in the USA…those are numbers. When I think about them, I feel a dull horror, and I imagine fields of the dead— but my mind puts faces on all those corpses. Faces that I know, and then, only then does it really reach me. And yet I'm burning, numbed, shaking, bleeding for one person." [37]

Those who had consumed some apocalyptic fiction, cited titles like Chuck Wendig's *The Wanderers*, Josh Malerman's *Bird Box*, and *A Single Yesterday*, by George R. R. Martin, as offering comfort by uplifting the readers in some way, through the portrayal of a character's resilience, a positive ending, or the possibility of preserving certain aspects of culture. However, one colleague read *I am Legend* by Richard Matheson, saying, "it made me feel more like humanity is doomed, and there's no reason to care if any of us live or die. There really isn't any redemption. It never purged my emotions; it just heightened them and dragged me down." [38]

The 'last man' narratives of Shelley's contemporaries are similarly bleak, whereas Shelley's own vision offers hope of sorts, since, even in his solitude, with humanity facing extinction, Verney seeks community, setting out on a voyage across the sea with his dog, his books, and driven by "a restless despair and a fierce desire of change" [39] in search of other survivors.

"Shelley reminds us through the heroic voice of Verney," writes Botting, [40] "that we should always act upon hope for retaining what makes us loving, humane, and connected to others, even in the face of total catastrophe." And Shelley reveals another unexpected silver lining of the apocalypse, because, even as the humans of Verney's world decline, the natural world around them flourishes—a cause for hope.

---

35 Anonymous
36 Vargo, 2020
37 Flinthart
38 Anonymous
39 Shelley, 1818
40 Botting, 2020

"I like to think that humanity (and by extension, me) is a resilient species," writes a fellow New Zealander. "There's little that we can't do within our knowledge base. But, it also reminds me that the world, as it is, will continue to turn with or without us. Death takes us all, but Life continues to roll forward. For some reason, knowing both those things makes me feel better." [41]

In the end, "Shelley shows that isolation is a human condition," claims researcher, G.R. Yadav. "Nobody can escape it, but finding a path to deal with it, depends on the will of man." [42] It seems likely that writing Verney's tale, *The Last Man*, was Shelley's own attempt to find that path.

ESCHATON

On the last day of the world
Rising with the blood-crimson sun I shall
seek the place where you have dwelled and
together we will break our fast among ruins
where the mighty hang from offal-laden
crucifixes at the pleasure of the multitudes
who at last their vengeful voice hath given tongue.

On the last day of the world
there will be honey-cakes and amber wine
slow kisses and blood-rich venison roasted
over paper fires; words of plausible madmen,
consigned at last, at long last to their proper fate,
and we will play upon violins and ancient harps
and the joyful music of forgotten lovers will ring
as the hateful pages one by one
turn to ash and rise into the rich and smoky air.

On the last day of the world
there shall come an end to the endless voices
which have walled us with their weary wisdom
And blood at last shall answer all the wrongs
of small and gentle people in the vanquished silent spaces
and the terrible, wondrous joy of knowing
no dread deed can ever be undone

---

41 Anonymous
42 Yadav, 2020

will rise like champagne bubbles
and we shall grow giddy and fall laughing
to lie in complicit innocence upon the ancient, dying earth.

On the last day of the world
you will paint your supple velvet skin with
ochre and crimson, and I shall don the warlike blue
dance barefoot to the music of breaking glass
baptise the flames in blood and melancholy
while the choir hymns the tide arising
and the waves reclaim the long-held forfeit
of our sea-enriched forefathers who
spurned the sullen, silent soil.

On the last day of the world
I will take you in my arms and
taste the mystery of your flesh
all the words between us lost
all our striving set at naught
arm in arm together we shall gravely,
joyously herald the long,
long night.

– Dirk Flinthart

Mary W and Mary S:
A Story with Objects

Lucy Sussex

"Hapless woman! what a fate is thine!"
Mary Wollstonecraft, *Letters*

Object: external

IT BEGINS WITH A BUS in Sydney, negotiating the crowded, humid summer streets. The destination is clearly marked, a route across the city. Those who board, swipe their transport card, use the name every day without reference to its resonance. Only a few, aware of the history of feminist thought, or fans via film or books of a very famous daughter, would look at it and wonder: what is the name Wollstonecraft doing on an Australian public transport?

In my mind, locked down physically as I am by covid regulations, I take the bus, following the route to the plush and affluent North Shore on my mobile via google as I go. Nothing is remarkable at the destination, a suburb, quiet, green, leafy and hilly, with its own eponymous railway station. I look around: no sign of any historical plaque or statue, far less a long skirt, a scarfed neck, a head decked with powder or a rakish top hat.

Mary Wollstonecraft is an absence here, though to anyone who knows her work the name gives thoughtful pause. The Wollstonecraft family arms, signifying gentility, were granted in 1765. On a shield, background bright green, three mermaids pose, each holding in her right hand a mirror and, in her left, a golden comb. On the crest, a mermaid, similarly preening, rises out of a crown of gold, described as naval, with ships and sails. It is an image of female, fishy narcissism not out of place on Sydney's beaches. The mermaids are half naked, the rest of their bodies clothed in scales. As such they reveal less flesh than Maggie Hambling's controversial 2020 silvery statue of Mary Wollstonecraft. Curiously, the family arms can also be rendered on silverware, another sign of gentility.

Neither Hambling's image nor the mermaids have any resemblance to the historical Mary Wollstonecraft.

Did she make use of these arms? Someone who could was her nephew Edward, and his sister Elizabeth, children of Mary's elder brother, Ned Wollstonecraft. The siblings emigrated to Australia, and thus brought their family name (if not also the family silverware) to this place. They departed this life, but left their name, written on the landscape.

What's in a name? Elizabeth Wollstonecraft was a real person who seems as undefined as her namesake Elizabeth Frankenstein. She has little public notice apart from her shipping record, marriage, and death. In contrast her younger brother Edward is well documented, featuring in colonial records and also the *Australian Dictionary of Biography*. The entry, written by M. D. Stephen in 1967, states: "Wollstonecraft resented the notoriety of his aunt and sought escape and fortune for himself and his sister in travel and trade." [1] The source for this remark is not given; but it has been repeated as gospel by Sydneysiders.

Brother and sister were orphaned in their early twenties, and unlike Mary and her brother Ned, remained close emotionally and geographically. Ned was a favoured son, a bully, who became a solicitor. Mary regarded him as inferior, especially mentally, and the dislike was mutual. If Edward inherited his father's bias, then his response to a query about his relationship to the famous Wollstonecraft comes as no surprise. He replied, in a slighting manner, 'She was an aunt of mine.' [2]

The date of this comment is 1812, when Mary had been dead 15 years, and her daughter Mary Godwin was only a teen, yet to meet Percy Shelley. Edward, who also had legal training, had become active in business. On a European voyage he met Alexander Berry, a Scot turned colonial entrepreneur. It was Berry who recorded Edward's comment. The encounter proved fateful: Berry employed Edward as his agent, and for four years shared a house with the Wollstonecraft siblings. In 1819 he made Edward his partner, and the two men set sail for New South Wales. There, Edward applied for and received from the colonial government a generous land grant, unceded territory of the Eora people. Both men further gained

---

1 Stephen, 1967
2 Berry, 1873

more land in the Shoalhaven river area (Jerrinja and Wandi Wandian nations), which they worked with large amounts of convict labour. They became rich and respected, with posts ranging from the magistracy to bank directorships to the colonial Parliament. The partnership extended to the familial when Berry married Elizabeth Wollstonecraft in 1827.

What has this to do with Aunt Mary Wollstonecraft? Well, it would not have happened without her. In old age, Berry wrote a memoir, detailing his first sight of Edward Wollstonecraft: a "tall, formal-looking young man, dressed in black."[3] Though the pair were Englishmen abroad, travelling by sea, Edward eyed Berry "askance". He did not seek his company, preferring to read his book alone. Berry, somewhat miffed, would not have bothered any further, were it not for this unsociable young man's surname. He was well-read, and it piqued his interest to persist. In a sentence mysteriously omitted from the *ADB* entry, Berry notes that he had read some of Mary Wollstonecraft's work, and Godwin's memoir of her. Despite what he would describe as Edward's "naturally defective temper", he sought acquaintance, which became friendship.

Edward Wollstonecraft's Australian wealth and status resulted from his association with Berry; which in turn resulted from Berry reading his aunt. In turn, Elizabeth gained a husband, likely a marriage less about passion than mature friendship and good financial estate planning: the bachelor Edward was increasingly sickly, and Elizabeth was his heir. Edward died five years after the marriage, a curmudgeonly in-law. Yet when Elizabeth died in 1845, Berry had the siblings interred together in an impressive monument, a pyramid of local stone.

Nobody ever traced its inscription of Wollstonecraft when learning to read, as is recorded Mary Shelley did with her mother's grave, under the guidance of Godwin. Yet the map of New South Wales is inscribed by the presence of Berry and the Wollstonecrafts. The Sydney suburb of Crow's Nest is stated to be named after Edward's home there, later Berry's (the brother-in-law is commemorated by Berry Island and the town of Berry). The adjoining suburb is said to be named for Edward.

Or was it? A 1908 letter begs to differ. It was written to a columnist for the *Sydney Stock and Station Journal*, an organ of settler colonisation. The unnamed journalist was a fan of Mary's, and termed her a "wonderful

---

3 Stephen, 1967

woman." [4] The letter-writer stated that Wollstonecraft was named after Berry's wife Elizabeth, "and so after your friend 'Mary'". Whatever the truth, the naming would not have occurred without Mary, and Berry, also a fan. Having married into the Wollstonecrafts, he happily corresponded in later life with Mary's famous daughter Mary Shelley, and after her death with her daughter-in-law and family archivist, Lady Jane Shelley.

The article concludes that Mary "wrote her name deep in the annals of the world." And prophetically and accurately: "she will be better known a century hence tha[n] she is today".

Representation

Should Mary then be commemorated at Wollstonecraft? With the rejected design for her memorial statue, by sculptor Martin Jennings, which shows her fully clothed, with pen and books, perhaps? Unlike her niece and nephew, she has numerous representations. The most controversial is the Hamill, and the most commonly used the last taken from life, the Opie portrait hung in the Godwin household. Here, she looks away demurely, an unremarkable if personable woman in mid-pregnancy. Her other images differ, with a clear gaze directed at the observer. John Keenan shows her looking up from a book, a study in greys. In an earlier Opie portrait, from 1790, she is similarly distracted from her reading.

Wollstonecraft's contemporary Jane Austen was much less of a public personality. She has only one genuine portrait, a sketch by Cassandra. It shows a woman with definite personality, sharp of nose, and beady of eye, her arms crossed, a gesture possibly defensive or defiant. The image would be softened, prettified for public consumption as Austen's audience grew. The result was doe-eyed, as pretty as a doll and similarly lacking a sense of the person. The final Opie portrait is the prettiest image of Mary Wollstonecraft, and also the most popular.

In contrast, possibly the least reproduced portrait of Wollstonecraft is one in which I have a personal interest. It is my Object Representation of Mary Wollstonecraft, with a link to my DNA. John Williamson's 1791 portrait of Mary Wollstonecraft was commissioned by my putative ancestor William Roscoe, a minor poet, Abolitionist, progressive activist, (briefly) Parliamentarian, and friend of both Godwin and Mary. His most popular work was the 1802 children's poem "The Butterfly's Ball and the Grasshopper's Feast." Coleridge termed him "natural, sweet and cheerful,

---

4 Berry, 1873

zealous in kindness, and a republican, with all the feelings of prudence and all the manners of good sense." At the time to be a republican was treason to the English monarchy.

Williamson's image is the most Gothic, masculine and also confronting representation of Mary Wollstonecraft. A study in black and white, black dress, white scarf, white hands, powdered hair, it has been compared to portraits of the major French revolutionaries. Yet not even her fellow feministas Olympe de Gouges and Théroigne de Méricourt, were depicted with such force. If the first Opie and the Keenan depicted her as a reader, then here is a woman who takes no prisoners. She looks fierce as the heraldic gryphon, even, perhaps, a vampire. The strongest impression is strength of personality, undeniable power. Here is a public intellectual, buoyed from writing the *Vindications*, to be published the next year.

As Roscoe, a noted art collector, commissioned the image, he approved the representation, held now in his native Liverpool's Art gallery. In his poetry he called Wollstonecraft an 'Amazon'. Only his bankruptcy and the sale of his collection saw it banished from his walls.

Part Object

One of the worthy causes shared by Roscoe and Wollstonecraft was breast-feeding. Roscoe translated from the Italian a poem, "The Nurse" by Luigi Tansillo, to great success. He dedicated it to his wife Jane, who had nursed all ten of their children.

> Once exil'd from your breast, and doom'd to bring
> His daily nurture from a stranger spring
> Ah, who can tell the dangers that await
> Your infant? Thus abandon'd to his fate [5]

Breastfeeding was then a class issue: women of the working class had no choice, but those of higher status hired wet-nurses, even sending their babies to live with the wet-nurse (the Austens did this with all of their children). Ned Wollstonecraft, as a valued eldest son, had unusually been fed by his mother Elizabeth; Mary had not. She believed in nurturing children in body and mind, so breast-fed her eldest, Fanny Imlay, referring to the baby in letters to Gilbert Imlay as "my animal". In another letter to a friend, she wrote: "My little Girl begins to suck so MANFULLY that her father reckons saucily on her writing the second part of the R[igh]ts of Woman".

---

5 Tansillo & Roscoe. 1804

A breast is a fetishized object, from the Saints such as the martyred Agatha, with her tray of breasts, or the Futurist dessert Fragomammella (Strawberry and ricotta breasts). In Ken Russell's *Gothic*, about the birth of *Frankenstein*, Claire Clairmont, Mary's step-sister, has her nipples transmogrified into eyes. In the lives of the Marys, mother and daughter, the breast functioned without fetish, that is, naturally.

Mary Wollstonecraft's legacy to her daughters was genetic and bodily, nurturing them in her womb, and with her milk. Mary jr had just enough time for the colostrum, the watery fluid rich in antibodies vital to the infant's immune system, before her mother's sepsis became apparent. With that, the vital milk became a health hazard, puerperal fever being thought to be caused by putrid milk, and so dangerous to infants too. As is well known, puppies were applied to her breasts to draw the milk out, nobody caring if they lived or died. She was also prescribed wine freely, a dying, drunken woman.

Formula in those days was unscientific, unhygienic, at worst bread soaked in water, known as pap. Mary Jr duly gained a wet nurse. When the time came with her own pregnancies and births, she fed her babies herself, but only son Percy, the male heir to Percy Shelley's baronetcy, survived. With him, she had the status of not only her famous parents, her own writing, her editing of her husband's work and careful nurturance of his posthumous fame, but also as the mother of an aristocrat.

The Internal Object

Mary Jr was an object internal to her mother, before her emergence as an 'animal'. Visceral links aside, she had no memory of her. What she knew of her mother was the Opie portrait, prominently displayed, and her books, frequently read and re-read. For Mary she had Object Constancy: the relationship with her mother was imagined, and never changed, unlike her sometimes difficult if loving relationship with her father. Her stepmother, Mary Jane Clairmont Godwin, mother of Claire, was no substitute. Though an intelligent woman, publisher, bookseller and translator of the *Swiss Family Robinson* into English, Mary claimed to 'shudder' at the thought of her, as if her stepmother was a horror.

There must have been more tangible artefacts, objects left behind: Wollstonecraft's personal possessions, her comb and mirror, her dresses. Some of these would have been handed down to her daughters, too valuable to discard with a household as straightened at times as Godwin's.

Yet what we hear of most is intimate, and very private. When Fanny Imlay committed suicide in 1816, a lonely death in Swansea from opiate poisoning, she was wearing stays marked with the initials M. W., her mother's underwear. The corpse being unclaimed, with a pauper's grave, the garments would have gone to a second-hand dealer, their significance lost. What Mary retained of her mother's worldly goods is unknown. Given her constant travels with Shelley, she likely retained little personal possessions. Yet the legacy of her mother remained a presence all her life.

The other reminder of Mary Wollstonecraft was the gravestone, frequently visited. That memory site was important to her daughter as a reader, her first primer being the funeral inscription cut into stone, memorial and memorable. It recurred in her life, when she took Shelley there, due homage and pilgrimage from a fellow Wollstonecraft fan. And there declared her love for him, a decision as wild and wilful as her mother's with Imlay.

Yet, in Mary Jr's writing is something hidden, but revealed via forensic linguistics. Language is like a fingerprint, a unique marker of identity, with literary style quantifiable at the level of grammar. In the nineteenth century it was particularly marked with writers with different levels of education, males from grammar or public school distinct from women and working-class men, even those who were autodidacts. Formal habits of prosody were literally beaten into them. Scholars, such as the late Professor John Burrows of the University of Newcastle, have put these works into machine-readable form, and analysed them. It has proved able to distinguish co-writers who are siblings, such as Henry and Sara Fielding.

Yet within the eighteenth and nineteenth century women writers Burrows examined, whose writing carried the traits of their more limited education than the males, are some anomalies. He discovered a small group actually wrote more like men than their female peers. They were: Mary (Perdita) Robinson, who knew both Godwins; Emily Brontë; crime-writer Mary Fortune, whose work I have examined with John Burrows; and Mary Shelley. It is worth noting that while Robinson's mother was a schoolteacher (as was Wollstonecraft), the others all lost their mothers very young. Quite why Anne Brontë, younger than Emily, is not a member of this group is unknown. But certainly, the mind that produced *Wuthering Heights* was as unusual as the mind that produced *Frankenstein* and the *Last Man*.

Godwin, while appreciating his daughter as a prodigy, has been described as not being as interested in female education as his first wife—here he was conventionally male, focussed on his son. Yet he wrote and published children's books, the latter with his second wife. If he guided Mary to read the inscription on the grave, he would likely not have stopped there. Another factor seems the formidable course of reading Mary put herself through with Shelley, a life otherwise marked by constant childbearing and nursing.

To say a woman wrote like a man was a compliment, now deeply suspect. Nonetheless, Mary Shelley wrote less like her mother, despite the latter's erudition and pedagogy, and more like a male.

Slut-shaming and Suicide

Nearly all of the women in Godwin's household had their sex life not entirely confined by the bond of wedlock. So, for that matter, was Mary Perdita Robinson, writer *and* mistress of the Prince Regent; and noblewomen such as the Duchess of Devonshire. The wages of such sin, if made public, was ostracism, shaming, a fate worse than death. What would have happened to Lydia Bennett if Wickham had not been bribed into marriage? The same fate as Maria Crawford in *Mansfield Park*, an adulterous wife sent into seclusion?

Loss of virtue was conventionally cited as a cause of female suicide, as if the latter was a desired outcome for a woman 'ruined' by a man. When rejected by Imlay, Mary Wollstonecraft made two unsuccessful attempts to kill herself. The manner of the first is unknown; the second was to throw herself in a river, a common choice for suicides: contemporary records reveal 306 bodies pulled from the Seine from 1795-1801 alone. Unlike the 'mermaids' and surfers of Sydney's beaches, these women's education had not included learning to swim. Neither had the otherwise well-educated Percy Shelley, who would drown in the ocean in 1822, no merman he.

In Godwin's memoir of his wife, he repeats what Mary told him of her second attempt:

> *The agony of her mind determined her; and that determination gave her a sort of desperate serenity. She resolved to plunge herself in the Thames; and, not being satisfied with any spot nearer to London, she took a boat, and rowed to Putney. Her first thought had led her to Battersea-bridge, but she found it too public. It was night when she arrived at Putney, and by that time had begun to rain with great violence. The rain suggested to her the idea of walking up and down the bridge, till her clothes were thoroughly drenched and heavy with the wet, which she did for half an hour without meeting a human being. She then leaped from the top of*

the bridge, but still seemed to find a difficulty in sinking, which she endeavoured to counteract by pressing her clothes closely round her. After some time she became insensible; but she always spoke of the pain she underwent as such, that, though she could afterwards have determined upon almost any other species of voluntary death, it would have been impossible for her to resolve upon encountering the same sensations again. I am doubtful, whether this is to be ascribed to the mere nature of suffocation, or was not rather owing to the preternatural action of a desperate spirit. [6]

At the time, Mary's daughter Fanny was an infant; and a motherless child was severely at risk. The loss of Mary when Fanny was three resonated through her short life. It was of Fanny that her mother wrote "Hapless woman!", something which proved deterministic. Suicides run in families, a fearful example to follow, as with Charmian Clift and the Johnstone children. Fanny would have known Godwin's account, and she planned carefully, in order to succeed. The reasons for the suicide remain unclear, as she does not seem to have been compromised. It has been suggested she had an unrequited love for Shelley.

Sister Mary wrote in her diary, in typically terse, cool mode:

Wednesday, October 9.—Read Curtius; finish the *Memoirs*; draw. In the evening a very alarming letter comes from Fanny. Shelley goes immediately to Bristol; we sit up for him till 2 in the morning, when he returns, but brings no particular news.

Thursday, October 10.—Shelley goes again to Bristol, and obtains more certain trace. Work and read. He returns at 11 o'clock.

Friday, October 11.—He sets off to Swansea. Work and read.

Saturday, October 12.—He returns with the worst account. A miserable day. Two letters from Papa. Buy mourning, and work in the evening.

Fanny was 22; and Mary then nineteen, her work being the writing of *Frankenstein*. She had lost one child, and given birth to a second, in the eyes of the law illegitimate, as was Fanny. Two months later her status changed, with the death of 21-year-old Harriet Westbrooke Shelley, abandoned by her husband. She too drowned herself in the rivers of London, described as being heavily pregnant at the time, by whom is unknown. She was

---

6 Godwin, 1798

buried as Harriet Smith, a name she had assumed at her lodgings, a name that may or may not have something do to with Austen's *Emma*, published earlier that year. The *Times* slut-shamed her: "a want of honour in her own conduct is supposed to have led to this fatal catastrophe". So did the Godwins/Shelleys, anxious to exonerate Shelley at his first wife's expense.

Had Mary Wollstonecraft succeeded, her second daughter would never have been born, and had Harriet *not* succeeded, Mary Jr could not have married Shelley, and become thus a respectable woman.

Mary Wollstonecraft was, like Harriet, subject to calumnies. Godwin has been blamed for writing his memoir of her when bereaved, and being brutally honest. From that the wider public learnt of Imlay, Fanny's birth, and the suicide attempts. William Roscoe, who knew Mary very well, was not impressed:

> Hard was thy fate in all the scenes of life
> As daughter, sister, parent, friend and wife
> But harder still in death thy fate we own,
> Mourn'd by that Godwin—with a heart of stone. [7]

Yet the narrative of Mary's reception/reputation undone by a grieving husband can be questioned. Eileen Hunt Botting, editor of the 2020 *Portraits of Wollstonecraft*, terms it a myth, albeit with some persistence. She has collected responses to Wollstonecraft's work over two centuries and finds that Wollstonecraft was not "*that* controversial [...] her global reception was strong and relatively positive from the start." She continued to be read, Alexander Berry being one example. Botting adds: "It was just the Napoleonic Era, mainly in Britain, where her reception went mainly underground."

Marriage did after all make a woman honest, as the writers George Eliot and Mary Braddon knew from personal experience. Braddon named a girl-child Mary Wollstonecraft in her 1880 crime novel *Just As I Am*, the joke being that the name is not deterministic, this Mary being unlearned. And Braddon knew better than to give this namesake character a fate worse than death. She herself, like Mary Shelley, had to wait for her lover's wife to die. It was something that only happened after six children and a number of best-selling novels.

Certainly a search of Trove for the two Marys in nineteenth-century Australian newspapers, shows no negative comments, rather the reverse,

---

7 Preedy, 1937

even if the pair are sometimes confused. Hardly surprising: Mary Wollstonecraft became Mary Godwin; Mary Wollstonecraft Godwin became Mary Shelley. The former's works are advertised from the 1830s, with in 1836 the *Hobart Town Courier* reporting Mary Shelley supervising her son's education at Harrow. The only reference to disapproval is in an article from the English *Chambers' Journal*, reprinted in the 1864 *Illawarra Mercury*. It bears the title "Mrs Grundy Moribunda", referring to the emblematic figure of the Victorian wowser/God's policewoman. The anonymous author has come to bury Mrs Grundy, and as evidence adduces a poem published in an 1863 collection, *Ballads and Songs*. Despite being anti-Grundy, he observes the Victorian propriety that women do not belong in the public sphere. Thus he does not identify the book nor the writer, except as "a well-known lady, one of the foremost of her sex" given to good works such as "Social Science" and "Women's Mission" (i.e. a feminist). The Poem is called "Two Graves", and describes a literary pilgrimage to Percy and Mary Shelley's graves:

> TWO graves within one year I saw,
> Where sleep, a thousand miles apart,
> Husband and wife, whose living law
> Was but to know one soul, one heart. [8]

The poet was Bessie Rayner Parkes, writer, activist, and friend of George Eliot. The *Chambers'* journalist quibbles with the word divine used with reference to Shelley's verse—the writer being a notorious atheist. Yet he takes heart from the poem not being controversial: "Not even the feeblest shriek has been set up by Mrs Grundy."

From the poem it can be seen that Shelley has become canonical. For Parkes, the graves are pilgrimage sites as much as Mary Wollstonecraft's had been for her daughter. Yet Mary Shelley's work was not yet part of the literary canon, as the manifestations of *Frankenstein* were still playing out (literally) in the popular genres of theatre. The following year, one of the odder manifestations was published in Melbourne: George Isaacs' "The Burlesque of Frankenstein."

Despite the title, Mary Shelley was not being slut-shamed, even if the title seems to anticipate *Flesh for Frankenstein*. At the time burlesque simply meant a pantomime, full of feeble jokes, puns, songs, and topical references.

A pantomime of *Frankenstein*? Oh no it's not! Oh yes, it is!

---

8 Parkes, 2010

George Isaacs came from a wealthy Sephardic family in England, and emigrated to the colonies with a gentile wife "to do a perish" as a man of letters. Burlesques of *Frankenstein* were nothing new, with from the 1820s the novel being pirated both as melodrama and comedy on the stage. Nor was localising/naturalising an English text for the Australian stage, with kangaroos featuring in Christmas pantomimes. Isaacs combined the two with an innovation: he linked the play with the new and controversial theory of Evolution, the subtitle being "The Man-Gorilla".

It is naturally very silly, with choruses of "Pop Goes the Weasel" and other popular songs. The topical references including the "Vagrant Act", New Zealand, and two Professors at Melbourne University, on opposite sides of the Darwin controversy, George Halford and William Thomson. The Monster has read Darwin; just as the Shelleys and Byron knew Erasmus Darwin, his grandfather, cited as scientific justification in the prefaces to *Frankenstein*.

When the Man-Gorilla requests a wife of Frankenstein, it is along these lines:

> Come, none of your soft sawder,
> I'll have a bran new woman—made to order.
> Something superior—a little fairy—
> My counterpart—perhaps not *quite* so hairy
> Of my own age and shape; with gentle eyes
> And nose like mine; but of a smaller size
> Swear such a *maid* you'll make, as me you *made*.

The play was never actually performed, but its publication makes it the first work of Australian science fiction. A Zoom reading is scheduled in 2022 by the Adelaide Critical Mass.

It is also worth noting that Isaacs makes Elizabeth Frankenstein a feminist. A character quotes: "The noblest study of man is man". Elizabeth's retort is: "Woman!"

One further comment on the Wollstonecraft/Shelley influence in Australia. Ada Cambridge was a noted novelist and poet, publishing in England while being a Melburnian vicar's wife. Her serials in colonial papers were under her initials, which enabled her freedom of expression. In the 1889 serial "A Woman's Friendship", reprinted in the prestigious Colonial Text series in 1995, two married women, Margaret Clive and Patty Kinnaird, form a Reform Club of three with the widowed Seaton McDonald. Their interests include reading and social change, including the enfranchisement of women. They read Mona Caird's controversial 1888 article on Marriage in the *Westminster Review*, and other works.

Though not as rigorous as Mary Shelley's reading program, theirs is certainly eclectic, including poetry by William Morris and Socialism. It is also indicative of the intellectual and social ferment which led to suffrage for women in the Austral colonies, beginning in 1893. Here they were far in advance of their English counterparts: when Cambridge returned to England with her husband in 1913, she was disenfranchised. Bessie Rayner Parkes, now the widowed Mrs Belloc, had to wait to be ninety before she could vote, in 1920.

In chapter seven of "A Woman's Friendship" the trio visit the Public Library (now State Library) in Melbourne. Here they read "Milton and Mary Wollstonecraft on *Marriage and the Rights of Women*." The juxtaposition shows Wollstonecraft's works being a pilgrimage site, rather than the person, in her grave. There is no mention of her personal life; she is on a par here with the canonical poet.

If we were, in some post-Covid time, to do a pilgrimage, beginning with Mary Wollstonecraft's grave, then to Mary Shelley's and then Percy's, it would end with Percy Jr, who died childless, bringing the line of Mary Wollstonecraft to an end. The Australian Wollstonecrafts also left no DNA, no issue, impressive though their pyramid memorial is. They leave their name, and letters in the Mitchell Library. As Ada Cambridge shows, Mary Wollstonecraft informed the debate which led to female suffrage. Mary Shelley via George Isaacs contributed to a founding text of Australian genre fiction, and *Frankenstein* continues to echo through our culture.

Should Wollstonecraft the suburb be part of the pilgrimage? Unlike the rest, it has no memorial, but then memorials and statues are contentious, easily vandalised, easily toppled. Mary Wollstonecraft was drawn from life, if somewhat differently, by various painters and engravers. If she is to be further represented as a material object, then the best exists already: her pile of books, still being published and read. As she wrote to Roscoe, during the sittings for her uniquely fierce portrait:

I do not imagine that it will be a very striking likeness; but, if you do not find me in it, I will send you a more faithful sketch—a book that I am now writing, in which I myself...shall certainly appear, hand and heart.

Contributor Biographies

Carina Bissett

Carina Bissett is a writer and poet working primarily in the fields of dark fiction and fabulism. Her work has been published in multiple journals and anthologies including Into the Forest: Tales of the Baba Yaga, Upon a Twice Time, Bitter Distillations: An Anthology of Poisonous Tales, and Arterial Bloom. Her poetry has been nominated for the Pushcart Prize and the Sundress Publications Best of the Net and can be found in the HWA Poetry Showcase, Fantasy Magazine, and NonBinary Review. She is also the co-editor of the award-winning anthology Shadow Atlas: Dark Landscapes of the Americas. Links to her work can be found at http://carinabissett.com.

Michele Brittany

Michele Brittany is the editor of 'Horror Literature from Gothic to Post-Modern: Critical Essays' (2020), 'Horror in Space: Critical Essays on a Film Subgenre' (2017) and 'James Bond and Popular Culture: Essays on the Influence of the Fictional Superspy' (2014). She's also a podcaster at H.P. Lovecast. Visit her at www.michelebrittany.com or Instagram @mbrittanywrites

Ciarán Bruder

I am an Irish writer, screenwriter, raconteur, and fan of the Oxford comma. I now live in Dublin after years spent in UAE, Australia, and New Zealand. I've published writing on major figures in the horror world before and hope to do it again.

Grant Butler

Grant Butler is an author from the US Midwest who writes in a variety of genres. Some of his literary influences include Stephen King, Ira Levin, Agatha Christie, and Thomas Harris. Cinema is also a big influence on his storytelling and some of his favourite films are Jaws, The Godfather, Goodfellas, and Psycho. He is the author of the novel The Heroin Heiress and his short fiction has been published in Sick Cruising and Mardi Gras Mysteries.

Octavia Cade

Octavia Cade is a New Zealand writer with an interest in science history and a PhD in science communication. A lot of her academic work looks at the way that science (and scientists!) are presented in speculative fiction. She's sold around 70 short stories to markets such as *Clarkesworld*, *Asimov's*, and *Strange Horizons*, and her latest book is *The Impossible Resurrection of Grief*, a climate fiction novella from Stelliform Press. She's a five-time Sir Julius Vogel winner and a Bram Stoker nominee, and she was the 2020 visiting writer in residence at Massey University. You can find her on Twitter as @OJCade.

Matthew R Davis

Matthew R. Davis is a dark fiction author and musician based in Adelaide, South Australia. He was shortlisted for a 2020 Shirley Jackson Award and the 2020 WSFA Small Press Award, and he won two categories in the 2019 Australian Shadows. His books are If Only Tonight We Could Sleep (collection, Things in the Well, 2020) and Midnight in the Chapel of Love (novel, JournalStone, 2021), with more on the slate for 2022. When not writing or working, he spends time with his photographer partner Meg and her eccentric cat, Juniper. Find out more at matthewrdavisfiction. wordpress.com.

Anthony P Ferguson

Anthony Ferguson is an author and editor living in Perth, Australia. He has published over sixty short stories and non-fiction articles in Australia, Britain and the United States. He wrote the novel Protégé, the non-fiction books, The Sex Doll: A History, and Murder Down Under, edited the short-story collection Devil Dolls and Duplicates in Australian Horror and coedited the award-nominated Midnight Echo #12. He is a committee member of the Australasian Horror Writers Association (AHWA), and a submissions editor for Andromeda Spaceways Magazine (ASM). He won the Australian Shadows Award for Short Fiction in 2020.

Claire Fitzpatrick

Claire Fitzpatrick is an award-winning author of speculative fiction, non-fiction, and poetry. She is the 2020 recipient of the Rocky Wood Memorial scholarship fund for this anthology, and the winner of the 2017 Rocky Wood Award for Non-Fiction and Criticism. She was also shortlisted for the 2022 William Atheling Jr. Award for Criticism or Review. Her 2019 debut collection 'Metamorphosis' (IFWG Publishing) was received with praise. She has been a panellist at various conventions and has been a regular contributor to Aurealis magazine since 2015. Visit her at www.clairefitzpatrick.com.au

Jason Franks

Jason Franks is the author of the novels *Bloody Waters, Faerie Apocalypse, X-Dimensional Assassin Zai*. He is also the writer of the *Sixsmiths* graphic novels, as well as many other comics and short stories. Franks' work has variously been short-listed for Aurealis, Ditmar and Ledger awards. By day he is a mild-mannered data scientist and engineer.

Franks lives in Melbourne, Australia. Find him online at www.jasonfranks.com.

Robert Hood

Robert Hood has been much published in Australia and overseas since his first professional sale in 1975—the award-winning short story "Orientation". His genres of choice are: horror/weird fiction, crime, fantasy and science fiction. He has published over 140 short stories, a number of novellas, a few novels, and lots of kid's books. He has won several major Australian awards, including the 1988 Australian Golden Dagger Award, the 2014 Ditmar Award (Best Novel) for Fragments of a Broken Land: Valarl Undead and the 2015 Australian Shadows Award (Best Collected Work) for Peripheral Visions: The Collected Ghost Stories. His latest is Scavengers, a crime/horror novel published by Clan Destine Press.

Nancy Holder

Nancy Holder is a New York Times best-selling author of approximately a hundred book-length projects and hundreds of short stories, essays, and articles. She received the Faust Grand Master Lifetime Achievement Award from the International Association of Media Tie-In Writers in 2020. In 2020, she won the Bram Stoker Award for Graphic Novel for Mary Shelley Presents Tales of the Supernatural, and has received five additional Stoker Awards for Novel, Young Adult Novel, and Short Story. She received the Lifetime Achievement Award from the Horror Writers Association in 2022. Go to @nancyholder, www.nancyholder.com and www.facebook.com/holder.nancy/

Sara Karloff

Sara Karloff was born on her father's 51st birthday, November 23, 1938. Boris Karloff was filming *Son of Frankenstein* at the time, and Sara jokes that she was "his most expensive birthday present ever."

In 1993, following the death of her step-mother, Evelyn Karloff, Sara formed Karloff Enterprises and took responsibility for the persona and licensing rights relating to her famous father. The company's goal is to maintain a standard of excellence and appropriateness when the name or likeness of her father is used. Through the licensing process she has been able to make merchandise and collectibles available to her father's fans.

Ms. Karloff helped lead a three-year effort to have her father and other iconic horror actors' images captured in a series of commemorative United States Postage Stamps. Eventually a set of stamps with four actors likenesses (Boris Karloff – two stamps; Bela Lugosi; Lon Chaney, Sr.; and Lon Chaney, Jr.) was issued in 1997. In 2003 Boris was honored once again on a third US commemorative stamp, an honour which heretofore has been reserved only for US Presidents.

Sara continues to attend conventions around the world speaking about her iconic father and his remarkable legacy, and she is a much-loved and respected ambassador for the tradition of the classic horror film.

Piper Mejia

Piper Mejia is an advocate for New Zealand writers and literature. Her short fiction has appeared in a range of publications including; *Room enough for Two* in Te Korero Ahi Ka (2018) and a collection of her short stories will be published by *Breach* in 2019. In addition to writing, Piper is a founding member of Young NZ Writers – a non-profit dedicated to providing opportunities for young NZ writers. As a child, Piper stayed up late laughing at horror films. As an adult, she spends a lot of time being disappointed by plot holes and yet somehow she has never lost her love for Science Fiction and Horror; two genres that continues to ask the question "What if…"

Leslie S. Klinger

Leslie S. Klinger is the editor of the highly-acclaimed *New Annotated Frankenstein, New Annotated Dracula*, and the two-volume *New Annotated H. P. Lovecraft* as well as the anthologies *In the Shadow of Dracula* and *In the Shadow of Edgar Allen Poe*, featuring 19th- century supernatural fiction. Together with Lisa Morton, he's also edited the anthologies *Ghost Stories, Weird Women, Weird Women* II, and *Haunted Tales*, all with extensive selections of Victorian horror. He co-edited (with Eric Guignard) the HWA's *Haunted Library of Horror Classics*. His latest book is *New Annotated Strange Case of Dr. Jekyll and Mr. Hyde* (Mysterious Press, 2022).

Lisa Morton

Lisa Morton is a screenwriter, author of non-fiction books, and prose writer whose work was described by the American Library Association's Readers' Advisory Guide to Horror as "consistently dark, unsettling, and frightening." She is a six-time winner of the Bram Stoker Award®, the author of four novels and over 150 short stories, and a world-class Halloween and paranormal expert. Her recent releases include the *Calling the Spirits: A History of Seances*; forthcoming in 2023 from Applause Books is *The Art of the Zombie Movie*. Lisa lives in Los Angeles and online at www. lisamorton.com.

Lee Murray

Lee Murray is a multi-award-winning author-editor, screenwriter, and poet from Aotearoa-New Zealand. A *USA Today* bestselling author and double four-time Bram Stoker Award-winner, Lee's titles include the Taine McKenna adventures, The Path of Ra series (with Dan Rabarts), and fiction collection *Grotesque Monster Stories*. Her most recent work is *Unquiet Spirits: Essays by Asian Women in Horror* (with Angela Yuriko Smith). Lee lives in the sunny Bay of Plenty with her well-behaved family and a naughty dog. Read more at leemurray.info.

Donald Prentice Jr

Donald Prentice Jr is a PhD student at the University of Canterbury where he is researching articulations of beauty in contemporary horror films.

H K Stubbs

Helen Stubbs lives on Australia's Gold Coast. She's an award-winning fiction and feature writer with stories published in anthologies and magazines, including "Motherdoll" in *Spawn* (IFWG), "Polymer Island" in *Kaleidotrope* and "Uncontainable" in *Apex Magazine*. She's a creative producer at Razor Gaze and interviews speculative fiction writers for the podcast Galactic Chat. For fun, she likes to bushwalk, climb rocks, read and write. Catch up with her at @superleni on Twitter or discover more about her work and adventures at helenstubbs.wordpress.com.

Lucy Sussex

Lucy Sussex is a New Zealand-born writer living in Australia. Her mother Marian was an artist, her father Ronald taught French. Her award-winning work ranges widely, from academic and critical writing, true crime to horror, with children's, adult and teenage audiences. It has also been translated into various languages. She began in science fiction in her teens, and attended a Writers' Workshop with Terry Carr and George Turner. Later she taught at Clarions West and South. Her bibliography includes books for younger readers and the novel, *The Scarlet Rider* (1996, St Martins; reissued Ticoderoga 2015). She has published five short story collections, *My Lady Tongue, A Tour Guide in Utopia, Absolute Uncertainty, Matilda Told Such Dreadful Lies* (a best of), and *Thief of Lives*. She has also edited anthologies of fiction for younger readers; and the World Fantasy award shortlisted anthology *She's Fantastical* (with Judith Raphael Buckrich). She has been an academic (La Trobe University), researcher, editor and weekly review columnist for newspapers including the Age and Sydney Morning Herald. Her literary archaeology (unearthing forgotten writers) work includes *Women Writers and Detectives in C19th Crime Fiction: the mothers of the mystery genre* (Palgrave). Her major discovery has been the crime writer/flaneuse Mary Fortune. In 2018 she was a State Library of Victoria fellow, as part of a Fortune biography in process with Megan Brown.

Her most recent book concerns Fergus Hume and his 1886 *The Mystery of a Hansom Cab*, the biggest selling detective novel of the 1800s. It has been released by Text publishing as *Blockbuster!* (2015), and won a history award.

She maintains an interest in women's writing, Victoriana, the Antipodes and genre fiction. In her free time she has written a novel based on a seventeeth-century case involving the first Englishwoman detective.

GODWIN-SHELLEY FAMILY TREE

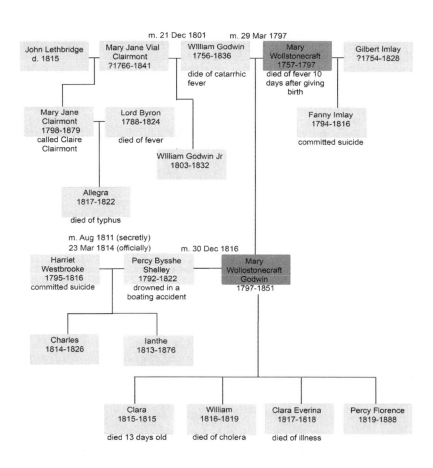

m. 21 Dec 1801   m. 29 Mar 1797

John Lethbridge
d. 1815

Mary Jane Vial
Clairmont
?1766-1841

WIlliam Godwin
1756-1836

dide of catarrhic
fever

Mary
Wollstonecraft
1757-1797
died of fever 10
days after giving
birth

Gilbert Imlay
?1754-1828

Mary Jane
Clairmont
1798-1879
called Claire
Clairmont

Lord Byron
1788-1824

died of fever

WIlliam Godwin Jr
1803-1832

Fanny Imlay
1794-1816

committed suicide

Allegra
1817-1822

died of typhus

m. Aug 1811 (secretly)
23 Mar 1814 (officially)   m. 30 Dec 1816

Harriet
Westbrooke
1795-1816
committed suicide

Percy Bysshe
Shelley
1792-1822
drowned in a
boating accident

Mary
Wollostonecraft
Godwin
1797-1851

Charles
1814-1826

Ianthe
1813-1876

Clara
1815-1815

died 13 days old

William
1816-1819

died of cholera

Clara Everina
1817-1818

died of illness

Percy Florence
1819-1888

THE VILLA DIODATI

The Villa Diodati is a mansion in the village of Cologny near Lake Geneva in Switzerland, notable because Lord Byron rented it and stayed there with John Polidori in the summer of 1816. Mary Shelley and Percy Bysshe Shelley, who had rented a house nearby, were frequent visitors. Because of poor weather, in June 1816 the group famously spent three days together inside the house creating stories to tell each other, two of which were developed into landmark works of the Gothic horror genre: *Frankenstein* by Mary Shelley and *The Vampyre*, the first modern vampire story, by Polidori.

After Byron's death, the Villa Diodati soon became a place of pilgrimage for devotees of Byron, and of Romanticism. The French writer Honoré de Balzac, who had become obsessed with the villa, had one of the characters in his 1836 novel *Albert Savarus* remark that the Villa Diodati is "now visited by everybody, just like Coppet and Ferney" (the homes of Madame de Staël and Voltaire respectively).

The villa has remained in private ownership. In 1945, the French artist Balthus moved into the property for a short period. The columnist Taki has written that when he visited the Villa Diodati in 1963 with the Belgian tennis player Philippe Washer it was then owned by the latter's family. As of 2011, the villa has been divided into luxury apartments.

PLACES OF INTEREST TO MARY WOLLSTONECRAFT

Paris

Wollstonecraft arrived in Paris at the end of 1792, just as the trial of Louis XVI and Marie Antoinette was beginning. She wrote that Louis being driven to the courthouse was one of the first sights she witnessed. In her early 30s, she met and fell in love with the notorious Gilbert Imlay, and had a baby out of wedlock. She kept on writing, but she had to be very secretive, because as an English person she could have been arrested and sent to the guillotine at any moment.

During her two and half years in France, she wrote. She had started with the intention of penning a series of letters for Johnson on her observations, but she decided instead to write a multi-volume history of the revolution. The first volume came out while she was in Le Havre. The others were never written.

Despite her initial disappointment when she witnessed the beginnings of the Terror, Wollstonecraft's stance on the Revolution remained positive. Mistakes had been made, which was inevitable; but France was nevertheless working towards the eradication of tyranny. Her book *An Historical and Moral View of the Origin and Progress of the French Revolution* (1795) was a critical study of a number of key documents written in the early years of the revolution by Mirabeau, Brissot, etc., and is concerned with the pursuit of liberty.

Portugal

Mary Wollstonecraft enjoyed travelling, and she spent time in Portugal with her close friend Fanny Blood. Fanny became ill with consumption, and the doctor recommended that she move to warmer climes, so she joined her fiancé in Portugal. They married, and within a few months, she was pregnant. Unfortunately the pregnancy did not relieve her tuberculosis. She became critically ill, so Wollstonecraft travelled to Portugal to help. She enjoyed the journey, and was one of the few passengers not to get ill during the crossing, helping to nurse others. She could not help Fanny, though, who died shortly after giving birth. Wollstonecraft stayed in Lisbon for a month, caring for Fanny's child. She used her time there to observe Portuguese customs, and came away convinced that Catholicism was not a healthy religion, and that the Portuguese were particularly bad in their treatment of women and of the lower classes.

Sweden, Norway, and Denmark.

'Letters Written During a Short Residence in Sweden, Norway, and Denmark' *(1796) is a personal travel narrative including twenty-five letters on a wide range of topics, from sociological reflections on Scandinavia and its peoples to philosophical questions regarding identity. It was the last work issued during her lifetime. Wollstonecraft's relationship with Imlay was a passionate but volatile one, and shortly after their daughter Fanny was born in 1794, Imlay abandoned the family. In the hopes of winning him back, Wollstonecraft soon agreed to undertake a trip to Scandinavia in search of a missing French cargo ship carrying a great deal of money owed to Imlay. Wollstonecraft travelled first to Gothenburg, where she remained for two weeks while Wollstonecraft investigated the missing ship.

Leaving Fanny and her nurse Marguerite behind, she embarked for Strömstad, Sweden, where she took a short detour to visit the fortress of Fredriksten, and then proceeded to Larvik, Norway. From there she traveled to Tønsberg, Norway, where she spent three weeks, and became increasingly suicidal. She also visited Helgeroa, Risør, and Kristiania (now Oslo) and returned by way of Strömstad and Gothenburg, where she picked up Fanny and Marguerite again. She returned to England by way of Copenhagen and Hamburg, finally landing at Dover in September 1795, three months after she had left England. Upon her return to England in September of 1795, only to find that Imlay had left her for another woman—an opera singer; it remains unclear whether Wollstonecraft succeeded in locating his ship. Despite the devastating loss of her lover, Wollstonecraft's experiences in Scandinavia brought her success in the form of her travelogue. Composed of twenty-five letters she wrote to Imlay during her travels, 'Letters Written During a Short Residence in Sweden, Norway, and Denmark' proved commercially successful, describing not only the natural and cultural landscapes of Scandinavia, but also Wollstonecraft's own mental state during this tumultuous period of her personal life.

PLACES OF INTEREST IN 'FRANKENSTEIN' BY MARY SHELLEY

Castle Frankenstein

The 13th-century Castle Frankenstein, in the Odenwald, where Johann Dippel (b. 1673), alchemist and grave robber, is said to have experimented with reviving corpses—and, some believe, inspired Shelley. Though it's unclear whether she knew about Castle Frankenstein, it's easy to see how Dippel conjures the image of a mad scientist. He was an avid dissector, claimed to have discovered an elixir of life, and peddled a variety of oils and potions concocted from animal flesh and bones.

Mount Tambora

The April 1815 eruption of Mount Tambora, which killed tens of thousands, spewed so much ash it cloaked Europe in gloom for many months. According to climate experts, the atmospheric debris even played a role in bizarre weather patterns that chilled the Northern Hemisphere through 1816. It was during that 'year without summer' that Shelley and friends enjoyed a haunting Swiss holiday.

Lake Geneva

Shelley places Victor Frankenstein's childhood in Geneva—a nod, perhaps, to where she first conjured him. In June 1816, Mary Wollstonecraft Godwin, then 18, joined her future husband, the poet Percy Shelley, her step sister Claire, Lord Byron and the physician John Polidori for a holiday here. In the narrative poem "Darkness," Byron described days where the "bright sun was extinguish'd" and people were "chill'd into a selfish prayer for light." The unseasonable rain and cold kept the group indoors, so they told one another ghost stories: Shelley's "creature" and Polidori's 'The Vampyre' were born.

London, England

The first edition of *Frankenstein; or, The Modern Prometheus* was published in London in 1818; five years later, the city saw the first stage adaptation, *Presumption; or, The Fate of Frankenstein*, written by Richard Brinsley Peake. The daughter of London intellectuals, Shelley made use of the city's early scientific explorations. In a journal entry from December 1814, she noted attending "Garnerin's lecture—on Electricity—the gasses—& the Phantasmagoria." The academic world's burgeoning interest in the supernatural clearly left an impression on the young writer.

Oxford, England

Mary visits Percy at Oxford in 1815, where his rooms were full of Leyden jars, a friction generator and various alchemical instruments. In the novel, Victor Frankenstein visits the city after meeting England's top scientists, describing his melancholy in a prophetic passage: " For an instant I dared to shake off my chains and look around me with a free and lofty spirit, but the iron had eaten into my flesh, and I sank again, trembling and hopeless, into my miserable self."

Bologna, Italy

In 1781, Luigi Galvani, a physician in Bologna, used an electrically charged knife to make a dismembered frog leg jump. The idea that electricity could "infuse a spark of being," as Victor puts it, impressed Shelley. Galvani's pioneering work led to a new field of science, electrophysiology, which became crucial to Alessandro Volta's invention of the electric battery at the turn of the century.

Chamonix, France

Victor hikes into Chamonix after the creature kills his brother. His descriptions of the valley as a 'glorious presence-chamber of imperial Nature' echo letters that Mary and Percy wrote on an 1816 trip. The region inspired Percy as well: during their trip, the "still and solemn power" of nature led him to write the epic poem *'Mont Blanc'*, which would be published in 1817.

Dundee, Scotland

Shelley spent two teenage years with the Baxter family, near Dundee, Scotland, arriving in 1812 looking for rest and recovery from an unexplained partial paralysis, and to escape the rising contentious conflicts with her stepmother, Mary Jane Godwin. Her father had become acquainted with William Baxter, himself a fellow radical thinker. Mary spent time with his four daughters exploring the Scottish hills, dabbling in youthful experiments in mysticism, and enjoying trips with the Baxters, the latter which introduced her to the North Sea tales of sailors which would later appear in the wraparound telling of the sea captain who picks up Victor from the icy waters in 'Frankenstein'. It was upon her return to England that she met Percy Bysshe Shelley, who idolised her father, and their relationship began.

Orkney Islands, Scotland

In the Orkneys, Victor abandons his effort to fashion a companion for the creature: "During my first experiment, a kind of enthusiastic frenzy had blinded me to the horror of my employment; my mind was intently fixed on the consummation of my labour, and my eyes were shut to the horror of my proceedings. But now I went to it in cold blood, and my heart often sickened at the work of my hands." After Shelley's novel was published, a Glasgow doctor named Andrew Ure tried to revive an executed convict.

Gulf of Spezia, Italy

Victor pursues the creature to "the blue Mediterranean " around Spezia. In a real-life Gothic twist, Percy drowned nearby when his boat capsized in a storm four years after the novel was published. His corpse washed ashore ten days later on the beach near Viareggio. In 'Notes on Poems of 1822', a widowed Shelley describes her grief: "hard reality brings too miserably home to the mourner all that is lost of happiness, all of lonely unsolaced struggle that remains."

Archangel, Russia

'Frankenstein' ends north of Archangel, where an explorer had found Victor, on the verge of death chasing the remorseful creature, who in the finale sets off to "the northern extremity of the globe" to destroy himself in a fire. "I shall die, and what I now feel be no longer felt," the creature says. "Soon these burning miseries will be extinct. I shall ascend my funeral pile triumphantly and exult in the agony of the torturing flames. The light of that conflagration will fade away; my ashes will be swept into the sea by the winds. My spirit will sleep in peace, or if it thinks, it will not surely think thus."

REFERENCES

Carina Bissett

Bride of Frankenstein, (1935). Universal Pictures.

Shelley, Mary Wollstonecraft, (1998). Frankenstein, or, The Modern Prometheus : the 1818 Text. Oxford ; New York :Oxford University Press.

Michele Brittany

Carey, E. (June 16, 2008) *Spotlight on Bernie Wrightson.* Available at: https://www.cbr.com/spotlight-on-bernie-wrightson/ (Accessed: 31 January 2022).

Cooke, J. B. (Summer 1999) *Like a Bat Out of Hell: Chatting with Bernie Wrightson, DC's Monster Maker.* Available at: https://www.twomorrows.com/comicbookartist/articles/05wrightson.html (Accessed: 10 February 2022).

Creepy Presents Bernie Wrightson (2011) Milwaukie, OR: Dark Horse Books.

Niles, S. (May, 8, 2012) *Frankenstein Alive, Alive! A Conversation with Bernie Wrightson.* Available at: https://www.steveniles.net/2002/05/frankenstein-alive-alive-a-conversation-with-bernie-wrightson.html (Accessed: 31 January 2022).

Niles, S. (July 2012) 'Niles Talks Frankenstein with Wrightson', in *Frankenstein Alive, Alive!* San Diego: IDW Publishing.

Pons, T. (April 19, 2011) *Berni Wrightson: Frankenstein Interview.* Available at: https://www.youtube.com/watch?v=btJ6CI5SiUM&t=6s (Accessed: 10 February 2022).

Shelley, M. S. (2020) *Frankenstein.* New York: Gallery 13.

Squires, J. (December 13, 2019) *The Late Bernie Wrightson's Original 'Frankenstein' Art for Marvel Cover Just Sold for Over $1 Million.* Available at: https://bloody-disgusting.com/news/3597790/late-bernie-wrights-original-frankenstein-art-marvel-cover-just-sold-1-million/ (Accessed: 31 January 2022).

Woerner, M. (March 25, 2017) *How Bernie Wrightson Uncovered the Soul of the Monster in His Work.* Available at: https://www.latimes.com/entertainment/herocomplex/la-et-hc-bernie-wrightson-20170320-htmlstory.html (Accessed: 31 January 2022).

Wrightson, B. (2011) 'The Muck Monster', in Creepy Presents Bernie Wrightson. Milwaukie, OR: Dark Horse Books, pp. 100-106.

Ciarán Bruder

Al Haidari, Ali Saaleh Ahmed & Bhanegaonkar, Dr. S. G. (2013) The Use and Creation of Myths in Major Works of P. B. Shelley: An Interpretation". Journal of Humanities and Social Science, Volume 7, Issue 1. 27-32.

Hoeveler, Diane. (1990) Shelley and Androgyny: Teaching The Witch of Atlas. Approaches to Teaching Shelley's Poetry. Ed. Spencer Hall. New York: Modern Language Association of America. 93-95.

Mukherjee, Marjana & Banerjee, Dr. Joydeep.(2014) Unveiling the Concept of Androgyny in Mary Shelley's Frankenstein. International Journal of Languages and Literatures, Volume 2, Issue 2. 2014. 307-322.

Pete, Alyssa. (2019). Swim the Warm Waters of Sins of the Flesh': Gender and Sexuality in Frankenstein and The Rocky Horror Picture Show". University of Oregon Undergraduate Research Symposium.

Shelley, Mary. (1818.) Frankenstein. Planet eBook, https://www.planetebook.com/free-ebooks/frankenstein.pdf.

Shelley, Percy Bysshe. (1824.) The Witch of Atlas. Penn State Project KNARF: Frankenstein, The Pennsylvania Electronic Edition. http://knarf.english.upenn.edu/PShelley/witch.html.

Walker, Victoria. (2018). Victor Frankenstein, Mary Shelley and Prometheus in the Role of Creator". Murray State University Scholars Week, Issue 3. 1-11.

Grant Butler

Ackerman, K.D., (2018). The Garfield Assassination Altered American History, But Is Woefully Forgotten Today. Smithsonian.com. Available at: https://www.smithsonianmag.com/history/garfield-assassination-altered-american-history-woefully-forgotten-today-180968319/ [Accessed May 4, 2021].

Anon, Joseph Lister and the use of antiseptics—Attempts to treat and cure illness and disease—WJEC—GCSE History Revision—WJEC—BBC Bitesize. BBC News. Available at: https://www.bbc.co.uk/bitesize/guides/zwkm97h/revision/5 [Accessed May 4, 2021].

Barry, E., (2019). Chloroform in Childbirth? Yes, Please, the Queen Said. The New York Times. Available at: https://www.nytimes.com/2019/05/06/world/europe/uk-royal-births-labor.html [Accessed May 3, 2021].

Eschner, K., (2017). It Didn't Take Very Long For Anaesthesia to Change Childbirth. Smithsonian.com. Available at: https://www.smithsonianmag.com/smart-news/it-didnt-take-very-long-anesthesia-change-childbirth-180967636/ [Accessed May 4, 2021].

Fulton, A., (2017). 'The Butchering Art': How A 19th Century Physician Made Surgery Safer. NPR. Available at: https://www.npr.org/sections/health-shots/2017/10/13/557367840/the-butchering-art-how-a-19th-century-physician-made-surgery-safer [Accessed May 4, 2021].

Hartnett, K., (2014). Anesthesia during labor? Thank Queen Victoria. The Boston Globe. BostonGlobe.com. Available at: https://www.bostonglobe.com/ideas/2014/09/05/anesthesia-during-labor-thank-queen-victoria/N9YYxvBqpcw3YLyLdoinyN/story.html [Accessed May 3, 2021].

Hill, A. (2010) John Keats was an opium addict, claims a new biography of the poet, The *Guardian*. Guardian News and Media. Available at: https://www.theguardian.com/books/2012/sep/21/john-keats-opium-addict (Accessed: March 17, 2020).

Jordison, S. (2009) The power of Shelley's Frankenstein lives on—but not in Cologny,

The Guardian. Guardian News and Media. Available at: https://www.theguardian.com/books/booksblog/2009/oct/21/mary-shelley-lord-byron-frankenstein (Accessed: March 17, 2021).

Lepore, J., (2018). The Strange and Twisted Life of "Frankenstein". The New Yorker. Available at: https://www.newyorker.com/magazine/2018/02/12/the-strange-and-twisted-life-of-frankenstein [Accessed May 4, 2021].

Magazine, S. (2018) Inside the story of America's 19th-century opiate addiction. Smithsonian Institution. Available at: https://www.smithsonianmag.com/history/inside-story-americas-19th-century-opiate-addiction-180967673/ (Accessed: May 17, 2021).

Mitchell, R., (2020). The president had been shot. Then the White House lied about his condition as he slowly died. The Washington Post. Available at: https://www.washingtonpost.com/history/2020/09/19/garfield-assassination-white-house-doctors-lied/ [Accessed May 4, 2021].

Radford, T. (2011) Frankenstein's hour of creation identified by astronomers, The Guardian. Guardian News and Media. Available at: https://www.theguardian.com/books/2011/sep/26/frankenstein-hour-creation-identified-astronomers (Accessed: March 17, 2021).

Zaleski, E. (2017) The summer storm that inspired Frankenstein and Dracula, The Daily Beast. The Daily Beast Company. Available at: https://www.thedailybeast.com/the-summer-storm-that-inspired-frankenstein-and-dracula (Accessed: March 18, 2021).

Octavia Cade

I, Frankenstein (2014), DVD, Lakeshore Entertainment, Beverly Hills & SKE Films, Los Angeles & Hopscotch Films, Glasgow, written by Kevin Grevioux and Stuart Beattie, directed by Stuart Beattie.

Saadawi, A., (2018). Frankenstein in Baghdad. Translated from the Arabic by Jonathan Wright. Penguin, New York.

Shelley, M. (2003). Frankenstein, Barnes & Noble Classics, New York.

Matthew R Davis

Bride of Frankenstein, (1935). Universal Pictures.

Doctor Who—The Haunting of Villa Diodati (2020). Emma Sullivan. BBC.

Gothic (1986) Virgin Films.

Nightmare on Joe's Street (2006). Time Warp Trio. Discovery Kids.

Rowing with the Wind, (1988) Ditirambo Films.

Summer of Monsters. (2014) Tony Thompson, Black Dog Books.

Sara Century (2018). The History of Mary Shelley in Pop Culture . SyFy Wire.

Christopher Frayling. (2017). Frankenstein: The First Two Hundred Years, Reel Art Press.

Glasfurd, G. (2020). The Year Without Summer. Two Roads/Hachette.

Glass, Adam and Cuartero-Briggs, Olivia. (2019) Mary Shelley Monster Hunter. Aftershock Comics.

Grant, Brea and Lee, Yishan. (2020). Mary: The Adventures of Mary Shelley's Great-Great-Great-Great-Great-Granddaughter. Six Foot Press.

Hay, Daisey. (2018). The Making of Mary Shelley's Frankenstein, Bodleian Library .

Mellor, Anne K. (1988). Mary Shelley: Her Life, Her Fiction, Her Monsters.

Morrison, Grant. et all. (1994-2000) The Invisibles. Vertigo/DC.

Winterson, Jeanette (2019). Frankisssstein: A Love Story. Jonathan Cape.

Anthony Ferguson

Canter, David. (1994). Criminal Shadows. London: Harper Collins,.

Matheson, Richard. (1954). I Am Legend. New York: Gold Medal Books,.

Seltzer, Mark. (1998) Serial Killers: Death and Life in America's Wound Culture. New York: Routledge.

Shelley, Mary. (2009). Frankenstein. Melbourne: Penguin, (first published 1818).

Stevenson, Robert Louis. (1886). The Strange Case of Dr Jekyll and Mr Hyde. London: Longman.

Vronsky, Peter. (2018) Sons of Cain. New York: Penguin,.

Wilson, Colin. (1995) A Plague of Murder. London: Robinson Publishing Ltd.

Wilson, Colin, and Seaman, Donald. (1996) The Serial Killers: A Study in the Psychology of Violence. London: Virgin Publishing.

Claire Fitzpatrick

Bowlby, J. (1982). Attachment and loss: Retrospect and prospect. American Journal of Orthopsychiatry, 52(4), pp.664–678.

Bretherton, I. (1992). The origins of attachment theory: John Bowlby and Mary Ainsworth. Developmental Psychology, 28(5), pp.759–775.

Gaughan, M. (2011). Children and Adolescents in Trauma: Creative Therapeutic Approaches edited by Chris Nicholson, Michael Irwin and Kedar Nath Dwivedi, Jessica Kingsley Publishers, London, 2010. 256pp. ISBN 978-1-84310-437-7, £22.99. Child Abuse Review, 21(3), pp.229–230.

Lerner, RM (1983) Child influences on marital and family interaction: a life-span perspective, Academic Press, New York.

Ozolins, Aija. (1975). Dreams and Doctrines: Dual Strands in "Frankenstein." Science Fiction Studies, 2(2), 103–112. http://www.jstor.org/stable/4238931.

Pabst-Kastner, C. (2015). A Biographical Sketch of Mary Wollstonecraft Shelley (1797-1851). [online] victorianweb.org. Available at: https://victorianweb.org/previctorian/mshelley/bio.html.

Shelley, Mary Wollstonecraft, (1998). Frankenstein, or, The Modern Prometheus: the 1818 Text. Oxford; New York :Oxford University Press.

Shemmings, D. and Shemmings, Y., (2011). Understanding disorganized attachment. London: Jessica Kingsley.

Williams, Valerie. (2019) Mary Wollstonecraft on Motherhood and Political Participation: An Overlooked Insight into Women's Subordination. Hypatia, vol. 34, no. 4, 29., pp. 802–8.

Wright, A. (2018). Mary Shelley. Cardiff: University of Wales Press.

Jason Franks

Clarke, Neil (2023). A Concerning Trend—Neil Clarke. url: http://neilclarke.com/a-concerning-trend/ (visited on 03/16/2023).

Curry, David (2023). ChatGPT Revenue and Usage Statistics (2023)—Business of Apps. url: https://www.businessofapps.com/data/chatgptstatistics/ (visited on 03/16/2023).

Franks, Jason (Sept. 2022). "Text Classification for Records Management". In: J. Comput. Cult. Herit. 15.3. ISSN: 1556-4673. DOI: 10.1145/3485846. url: https://doi.org/10.1145/3485846.

Ham, Fredric M. and Ivica Kostanic (2000). Principles of Neurocomputing for Science and Engineering. 1st. McGraw-Hill Higher Education. ISBN: 978-007-025966-9.

Heaven, Will (2022). Why Meta's latest large language model only survived three days online — MIT Technology Review. url: https://www.technologyreview.com/2022/11/18/1063487/meta-large-language-model-ai-onlysurvived-three-days-gpt-3-science/ (visited on 03/17/2023).

James, Gareth et al., eds. (2013). An introduction to statistical learning: with applications in R. en. Springer texts in statistics 103. OCLC: ocn828488009. New York: Springer. ISBN: 978-1-4614-7137-0.

Kingma, Durk P et al. (2014). "Semi-supervised Learning with Deep Generative Models". In: Advances in Neural Information Processing Systems 27. Ed. by Z. Ghahramani et al. Curran Associates, Inc., pp. 3581–3589. url: http://papers.nips.cc/paper/5352-semi-supervised-learning-withdeep-generative-models.pdf (visited on 10/23/2019).

Kirkpatrick, Keith (2023). "Can AI Demonstrate Creativity?" In: Commun. ACM 66.2, pp. 21–23. DOI: 10.1145/3575665. url: https://doi.org/10. 1145/3575665.

Shelley, Mary Wollstonecraft (2008). Frankenstein, or, The modern Prometheus: the original two-volume novel of 1816-1817 from the Bodleian Library manuscripts. eng. Oxford [England: Bodleian Library. ISBN: 9781851243969.

Thomas, Patrick (2022). Google Suspends Engineer Who Claimed Its AI System Is Sentient; Tech company dismisses the employee's claims about its LaMDA artificial-intelligence chatbot technology. English.

Thorbecke, Catherine (2023). Plagued with errors: A news outlet's decision to write stories with AI backfires — CNN Business. url: https://edition.cnn.com/2023/01/25/tech/cnet-ai-tool-news-stories/index.html (visited on 03/17/2023).

Upward, Frank et al. (Mar. 2013). "Recordkeeping informatics: re figuring a discipline in crisis with a single minded approach". en. In: Records Management Journal, pp. 37–50. ISSN: 0956-5698. doi:10.1108/09565691311325013. Url: https://www.emerald.com/insight/content/doi/10.1108/ 09565691311325013/full/html (visited on 08/10/2019).

Vaswani, Ashish et al. (2017). "Attention Is All You Need". In: CoRR abs/1706.03762. arXiv: 1706.03762. url: http://arxiv.org/abs/1706.03762.

Nancy Holder

AbeBooks. "Frankenstein, or The Modern Prometheus. Shelley, Mary Wollstonecraft, Lynd Ward." https://www.abebooks.com/servlet/BookDetailsPL?bi=31393827672 Accessed December 28, 2022.

Bryne, John. (2009) *Angel vs. Frankenstein I (The Heir)*. IDW.

---. *Angel vs. Frankenstein II*. IDW, 2009.

del Toro, Guillermo. (2017) "Introduction: Mary Shelley, or the Modern Galatea." *The New Annotated Frankenstein*. Ed. and with a Foreword and Notes by Leslie S. Klinger. Norton.

"Frankenstein Becomes a Star." (2018) *Frankenstein: the Man, the Monster, the Legacy*. Life Books, 29.

Frayling, Christopher. (2017) *Frankenstein: The First Two Hundred Years*. Reel Art Press, 89

Hawcock, David and Claire Brampton. (200)9*Frankenstein: A Classic Pop-Up Tale*. UK: Allcloud/Cowley Robinson Publishing; US: Universe, 2010.

Ita, Sam. (2010) *Frankenstein: A Pop-Up Book*. Union Square & Co.; Pop edition.

Holder, Nancy. (2020) *Mary Shelley Presents Tales of the Supernatural*. Kymera Press.

Judge, Lita. (2018) *Mary's Monster: Love, Madness, and How Mary Shelley Created FRANKENSTEIN*. Roaring Brook Press.

Laneri, Rachel. "How this makeup whiz created the most recognizable monster of all time." *New York Post. nypost.com/2018/04/11/how-this-makeup-whiz-created-the-most-recognizable-monster-of-all-time/* April 18, 2018. Accessed Dec. 12, 2022.

Mignola, Mike, et. al. *Frankenstein: New World*. Dark Horse, August 2022—December 2022.

Niles, Steve. (May 08, 2012) "Frankenstein Alive, Alive! A Conversation with Bernie Wrightson." *Steve Niles Horror Writer. https://www.steveniles.net/2012/05/frankenstein-alive-alive-a-conversation-with-bernie-wrightson.html*. Accessed December 28, 2022.

Niles, Steve, and Bernie Wrightson. (2018) *Frankenstein Alive Alive! The Complete Collection*. IDW.

Ruditis, Paul. (2018) *The Vault of Frankenstein: 200 Years of the World's Most Famous Monster*. becker&mayer! books, 156.

Shelley, Mary, and Bernie Wrightson. (1983) *Bernie Wrightson's Frankenstein*. Marvel Comics.

Shelley Mary. (1934) *Frankenstein* illustrated by Lynd Ward. Harrison Smith and Robert Haas.

Shelley, Mary. (2018) *Frankenstein: Manuscript*. SP Books – Editions des Saints Pères.

Shelley, Mary. (2017) *The New Annotated Frankenstein*, edited and with a Foreword and Notes by Leslie S. Klinger, Introduction by Guillermo del Toro. Norton.

Shelley, Mary. (1986) *Frankenstein Or the Modern Prometheus*. Introduction by Elizabeth Kostova. Penguin Books, ix.

Robert Hood

A Nightmare Wakes (2020). America: Shudder.

Edwards, A. (1988) Haunted summers. London: Coronet.

Excerpts from Bride of Frankenstein (1935). Universal Pictures. Gothic (1986) Virgin Films.

Peake, R.B. (1824) "Presumption; or, The Fate of Frankenstein." New York City.

Shelley, M.W. and Klinger, L.S. (2017) The new annotated Frankenstein. New York: Liveright Publishing Corporation.

Shelley, Mary Wollstonecraft, (1998). Frankenstein, or, The Modern Prometheus: the 1818 Text. Oxford; New York: Oxford University Press.

Thompson, T. (2014) Summer of monsters: The scandalous story of Mary Shelley. Newtown, NSW, Australia: Black Dog Books, an imprint of Walker Books Australia Pty Ltd.

Piper Mejia

Frank, Anne. (1947) The Diary of Anne Frank. Contract Publishing.

Wollstonecraft, M. (1787) Thoughts on the education of daughters with reflections on female conduct, in the more important duties of life. New York: Garland.

Shelley, Mary Wollstonecraft, (1998). Frankenstein, or, The Modern Prometheus: the 1818 Text. Oxford; New York: Oxford University Press.

UNICEF. (2020). Girl's Education. Available at https://www.unicef.org/education/girls-education.

Lee Murray

Anonymous authors quoted by kind permission.

Barr, R. (2020). 'Pandemic and the Horrors of Solitude', Solitudes: Past and Present. https://solitudes.qmul.ac.uk/blog/pandemic-and-the-horrors-of-absolute-solitude/.

Battersby, L. (2021). Personal communication.

Baxter, A. (2021). Personal communication.

Eileen Hunt Botting, 'Mary Shelley Created 'Frankenstein,' and Then a Pandemic', The New York Times, March 13, 2020. https://www.nytimes.com/2020/03/13/opinion/mary-shelley-sc-fi-pandemic-novel.html.

Flinthart, D. (2021). Personal communication.

Goody, H. (2021). Personal communication.

Green, J. (2020). 'Pandemic Panic: Mary Shelley's The Last Man', The Library Company of Philadelphia. https://librarycompany.org/2020/05/26/pandemic-panic-maryshelleys-the-last-man/.

Joelson, M. (2020). 'The Last Woman: Mary Shelley's Apocalyptic Vision', Peter Harrington, London, UK. https://www.peterharrington.co.uk/blog/mary-shelleys-thelast-man/.

Murray, L. (2020). 'Writing From My Bubble', Join Me in the Madhouse, by Stephanie Wytovich, May 14, 2020. http://stephaniewytovich.blogspot.com/2020/05/writingfrom-my-bubble-guest-post-from.html.

Murphy, O. (2020). 'Guide to the Classics: Mary Shelley's The Last Man is a prophecy of life in a global pandemic', The Conversation: Arts and Culture. https://theconversation.com/guide-to-the-classics-mary-shelleys-the-last-man-is-a-prophecy-of-life-in-a-globalpandemic-136963.

Shelley, M. (1826). The Last Man, Henry Colburn, London.

Stred, S. (2021). Personal communication.

Yadav. G. R. (2020). Mary Shelley's The Last Man: Alienation in the Time of Global Pandemic, IJCRT Volume 8, Issue 5 May 2020. https://ijcrt.org/papers/IJCRT2005236.pdf.

Vargo, L. (2020). 'Mary Shelley's The Last Man and COVID-19', Fifteen Eighty-Four, Academic Perspectives from the University of Cambridge, Cambridge University Press. http://www.cambridgeblog.org/2020/05/mary-shelleys-the-last-man-and-covid-19/.

Yadav. G. R. (2020). Mary Shelley's The Last Man: Alienation in the Time of Global Pandemic, IJCRT Volume 8, Issue 5 May 2020. https://ijcrt.org/papers/IJCRT2005236.

Donald Prentice Jr.

Austin, JL. (1962). *How to Do Things with Words.* London: Oxford University Press, p. 132.

Butler, Judith. "Performative Acts and Gender Construction: An Essay in Phenomenology and Feminist Theory," *Theatre Journal*, vol.40, no. 4 (Dec. 1988), pp.520-521.

Colebrook, Claire. (2003). Gender. London: Bloomsbury Publishing, 2003, p. 244.

Foucault, Michel. 1977. *Discipline and Punish: The Birth of the Prison.* New York: Random House, p. 183.

Salih, Sarah. "Judith Butler," (London: Routledge, 2002), p.84.

Shelley, Mary. "Frankenstein," (Global Grey, 1818 [2021]), p.35.

Mary Shelley's Frankenstein. (1994). [video] Directed by K. Branagh. USA: TriStar Pictures.

HK Stubbs

Gordon, Charlotte. (2015). Romantic Outlaws, Great Britain: Windmill Books.

Kegan Paul, Charles. (1876) William Godwin: His Friends and Contemporaries. London.

Kelly, Gary. (1992). Revolutionary Feminism: The Mind and Career of Mary Wollstone-craft. New York: St. Martin's Press.

Lepore, Hill. (2018). 'The Strange and Twisted Life of "Frankenstein,"' The New Yorker, 5 February.

Mellor, Anne K. (2002). Mary Wollstonecraft's A Vindication of the Rights of Woman and the Women Writers of Her Day." In The Cambridge Companion to Mary Wollstonecraft, edited by Claudia L. Johnson, 141–59. Cambridge: Cambridge University Press, doi:10.1017/CCOL0521783437.009.

Shelley, Mary. (1818). Frankenstein. London: Lackington, Hughes, Harding, Mavor & Jones: 1818.

Lucy Sussex

Berry, Alexander (1873). "Passages in the life of a Nonagenarian", Sydney Morning Herald 29 September.

Anon.(1864). "Mrs Grundy Moribunda", Illawarra Mercury 20 December.

Black, Anne. (2020) Pendragon: The Life of George Isaacs, Colonial Wordsmith, Adelaide, Wakefield.

Botting, Eileen. (ed.) (2020). Portraits of Wollstonecraft, London, Bloomsbury.

Braddon, Mary. (1880). Just as I am, London, Tauchnitz.

Cambridge, Ada. (1889) A Woman's Friendship.

Chandler, George. (1953) William Roscoe of Liverpool, 1753-1831, London, Batsford.

Godwin, William (1798) Memoirs of the Author of A Vindication of the Rights of Women. Available at: https://www.gutenberg.org/ebooks/16199.

Sydney Stock and Station Journal, (1908). 'Gossip'.

Hunt, E.M. (2002) "The family as cave, Platoon and prison: The Three stages of Wollstonecraft's philosophy of the family," *The Review of Politics*, 64(1), pp. 81–119. Available at: https://doi.org/10.1017/s0034670500031624.

Isaacs, George. (1865). The Burlesque of Frankenstein. Rhyme and Prose: and, a Burlesque. And its History, Melbourne, Clarson, Shallard, Bessie Rayner. Ballads and Songs.

Stephen, MD. (1967). "Edward Wollstonecraft" https://adb.anu.edu.au/biography/wollstonecraft-Edward-2812.

Tansillo, Luigi. & Roscoe, William. (1804) *The nurse / a poem. Trans. from the Italian by Luigi Tansillo by William Roscoe* Printed by J. M'Creery, for Cadell and Davies Liverpool.

INDEX